LEARNING FROM THE MESS: METHOD/OLOGICAL PRAXIS IN RHETORIC AND WRITING STUDIES

T0356512

PERSPECTIVES ON WRITING
Series Editors: Rich Rice and J. Michael Rifenburg
Consulting Editor: Susan H. McLeod
Associate Editors: Johanna Phelps, Jonathan M. Marine, and Qingyang Sun

The Perspectives on Writing series addresses writing studies in a broad sense. Consistent with the wide ranging approaches characteristic of teaching and scholarship in writing across the curriculum, the series presents works that take divergent perspectives on working as a writer, teaching writing, administering writing programs, and studying writing in its various forms.

The WAC Clearinghouse and University Press of Colorado are collaborating so that these books will be widely available through free digital distribution and low-cost print editions. The publishers and the series editors are committed to the principle that knowledge should freely circulate and have embraced the use of technology to support open access to scholarly work.

Recent Books in the Series

Diane Kelly-Riley, Ti Macklin, and Carl Whithaus (Eds.), *Considering Students, Teachers, and Writing Assessment: Volumes 1 and 2* (2024)

Amy Cicchino and Troy Hicks (Eds.), *Better Practices: Exploring the Teaching of Writing in Online and Hybrid Spaces* (2024)

Diane Kelly-Riley, Ti Macklin, and Carl Whithaus (Eds.), *Considering Students, Teachers, and Writing Assessment: Volumes 1 and 2* (2024)

Genesea M. Carter and Aurora Matzkel (Eds.), *Systems Shift: Creating and Navigating Change in Rhetoric and Composition Administration* (2023)

Michael J. Michaud, *A Writer Reforms (the Teaching of) Writing: Donald Murray and the Writing Process Movement, 1963–1987* (2023)

Michelle LaFrance and Melissa Nicolas ((Eds.), *Institutional Ethnography as Writing Studies Practice* (2023)

Phoebe Jackson and Christopher Weaver (Eds.), *Rethinking Peer Review: Critical Reflections on a Pedagogical Practice* (2023)

Megan J. Kelly, Heather M. Falconer, Caleb L. González, and Jill Dahlman (Eds.), *Adapting the Past to Reimagine Possible Futures: Celebrating and Critiquing WAC at 50* (2023)

William J. Macauley, Jr. et al. (Eds.), *Threshold Conscripts: Rhetoric and Composition Teaching Assistantships* (2023)

Jennifer Grouling, *Adapting VALUEs: Tracing the Life of a Rubric through Institutional Ethnography* (2022)

LEARNING FROM THE MESS: METHOD/OLOGICAL PRAXIS IN RHETORIC AND WRITING STUDIES

Edited by Ashley J. Holmes and Elise Verzosa Hurley

The WAC Clearinghouse
wac.colostate.edu
Fort Collins, Colorado

University Press of Colorado
upcolorado.com
Denver, Colorado

The WAC Clearinghouse, Fort Collins, Colorado 80523

University Press of Colorado, Denver, Colorado 80203

ISBN 978-1-64215-218-0 (PDF) | 978-1-64215-219-7 (ePub) | 978-1-64642-618-8 (pbk.)

DOI 10.37514/PER-B.2024.2180

Produced in the United States of America

Library of Congress Cataloging-in-Publication Data

Names: Holmes, Ashley J. editor. | Verzosa Hurley, Elise editor.
Title: Learning from the mess : method/ological praxis in rhetoric and writing studies / edited by Ashley J. Holmes and Elise Verzosa Hurley.
Description: Fort Collins, Colorado : The WAC Clearinghouse ; Denver, Colorado : University Press of Colorado, [2024] | Series: Perspectives on writing | Includes bibliographical references.
Identifiers: LCCN 2024021756 (print) | LCCN 2024021757 (ebook) | ISBN 9781646426188 (pbk.) | ISBN 9781642152180 (pdf) | ISBN 9781642152197 (epub)
Subjects: LCSH: English language—Rhetoric—Study and teaching. | English language—Rhetoric—Research—Methodology. | English language—Composition and exercises—Research—Methodology. | LCGFT: Essays.
Classification: LCC PE1404 .L37 2024 (print) | LCC PE1404 (ebook) | DDC 808/.042071—dc23/eng/20240718
LC record available at https://lccn.loc.gov/2024021756
LC ebook record available at https://lccn.loc.gov/2024021757

Copyeditor: Annie Halseth
Designer: Mike Palmquist
Cover Photo: RawPixel Image 79563. Licensed.
Series Editors: Rich Rice and J. Michael Rifenburg
Consulting Editor: Susan H. McLeod
Associate Editors: Johanna Phelps, Jonathan M. Marine, and Qingyang Sun

The WAC Clearinghouse supports teachers of writing across the disciplines. Hosted by Colorado State University, it brings together scholarly journals and book series as well as resources for teachers who use writing in their courses. This book is available in digital formats for free download at wac.colostate.edu.

Founded in 1965, the University Press of Colorado is a nonprofit cooperative publishing enterprise supported, in part, by Adams State University, Colorado State University, Fort Lewis College, Metropolitan State University of Denver, University of Alaska Fairbanks, University of Colorado, University of Denver, University of Northern Colorado, University of Wyoming, Utah State University, and Western Colorado University. For more information, visit upcolorado.com.

Citation Information: Holmes, Ashley J., and Elise Verzosa Hurley. (2024). *Learning from the Mess: Method/ological Praxis in Rhetoric and Writing Studies*. The WAC Clearinghouse; University Press of Colorado. https://doi.org/10.37514/PER-B.2024.2180

Land Acknowledgment. The Colorado State University Land Acknowledgment can be found at landacknowledgment.colostate.edu.

CONTENTS

Contents

PART 4. RECONSTRUCTING METHOD/OLOGICAL TENETS

ACKNOWLEDGMENTS

First, we would like to offer a huge thank you to all of our contributing authors: Stephanie, Will, Sarah, Crystal, Sonia, Jerry, Meagan, April, Stephanie, Bridget, and Aja. Thanks to each of you for responding to our call, for bravely sharing your messy research stories, and for challenging us and the field to embrace more diverse and capacious approaches to method/ologies in rhetoric and writing studies. We are grateful for your insights and honored to feature your compelling work in these pages.

We would also like to extend our thanks to the 75+ contacts for graduate programs listed on the Consortium of Doctoral Programs in Rhetoric and Composition (https://ccccdoctoralconsortium.org/), most of whom very kindly responded to our early inquiry about examples of methods texts that they assign in their graduate courses. These suggestions of sample articles and books helped advance our thinking about *Learning from the Mess* in its early stages, and we appreciate the replies and suggestions offered.

We are also indebted to the WAC Clearinghouse Perspectives on Writing series editors—Rich Rice, Heather MacNeill Falconer, and J. Michael Rifenburg—who reviewed an earlier version of the book proposal, offered extremely valuable suggestions for reframing, and later supported our revised proposal. Your support, guidance, and professionalism throughout this process have been fantastic, and we are thrilled that *Learning from the Mess* found a home in the Perspectives on Writing series. Thank you also to our two anonymous external reviewers, whose review feedback meaningfully contributed to our revisions in the final preparations for this collection. Many thanks also to Mike Palmquist and the WAC Clearinghouse for your support in the production and publication processes.

Finally, we would like to thank our families and friends who have supported us during our work on this project. We thank Rebecca Richards, a friend and colleague, who reviewed and gave feedback on an earlier version of this book's proposal. Ashley would like to thank Dan, Walter, and Graham, as well as acknowledge the support of two internal grants from Georgia State University that provided release time from teaching to finish the work on *Learning from the Mess*: the Provost's Faculty Fellowship and a College of Arts and Sciences Research Intensive Semester (RISe). Elise would like to thank Jeremy and their two pups, Pearl and Violet, in addition to her colleagues Angela Haas, Julie Jung, and Derek Sparby, who graciously offered their thoughts in the project's early stages.

LEARNING FROM THE MESS: METHOD/OLOGICAL PRAXIS IN RHETORIC AND WRITING STUDIES

INTRODUCTION.

BEYOND PLURALISM IN RESEARCH METHODS AND METHODOLOGY

Ashley J. Holmes
Georgia State University

Elise Verzosa Hurley
Illinois State University

In the last five years, the contexts in which we do the work of rhetoric and writing studies have changed drastically, including how and where we teach, write, and conduct research. We've seen a volatile political climate where facts are constantly called into question, lived and worked while a pandemic raged across the globe illustrating ever-deepening inequalities, and witnessed relentless state violence against Black bodies and attacks on other people of color. To do research, today, means to grapple with the complexities of everything going on around us—news headlines and sound bytes about what can and can't be taught in educational contexts, legislation meant to exclude and harm the most vulnerable populations, and safety in public spaces. To do ethical and humane research today also means prioritizing issues of equity, justice, and accountability, and reflecting on how research affects us as scholars and, perhaps more importantly, as human beings. Numerous calls from leadership in the field have illustrated the necessity to disrupt the status quo and take action against outdated, long-held beliefs and exclusionary standards that are institutionalized, in multiple ways, in the very pillars that constitute our discipline, pillars that shape our practices and, thus, how we come to knowledge (Inoue, "Framework" and "Why"; Baker-Bell et al.). This collection takes up this call by revising, resisting, rethinking, and reconstructing the method/ologies that both ground and guide research in a field as capacious as ours. If the last few years have taught us anything, it's that our lives and the challenges we face aren't bound within neat and tidy categories; and neither is our research.

The research process—from formulating research questions, operating within a methodological framework, designing a study, deliberating on appropriate methods, conducting the research, analyzing the results, and writing up the

DOI: https://doi.org/10.37514/PER-B.2024.2241.1.3

findings—is complex, relational, distributed, circuitous, and very often messy (Dadas; Rickly and Cargile-Cook; Banks, Cox, and Dadas). And yet, our first encounters with research in rhetoric and writing studies, often through graduate courses on research methods or undergraduate research experiences, are assigned readings of polished, published works in well-regarded journals and collections which often make it *seem* that *writing about* the research process is fairly straightforward and linear. As Rickly and Cargile-Cook ask: "When we look at virtually any published research, something is missing: Where's the mess?" (119). If the research process is messy and makes use of overlapping method/ologies, how do researchers create a sense of coherence when writing and publishing about research methods and methodologies? And, when coherence isn't possible or desirable, how can researchers show the value of messy method/ological frameworks, advocate for disruption to tradition, and convince stakeholders in our discipline that alternate ways of knowing and doing research in rhetoric and writing studies are valid and, in fact, often necessary?

We argue that there is, indeed, a lot to be learned from the messiness of research contexts and we believe that it's valuable to revisit and reflect on research method/ologies, to shed light on the processes commonly elided between research design and publication, and to make explicit that the method/ologies we use in our research require praxis. In this introduction, we situate the chapters featured in the collection as informed by a reexamining, critical questioning, and expanding of method/ologies in rhetoric and writing studies; this expansion has largely been spearheaded by conversations in cultural rhetorics, feminist rhetorics, queer rhetorics, and linguistic justice. We also highlight the ways contributors to this collection are already committed to and doing this work, demonstrating multiple pathways toward more equitable research practices. Among these chapters, we read about how researchers revisit their methods and findings over time and how they resist traditional approaches to method/ologies that curtail innovation and inclusion: in short, we get to read the often untold stories behind published research and track trajectories of method/ological change and progress in the field of rhetoric and writing studies.

THE CONCEPT FOR THIS COLLECTION

We come to this project bringing our experiences as advisors of graduate and undergraduate student research, as teachers of research methods, and as manuscript reviewers and editors considering the efficacy and merits of various method/ological approaches. Advising and teaching graduate students about research methods since 2012 and 2013, we have both witnessed students struggling to design method/ologically sound research projects. Moreover, even when there is a firm grasp of research design and coding, many novice researchers have a difficult time knowing how to write about their research method/ologies for their theses and dissertations, as well as for peer-reviewed publications. In a discussion about how positively graduate students responded to "model methods" readings Ashley assigned in a graduate seminar, we began forming the ideas for this edited collection. While exploring scholarly models and exemplars is a common strategy in graduate programs, method/ology sections in dissertations are vastly different from those in published articles and essays, primarily because their inclusion in a dissertation functions "as a sort of proof and a performance" as well as a "reflection" of a graduate student's first major research project (Pantelides 198–99). Extended sections on method/ology are rare in journal articles and edited collection chapters—often reduced to a brief paragraph, a few footnotes, or edited out entirely, further contributing to the seeming "tidiness" of an often-messy process of research.

Both novice and experienced researchers have likely experienced the challenges with research method/ologies, perhaps feeling lost, overwhelmed, or boxed-in; yet, in rhetoric and writing studies, there are too few examples of what to do with the method/ological mess to help researchers navigate resisting, rethinking, and revising our methods. We also acknowledge that the naming and labeling of "sound" method/ologies is very much indicative of values and existing power structures that legitimate what "counts" as research or as knowledge more broadly within any given discipline. Thus, in compiling this collection, we sought to explicitly include chapters that not only acknowledge the ways in which research method/ologies are messy, but also pieces that explore the ways in which method/ologies can change over time, push against traditional method/ological approaches and definition, reflect on method/ological dispositions, and chart avenues for building new method/ological tenets. In so doing, then, this collection is informed by our own method/ological commitments to making our discipline more inclusive by highlighting the diversity of research method/ology scholars use; examining research sites that are often overlooked or undervalued; and challenging the traditional frames that guide the subjects and sites of inquiry that more established and traditional method/ologies have served.

Our early discussions about this edited collection focused on supporting graduate student and early-career researchers—a commitment we continue to hold at the center of this work. To get a sense of the current state of affairs, we went to the source of where we and others first learned about research methods: graduate programs. We began by informally surveying via email the main points of contact for each of the 75+ programs listed as members of The Consortium of Doctoral Programs in Rhetoric and Composition (https://ccccdoctoralconsortium. org/). We asked for recommendations of journal articles or book chapters, and we received overwhelming responses and suggestions from the very teacher-scholars who often teach graduate courses in research method/ology, including the kinds of pieces that they liked to assign as well as what they would like to see more of. As we pored over their suggestions, we realized that while our field has several excellent handbooks that walk novices through the research process along with copious published research that deploys a particular methodological approach, there were fewer resources that explicitly addressed the messiness and the hard intellectual labor of grappling with the complexity of method/ologies. In other words, what novice researchers were likely to encounter in a graduate course was a straightforward "how to" primer on beginning a research project, and tidy, polished pieces that may (or may not) have a brief paragraph about method/ology before moving on to the results and analysis of any given study. To echo Rickley and Cargile-Cook once more: "Where's the mess?" (19). Each of the chapters makes the mess visible through questioning, disruption, and/or innovation in method/ologies.

Central to this collection is the relationship between the featured chapter and paired readings. Each author's chapter responds to or builds from at least one of their recently published articles, chapters, and/or books. The chapters in *Learning from the Mess* extend the research stories that began in these earlier publications, and reading them alongside one another highlights the powerful research interventions by these contributing authors. Their work embraces the unwieldy and the capacious, moving beyond mere pluralism in research method/ologies. .

BEYOND PLURALISM IN RESEARCH METHODOLOGIES AND METHODS

The terms "methodology" and "method" have traditionally been defined as the frame through which research is guided (methodology) and the tools used to collect data (method) (Harding 2–3). The actual practices these two terms connote are not fixed and, as collections on method/ology in rhetoric and writing studies emphasize, are constantly being adapted to be applicable to a wide range of contexts and new ways of dissemination. In their 1992 collection *Methods and Methodology in Composition Research*, Gesa Kirsch and Patricia A. Sullivan embrace "methodological pluralism" and take a "self-questioning" stance (2). The structure of Sullivan and Kirsch's collection from thirty years ago already suggests a tension between traditional and innovative approaches—between what we see as a kind of tidiness and messiness—as they organize Part I to highlight method/ologies "gaining prominence" at the time and Part II to identify "research problems and issues" (Kirsch and Sullivan 5). In our approach to this collection, we found guidance and support from the arguments made by contributors to Kirsch and Sullivan's *Methods and Methodology*. For example,

Kirsch's chapter-length contribution argues that critical self-awareness is central to methodological pluralism because it reveals that "all methodologies are culturally situated and inscribed, never disinterested or impartial" (248). New approaches to research in any field of study will understandably result in disruption and dissonance as they call into question how we know what we know and whether our method/ologies are valid, just, and ethical. As Kirsch reminds us, these new approaches may not "produce a coherent or unified body of knowledge but, instead, may reveal contradictions, fissures, and gaps in our current knowledge of composition" (248). The challenge we take up in this collection is to embrace these fissures by exploring research studies that push the boundaries of knowledge production through methodological pluralism and innovative methods in ways that acknowledge this work as "a continuously changing enterprise" (Kirsch 248).

The value of methodological pluralism in the field of rhetoric and writing studies has made space for alternative research approaches and an expansion of the sites for research over time. Writing twenty years later in her preface to *Writing Studies Research in Practice*, Kirsch celebrated the broader contexts in which we study rhetorical activities and literate practice, naming ". . . after-school settings; . . . service learning and community organizations; . . .social networking sites; historical contexts; . . . among groups often considered to reside at the margins of society; . . . [and in] international and transnational contexts" (xi). These new contexts, she asserts, "challenge researchers to adapt and refine research methods and to develop new ones (Kirsch xi). Making similar claims about the evolution of research design and methodological pluralism, Janice Lauer, in a 2014 interview, revisits her work "A Dappled Discipline" after 30 years to argue that the discipline has retained traditional modes of inquiry (e.g., theory, history, and empirical research) but that "these modes have expanded their types of investigation, theoretical assumptions, scholars, epistemic courts, and hence their bodies of knowledge" (Vealey and Rivers 170).

While methodological pluralism has laid an important foundation for researchers in the field to be more expansive in their approach to method/ology, we believe it's important at this time that the field move beyond only pluralism. Pluralism, like common tropes around diversity, can easily slide into an equalizing or neutralizing force that is co-opted by institutions to maintain the status quo under a new, more politically correct name. We invite readers of this collection to critically question why our field has traditionally valued some method/ologies while casting others aside; we challenge researchers not only to acknowledge difference in method and methodological frameworks but also to actively listen to and reflect on method/ological commitments while also seeking approaches that are more equitable, ethical, and just.

RETHINKING METHODOLOGIES AND METHODS

Moving beyond methodological pluralism requires that we rethink our relationship to knowledge work and research practice; after all, method/ologies are never neutral, a point especially illuminated by recent conversations in cultural rhetorics. Seeking to challenge and decolonize the dominant paradigm of Western approaches to knowledge-making—including how knowledge comes to be via research—cultural rhetorics scholars explicitly question why certain method/ologies and methods are used in the first place, insisting that we must move "beyond simply applying frames from one culture/tradition to another culture's rhetorical practices" (Bratta and Powell). Key to a cultural rhetorics "orientation to a set of constellating theoretical and methodological frameworks" (Cultural Rhetorics Theory Lab 2) is relationality and the ways in which cultural communities, beliefs, and practices—including knowledge-making practices—are enmeshed in a specific community's own intellectual traditions and histories, rather than relegating them as a response to and resulting from Western thought as *the* origin of intellectual production. As Riley Mukavetz explains, "To do cultural rhetorics work is to value the efforts and practices used to make and sustain something and use that understanding to build a theoretical and methodological framework that reflects the cultural community a researcher works with" (110). In addition to an emphasis on reciprocity and responsibility in research, cultural rhetorics method/ologies also find value in weaving together seemingly disparate and messy lines of inquiry, explicitly recognizing that meaning-making comes from a "compendium of theories, ideas, experiences, tangible tools, and intangible epistemologies" (Medina-Lopez). "Data" then, can come from storytelling, from embodied and emplaced interactions with research sites and participants, and from multiple literate acts beyond the textual (Powell et al.). Perhaps more important when thinking about our field's method/ologies, however, is that a cultural rhetorics orientation to research is explicitly interventionary and makes visible the "web of relations" within which our locations, institutions, and research practices are complicit in colonialism (Powell et al.). Among the hard questions cultural rhetorics scholars ask us to consider are: Why is a particular method/ology being used? What other possibilities exist for method/ologies to be more relational and reciprocal? And who does the research serve?

The need to intervene and disrupt traditional research practices in rhetoric and writing studies has also been echoed by others in the field, evidenced by the publication of edited collections focused squarely on research methods and methodologies. William P. Banks, Matthew B. Cox, and Caroline Dadas' 2019 collection *Re/Orienting Writing Studies: Queer Methods, Queer Projects* calls on us to examine the heteronormative orientations that undergird our research. Moreover, the essays in the collection purposefully make messy the seemingly clean lines between method/ologies, calling on us to recognize the value of "queer rhetorics and queer method/ologies . . . in rethink[ing] the work of traditional data-collection methods and frames of inquiry" (6). Noting that anything labeled *queer* begins its work in a complicated, in fact quite 'messy' place (6), the contributors explore the value of complicating overly tidy methodological frameworks and methods—that in fact, research practices *shouldn't* be forced into tidy categories because doing so more often than not hampers inclusivity, and may actually perpetuate oppression, thus limiting what's possible for knowledge-making.

Other recent publications on method and methodology not only call for more inclusive and diverse frames to guide our research, but also ask us to examine the ethical imperatives that undergird *why* we do research, as the 2021 edited collection *Race, Rhetoric, and Research Methods* argues. Calling attention to the ways in which racism is embedded in our discipline's research practices, Alexandria L. Lockett, Iris Ruiz, James Chase Sanchez, and Christopher Carter emphasize that texts commonly encountered during graduate study present a dominant narrative (read: white) without "sufficient attention to structural racism. Consequently, students and faculty lack models for designing research about this very problem" (19). By foregrounding how race and racism impact the work of teaching and learning in our field, the authors deploy antiracism as methodology and illustrate how methods such as critical historiography, autoethnography, visual rhetorical analysis, and critical technocultural analysis can innovate and actively disrupt existing research practices in service of justice (22). As this brief review of recent conversations in our discipline demonstrates, reexamining the methodologies that drive our research as well as the methods we use can be a starting point to reimagining new and more just research practices.

To that end, this collection features ten chapters that challenge readers to rethink and reflect upon their own method/ological choices in the past and to envision new possibilities for their future research designs. We have clustered these chapters around the following themes: (1) Revising Method/ologies over Time, (2) Resisting Method/ological Definitions and Norms, (3) Rethinking Method/ological Dispositions, and (4) (Re)Constructing Method/ological Tenets. As noted previously, we have asked each contributor to connect their reflections about method/ologies to a specific or series of paired reading(s) previously published by the chapter author. We invite readers to consult the referenced paired readings, placing them in conversation with the chapters in this collection; we see this as a valuable opportunity to document a researcher's journey over time and how contributors to this collection arrived at the necessity to revise, resist, rethink, and/or (re)construct their method/ologies. While we have grouped chapters around key themes in research method/ologies, we encourage readers to jump around and explore various chapters of interest in any order, dipping into topics here and there to follow their curiosities. Knowing also that readers of this collection will be at different stages as researchers and in varying professional positions and trajectories, we want to acknowledge the risks and challenges, as well as the opportunities and rewards, of employing non-traditional method/ologies. We hope that the chapters herein provide space for reflective praxis, as they have for us as researchers, and inspiration for seeking more just and equitable approaches to research and writing method/ologies.

REVISING METHOD/OLOGIES OVER TIME

The collection begins with a series of chapters that highlight researchers reflecting on how they changed, revised, or reconsidered their method/ologies over time. In the opening chapter "Toward a Queer Validity: Delighting in the Messy Methods of Writing Research," Stephanie West-Pucket and William P. Banks narrate their journey toward building a method/ology "to help us orient the messiness of story and create research trajectories that bumble and blunder around through the chaos." West-Pucket and Banks articulate the necessity of representing the complexity of research participants' experiences and stories and how, to do that well, researchers may need to critically question and break out of traditional method/ological models. Their chapter also compellingly speaks to the hurdles graduate student researchers may face when implementing non-traditional methods, as well as the difficulties graduate faculty face in growing beyond the possibly limiting traditional methodologies learned in graduate school. Their chapter forwards queer phenomenology as a valuable approach to research methods that welcomes movement, change, and repositioning over time—a queering of "preplanned research trajectories" that prompts researchers to "speed up, to slow down, and to change course in ways that allow alternative stories, patterns, practices, and experiences to emerge."

Sarah Riddick similarly finds value in revisiting method/ologies in her chapter "Deliberative Drifting Over Time: A Critical Reflection on Designing Social Media Methods for Longevity." This chapter is a direct response to and extension of Riddick's 2019 *Computers and Composition* article that theorized deliberative drifting as a method. Riddick describes how deliberative drifting developed, but she uses this chapter as an opportunity to more fully explore themes of "engagement, positionality, and feasibility" that she has been reflecting on and wrestling with since she conducted her initial research. Riddick models and demonstrates the critical questioning all researchers should be doing of their own scholarship and others', concluding by helpfully providing a list of questions for future users of deliberative drifting and related social-media methods to consider.

Another approach to revising method/ologies over time may involve revisiting previously collected data and examining it from a new theoretical perspective or methodological lens. Crystal VanKooten does precisely this in her chapter contribution "Voicing Transfer: Examining Race, Identity, and Student Learning through Video." VanKooten's chapter recounts how her decision to "ignore race in writing research" and within her own prior research resulted in a "'color blind' stance" that has consequences. VanKooten revisits data she collected for a prior study and publications to more explicitly foreground issues of race in the analysis; her work in this chapter focuses on the students of color in the study, reflecting on the loss of their representation and voices in the original analysis. VanKooten questions the series of choices that originally led her to dismiss questions of race and identity, and she ultimately argues for the significance of revisiting prior research, as she does here, in order to "disrupt comfortable whiteness."

RESISTING METHOD/OLOGICAL DEFINITIONS AND NORMS

Diverse sites of research and diverse perspectives often require that we adopt new or revise existing method/ological approaches, including *how* that research is composed and delivered. This section opens with Sonia Arellano's "Revising Textile Publications: Challenges and Considerations in Tactile Methods," where she explores "the relationship between the research method we employ and our revision processes" (2), particularly in relation to a new, tactile mode of research: Quilting as Method (QAM). Synthesizing two previous publications wherein Arellano lays out the potentials of QAM prior to composing a tactile research argument via a quilt, Arellano describes the challenges of doing research that not only uses a new method but also takes shape in a new mode. She asks us to resist the commonplaces that typically undergird written revision processes, including the typical norms for what academic publications look like and do, as well as the institutional standards by which such intellectual work is judged.

Innovative methods and approaches, however exciting they may be, also run the risk of establishing new norms and new inequalities, as Jerry Lee's "Messy Language, Messy Methods: Beyond a Translingual 'Norm,'" reminds us. Responding to calls concerning the translingual turn in composition studies, Lee cautiously resists the invocation of "a linguistic 'norm,' ... even if the norms were established through well-intended action, the very question of who gets to decide on the norm is a power-laden process which in turn exacerbates all kinds of social and educational inequalities" (6). Instead, Lee argues for a method/ological disposition that embraces the messiness of language research. After all, language use is always fluid, thus language use researchers should remain open to the dynamic and unexpected uses of language without immediately codifying a set of standards or norms.

The chapters in this section open up provocative questions about the norms and definitions that underlie our research, ultimately arguing that all researchers ought to think deeply about why certain standards have been set, by whom, and for whom, as well as where there are spaces of resistance so that we can work toward more accountability and justice in our research designs and practices.

RETHINKING METHOD/OLOGICAL DISPOSITIONS

Drawing from one of our contributors Meagan Malone, we clustered the set of chapters in this section around the concept of rethinking "method/ological dispositions"—the styles of thinking about and doing research that we develop based on our past experiences, our field of study, and adjacent disciplines. Malone's chapter "Embracing the Potentials and Navigating the Pitfalls of Inter-disciplinary Method/ologies" reflects on some of the method/ological choices she made in her published analysis of Natalie Wynn's YouTube channel Con-trapoints. Malone narrates challenges she faced as a graduate student working with some method/ologies in rhetorical studies that were ultimately limiting her research and analysis. Like other contributors to this edited collection (e.g., Martinez; Abraham), Malone draws inspiration from her prior experiences in a different field of study. Malone argues for the necessity of continuously examin-ing our method/ological assumptions throughout our research processes.

Continuing to identify differences in doctoral and post-graduate research experiences, April O'Brien's "Shifting Method/ologies: My Journey with Coun-termapping" narrates her experiences with moving toward countermapping as a method. O'Brien tells the story of how her research method/ologies evolved over time, describing specific "aha," or what she calls "punctum," moments. O'Brien's chapter reflects on how she had to face "hard truths about the injustices in [her] own anti-racist work," and her choice to move toward countermapping. O'Brien argues for the valuable lesson she learned from her experience: the necessity of embracing (even when difficult) a shift in method/ologies.

In the final chapter in this section, Stephanie Abraham describes her journey of "becoming, and sometimes unbecoming a qualitative researcher." In "Doing, and Undoing, Qualitative Research: A Story of Theory, Method, and Failure," Abraham reflects on her experiences as an elementary educator, on her work with multilingual and Latinx students, and her prior research and publications related to translanguaging and literacy practices. Drawing on her own experiences as a researcher, Abraham calls for more research that "undos and unbecomes" and that ends with "more questions than answers" as a way of documenting and attending to the messiness of research method/ologies.

RECONSTRUCTING METHOD/OLOGICAL TENETS

Just as revisiting our method/ological dispositions can help us see why we use the method/ological approaches that we do, they can also help us reconstruct new method/ological tenets that reflect our personal, intellectual, and embodied commitments as researchers. The latter is particularly important when there's a seeming dearth of resources to turn to. For example, while prioritizing research participant safety is a common tenet of research with human subjects, what method/ologies are in place to ensure researcher safety? Bridget Gelms grapples with this very question in the opening chapter of this section, "Risky Projects & Researcher Well-Being: Locating New Methodological Traditions in Rhetoric & Writing Studies." As a digital rhetoric scholar who studies online harassment, Gelms narrates and reflects on "the hidden costs [researchers] face when pursu[ing] the sort of high stakes, risky, and emotionally challenging topics that can inspire upset or damage to the researcher." Writing in conversation with a previously published piece, Gelms points to the ways in which researchers can become entangled with explicit threats to their well-being and safety along with second-hand trauma—issues that are complicated by "methodological traditions that privilege rigidity and present objectivity as a gold standard." Thus, she argues for the value of methodologically locating the researcher within a project, foregrounding researcher well-being—physically, intellectually, and emotionally—as a means of leveraging the complications that can arise from risky research projects.

The final chapter in the collection, "What We Thought We Knew: Snapshots Along the Development of a Cultural Rhetorics Methodological Philosophy," also demonstrates how method/ological tenets that guide our research are constructed over time and in different contexts. Here, Aja Martinez weaves together seemingly disparate method/ological dispositions cultivated over timespans of learning across disciplines and different settings—personal, familial, educational—to illustrate *how* method/ological philosophies are interdependent, connected, and can be built to guide research questions that explicitly foreground the stories of multiply minoritized and marginalized peoples. Martinez locates how her values as a researcher came to be, laying down the groundwork for the method/ological philosophy informed by cultural rhetorics from which all her work is built upon. Pedagogically, Martinez also calls on rhetoric and writing studies teachers to reconsider how we read and teach rhetorical texts—that we should do so not simply as rhetorical artifacts but as rhetorical methods—even when the method/ologies are not explicit. Doing so can open up new ways of looking and understanding what method/ologies do and the values they espouse.

EMBRACING THE MESS: CRITICALLY REVISITING METHODS AND METHODOLOGIES

This critical moment, we believe, is especially ripe for embracing the interventionary work that messy, and sometimes disruptive, method/ologies can do for rhetoric and writing studies. The chapters in *Learning from the Mess* collectively represent what we believe to be an incredible research intervention. While each author takes a different approach to these method/ological disruptions, the chapters demonstrate and enact what it takes for a field to critically question how it produces knowledge and to begin making changes. In contrast to scholars who want to discipline the field and mark off its boundaries and approaches, *Learning from the Mess* offers an alternate, revolutionary trajectory that embraces the field's capaciousness.

We see this collection as a starting point to embracing our field's shifting values in order to have a ready-set of method/ological readings from which graduate students and novice researchers, going forward, can draw upon in thinking expansively about just research designs. While some of our contributors call for new method/ological approaches, we see as equally important the calls for revising and rethinking our prior research, questioning our choices, and providing space—as we hope this collection does—for reflective praxis on our method/ologies, perhaps most especially when reflective distance and evolution over time demands that we pursue more just, nuanced, or critical positions as researchers. We hope that the stories researchers have bravely shared here will encourage other researchers and publication venues to make space for the mess, to embrace the untidy findings and processes, and to see those as valuable (indeed, publishable) lessons for other researchers and for the field of rhetoric and writing studies.

WORKS CITED

Baker-Bell, April, Bonnie J. Williams-Farrier, Davena Jackson, Lamar Johnson, Carmen Kynard, and Teaira McMurtry. "This Ain't Another Statement! This is a DEMAND for Black Linguistic Justice!" CCCC Position Statement, July 2020, https://cccc.ncte.org/cccc/demand-for-black-linguistic-justice/.

Banks, William P., Matthew B. Cox, and Caroline Dadas, editors. *Re/Orienting Writing Studies: Queer Methods, Queer Projects*. Utah State UP, 2019.

Bratta, Phil and Malea Powell. "Introduction to the Special Issue: Entering the

Cultural Rhetorics Conversations." *enculturation: a journal of rhetoric, writing, and culture*, vol. 21, no. 1, 2016, http://enculturation.net/entering-the-cultural-rhetorics-conversations.

Cultural Rhetorics Theory Lab. "What is Cultural Rhetorics?" 2012, Brochure.

Dadas, Caroline. "Messy Methods: Queer Methodological Approaches to Researching Social Media." *Computers & Composition*, vol. 40, 2016, pp. 60–72.

Harding, Sandra. "Introduction: Is There a Feminist Method?" *Feminism and Methodology*, edited by Sandra Harding, Indiana UP, 1988, pp. 1–14.

Inoue, Asao B. "2019 CCCC Chair's Address: How Do We Language So People Stop Killing Each Other, or What Do We Do About White Language Supremacy?" *College Composition and Communication*, vol. 71, no. 2, 2019, pp. 352–69.

———. "Why I Left the CWPA (Council of Writing Program Administrators)." *Asao B. Inoue's Infrequent Words*, 18 Apr. 2021, http://asaobinoue.blogspot.com/2021/04/why-i-left-cwpa-council-of-writing.html.

Kirsch, Gesa. "Foreword: New Methodological Challenges for Writing Studies Researchers." *Writing Studies Research in Practice: Methods and Methodologies,* edited by Lee Nickoson and Mary P. Sheridan, Southern Illinois UP, 2012, pp. xi–xvi.

———. "Methodological Pluralism: Epistemological Issues." *Methods and Methodology in Composition Research*, edited by Gesa Kirsch and Patricia Sullivan, Southern Illinois UP, 1992, pp. 247–69.

Kirsch, Gesa, and Patricia Sullivan, editors. *Methods and Methodology in Composition Research*. SIUP, 1992.

Lockett, Alexandria L., Iris Ruiz, James Chase Sanchez, and Christopher Carter. *Race, Rhetoric, and Research Methods*. WAC Clearinghouse/UP of Colorado, 2021. https://doi.org/10.37514/PER-B.2021.1206.

Medina-Lopez, Kelly. "Rasquache Rhetorics: A Cultural Rhetorics Sensibility." *Constellations: A Cultural Rhetorics Publishing Space*, vol. 1, no. 1, 2018, https://constell8cr.com/issue-1/rasquache-rhetorics-a-cultural-rhetorics-sensibility/.

Nickoson, Lee, and Mary P. Sheridan, editors. *Writing Studies Research in Practice: Methods and Methodologies*. Southern Illinois UP, 2012.

Pantelides, Kate L. "Graduate Students 'Show Their Work': Metalanguage in Dissertation Methodology Sections." *Journal of Technical Writing and Communication*, vol. 47, no. 2, 2017, pp.194–214.

Powell, Malea et al. "Our Story Begins Here: Constellating Cultural Rhetorics." *enculturation: a journal of rhetoric, writing, and culture*, vol. 18, no. 1, 2014, http://www.enculturation.net/our-story-begins-here. .

Rickly, Rebecca, and Kelly Cargile-Cook. "Failing Forward: Training Graduate Students for Research—An Introduction to the Special Issue." *Journal of Technical Writing and Communication*, vol. 47, no. 2, 2017, pp. 119–29.

Riley Mukavetz, Andrea M. "Toward a Cultural Rhetorics Methodology: Making Research Matter with Multi-Generational Women from the Little Traverse Bay Band." *Rhetoric, Professional Communication, and Globalization*, vol. 5, no. 1, 2014, pp. 108–25.

Vealey, Kyle, and Nathaniel Rivers. "Dappled Discipline at Thirty: An Interview with Janice M. Lauer." *Rhetoric Review*, vol. 33, no. 2, 2014, pp. 165–80.

PART 1.
REVISING METHOD/OLOGIES OVER TIME

CHAPTER 1.

TOWARD A QUEER VALIDITY: DELIGHTING IN THE MESSY METHODS OF WRITING RESEARCH

Stephanie J. West-Puckett
The University of Rhode Island

William P. Banks
East Carolina University

Paired readings:

- West-Puckett, Stephanie J., Nicole I. Caswell, and William P. Banks. *Failing Sideways: Queer Possibilities for Writing Assessment.* Utah State UP, 2023.

- West-Puckett, Stephanie J. 2017. *Materializing Makerspaces: Queerly Composing Space, Time, and (What) Matters.* (Doctoral Dissertation, East Carolina University).

In this chapter, we look back at research projects that challenged our pre-existing notions of research method/ologies and our assumptions about validity in research in order to demonstrate how we developed a Queer Validity Inquiry (QVI) paradigm that seeks to engage the "messiness" of qualitative and social research. In unpacking our queer methodological model, we "lean in" to the embodied complexities of writing research, particularly the excesses of bodies making meaning in the world and our attempts to understand those practices. In this process, we seek to capture the stories that contradict, that don't cohere, that defy interpretation. Ours is a story of messiness and chaos, of trying to figure out a meaningful or meaning-making research method/ology that would honor the writing practices of participants and still make some sort of sense to those reading about our studies. As an approach to thinking about how to validate our messy research practices, we believe our QVI model foregrounds relationships,

DOI: https://doi.org/10.37514/PER-B.2024.2241.2.01

connectivity, and the affective flows that make up constellated mean-
ing-making networks, and in doing so, points to ways that writing
studies researchers can enact more critically aware methodological
pluralisms.

In writing studies, as in much contemporary social science research, "messiness" has become a commonplace. Experienced researchers recognize that our work grows out of complex contexts of meaning making and that trying to organize and order that chaos is difficult. We talk with graduate student researchers about those complexities, and we try to help them manage their endless pages of data and field notes into something that their dissertation committees (and the field at large) will recognize as "research." As such, we believe that writing studies has somewhat come to terms with the idea that research is fundamentally a storytelling project, a set of practices for mediating lived experiences, contexts, actions, and materials in such a way that we create meaning out of the people, objects, and spaces we study. In fact, quite regardless of method/ology, writing studies researchers know that narrative/story is inescapable, not a "limitation" to be explained or justified, necessarily, but a central element of our knowledge making practices. Whether we are exploring how people compose/communicate their stories or we are framing the data we collect (e.g., statistics, case studies, interviews, and ethnographic data sets), we are ultimately creating a story of our research. Meaning-making is fundamentally world-building, and worlds require narrative structures for coherence (Holland et al.). How reflectively and critically we do that work, however, has been an issue that our field continues to struggle with.

Early on, this lack of critical self- and methodological awareness was something Gesa Kirsch expressed concern about when she wrote "Methodological Pluralism: Epistemological Issues." Rather than engage in pluralistic methods just to collect more data, Kirsch argued that researchers must engage with the epistemological distinctions among the methods and methodologies they choose: "Such a critical self-awareness reveals that all methodologies are culturally situated and inscribed, never disinterested or impartial. I suggest that methodological pluralism demands a rethinking of all methodologies and new ways of conducting and interpreting research" (248). Of course, Kirsch was also quick to note that pluralism alone will not "fix" the chaos of research nor solve all of our thorny research problems, "but, instead, may reveal contradictions, fissures, and gaps in our current knowledge of composition" (248). "The strength of new approaches," continued Kirsch, "will lie in the ability to invite new questions, to encourage dialogue and inquiry, and to define knowledge making as a continuously changing enterprise" (248). Rather than clean up or streamline our work, pluralistic research practices have contributed significantly to the "messy methods" (Dadas) that researchers may tend to avoid in favor of the seemingly more ordered models that 20th century qualitative work provided. While our field was perhaps quick to welcome plural method/ologies, prevailing paradigms about what counts as knowledge, what are valid collection practices, and how we should make sense of our data have often caused us either to return to simpler systems or to run our new pluralistic models through more linear and traditional frameworks. These moves, we believe, run the risk of silencing dissenting voices, experiences, and stories in our data.

In our work together on teacher research projects as part of our local site of the National Writing Project and then through Stephanie's dissertation study (West-Puckett, "Materializing"), it has been this latter problem of methodological purity that we have often run up against. While we were advocating for "mess that matters" in our inquiry practices, we found editors, reviewers, and—where the dissertation was concerned—colleagues and graduate school leadership all pushing back in small but meaningful ways on what we could do. In every case, this pushback was intended to be helpful, to put meaningful boundaries around the project or to help us articulate results in a way that these various reader proxies assumed necessary for "the field." And, of course, they have probably been right in terms of how others might read and engage these different research projects. In this chapter, however, we want to return to a couple of those projects and unpack some of the ways we had conceived of the "messiness" of research from a queer methodological position. When we talk about mess in the research context, particularly writing studies research contexts, what exactly are we talking about? In part, it is the excess of bodies making meaning in the world and our attempts to understand those practices. It is the stories that contradict, that don't cohere, that defy interpretation. It is the affective currents that swirl and pull us along, the identities that shift and persist, the meaning-making materials (conceptual, digital, and physical) that get tangled and knotted together, that unravel, and rub on our fingers—and the failures of language or rhetoric or research to capture a totalizing "Truth" that unifies experience or our understanding of it. It's the shame and stigma we may feel when we realize that we often fail to honor the plenitude and complexity of our research participants' experiences and stories.

In this chapter, we do not attempt to clean up that mess. In other words, we are not going to help you sterilize, sanitize, or scrub your research paradigms, processes, or the stories that issue forth from them. Instead, over the last several years, we have worked to build a method/ology to help us orient toward the messiness of story and create research trajectories that bumble and blunder around through the chaos so that we might tell different kinds of stories. This method, which we first conceived of in response to the controlling logics of assessment, is called Queer Validity Inquiry (QVI). As a method of ongoing resistance to the normative and normalizing practices of methodological colonialism (Patel; Tuhiwai Smith; Bratta and Powell), Queer Validity Inquiry (QVI) is a methodology for dwelling in messy spaces, for holding and engaging with experiences—those that belong to us and those that don't—and a way of making meaning, stories, and knowledge laterally (West-Puckett, Caswell, and Banks). As an approach to thinking about validity beyond top-down notions of positivism and objectivism (Knoblauch), QVI foregrounds relationships, connectivity, and the affective flows that make up constelled meaning-making networks, and in doing so, points to ways that writing studies researchers can enact more critically aware methodological pluralisms.

UNBINDING THE DATA DEMONS: ON THE MESSINESS OF TEXTS, BODIES, AND MOTION

Metaphors for research are undoubtedly as varied as the number of researchers out there, each of us encountering the research site with a creative way to make sense of what we find. Some researchers "herd cats" while others "wait for spring" to see whether flowers, weeds, grass, or all three emerge from a small plot of earth they haven't themselves cultivated. Some "sift for gold" while others work "to separate the wheat from the chaff" among their data. One of the ways we (the authors) have jokingly talked about data has been as unruly imps and demons, each with its own particular interests and desires. Our data are not simply there to do what we want them to; they have their own goals. Reigning them in requires a binding spell, perhaps a pentagram on the floor to trap them and hold them still so we can decide which ones need vanquishing, which ones we might reform, which ones might be useful just as they are. Seeing the triangular points of the pentagram in our minds, it's no surprise that we then began to riff on the ways that certain methodologies have advocated for triangulation as a way to create meaningful or valid data. Those triangulations evince their own binding ritual on our data, keeping certain elements in and vanquishing others. But what happens if we eschew those binders, embrace the mess, and explore methodologies that "delight in disorder," that revel in the chaos itself?

Over many years of research in different contexts, we have found ourselves increasingly working toward and eventually through queer methodologies that embrace the messiness of writing research. Our thinking here is indebted to the ways that Caroline Dadas has taken up and expanded John Law's initial theme of "messiness" in social science methods and framed it as queer project. Central to Dadas' work is an understanding of the ways that "the term *queer* ... invoke[s] complication" in order to "trouble the production of knowledge" (63). Queer methodologies, she contends, "encourage us to reconsider and, when needed, disrupt previous research practices" (69). To demonstrate that movement in our thinking, we want to unpack what we mean by queer methodologies for writing research and explore briefly how some of our previous work helped us to become more comfortable with relaxing the grip that normative research paradigms were having on our processes. In sharing this trajectory of our work, however, we do not mean to suggest that other paradigms are not important or useful — there is much to be learned from more traditional models of inquiry; rather we believe that researchers in writing studies would benefit significantly from methodologies that "lean in" to complication and foreground the tentative nature of the knowledge we are often making about writing.

Similarly, in *Re/Orienting Writing Studies: Queer Methods, Queer Projects*, William P. Banks, Matthew B. Cox, and Caroline Dadas frame queer methodologies through the practice of orientation. Based on Sara Ahmed's phenomenological project of understanding orientation as a practice of turning both toward and away from certain bodies and objects—and how those orientations then establish the paths we walk, the ways we understand ourselves, and the ways that we engage both human and non-human matter(s) —Banks, Cox, and Dadas challenge traditional thinking about methods as practices that generate valid or reliable research by highlighting how *method-as-orientation* does intellectual work through its recognition that accepted (and acceptable) practices for data collection can never be value-neutral:

> Rather, each represents a way of orienting a researcher toward an object, a people, or a space. Where these practices—surveys, focus groups, observations, rhetorical analyses, and so forth—become commonplace, where they represent normative/unquestioned activities or epistemologies, they demonstrate not only the ways that each has become an active method for orienting a researcher (and thus also preventing other orientations, other views from taking the foreground) but also how each has become a normative orientation for the field, a well-trodden path whose existence actively replicates itself from researcher to researcher, from discipline to discipline. (4)

Likewise, in *After Method: Messiness in Social Science Research*, John Law has argued that "If 'research methods' are allowed to claim methodological hegemony or (even worse) monopoly . . . then when we are put into relation with such methods we are being placed, however rebelliously, in a set of constraining normative blinkers" (4). To disrupt those blinkers and the "reproductive futurism" (Edelman 2) that replicating existing models embraces, Banks, Cox, and Dadas argue that queer methodologies focus instead on rhetorics of intentionality (over outcome), failure (over success), and forgetting (over memory/memorialization). These are all rhetorics that resist closure and finitude and, as such, do little to help us bind or contain the messiness of our work. As we demonstrate below, such resistance is important if we want to move away from simply retelling the stock stories of our research.

In what follows, we center a story of Stephanie's dissertation research and how we—as doctoral student and dissertation advisor—worked inter/intra-actively to develop an analytical framework for understanding a fundamentally messy and complex scene of writing. This is a story of messiness and chaos, of trying to figure out a meaningful or meaning-making research method/ology that would honor the writing practices of participants and still make some sort of sense to those reading about the study. At the heart of this project was the desire to make sure that Stephanie's data collection and analysis practices did not enact violence on her participants or their materials by too quickly trying to push them through a pre-made methodological meat grinder. What emerges, we contend, is a new way of understanding methodological "messiness" that does not simply acknowledge the chaos of our work, but which provides a theoretical and practical justification for this work that has been missing from writing studies. To do that, we close this chapter with a brief look at how our current work on Queer Validity Inquiry (QVI) in writing assessment (in part) grew out of and was influenced by the methodological frustrations we felt trying to manage the messiness of Stephanie's dissertation project.

WHEN DATA FAILS TO CONVERGE

To some scholars in the field, both in- and outside of the Writing, Rhetoric, and Professional Communication program at East Carolina University, Stephanie's dissertation questions were, well, weird. Informed by Malea Powell's notion of constellating, as well as queer and feminist-inflected new materialisms (Payne; Chen; Stewart; Ahmed; Halberstam, Cvetkovich; Coole and Frost), Stephanie was interested in how composing networks emerge. For several years prior to and during her doctoral study, Stephanie and Will had served as co-principal investigators (Co-PIs) and project directors on several National Writing Project initiatives that brought together K–12 classroom teachers; informal educators working in museums, afterschool programs, libraries, and community centers; and youth learners. These initiatives were intended to build production-centered learning experiences to support and deepen student interest, develop mentoring relationships across educational contexts, and create opportunity ladders for students, especially those from minoritized backgrounds. With each new project, Stephanie had seen networks emerge that enabled the production of new texts, objects, relationships, and identities. She began calling these networks safety *nets* capable of doing the transformative *work* of composition writ large. What she wanted to better understand, however, was how disparate nodes or bodies (both human and non-human) came to be caught up in such net/works and developed the intra-active capacity to compose a complex array of rhetorics and materials. Thus, her primary research question was, "How do maker networks materialize, and what might we learn about composing from those networks?" and her sub-questions included, "Who and what gets to make? Who and what gets made? What drives composition (as process and product) in the network?" Weird, indeed, at a time when few had considered what making and makerspaces had to do with writing and how non-humans might have the agency to co-produce, write, and make.

Stephanie was, at the time, co-leading two particular NWP projects, a high-school makerspace development initiative (West-Puckett, "Remaking") and a science literary initiative that brought together spoken word poets, science museum educators, and K–12 teachers in a massive open online making and learning collaboration (West-Puckett, "Crash"). She chose to focus on these particular initiatives because they were sustainable projects meant to develop long-term learning relationships, and they were both built from principles and practices of Connected Learning (Ito et al.). In each network, Do-It-Yourself (DIY)/Do-It-Together (DIT) was a pervasive ethos, and making with physical, digital, and conceptual tools was a central practice of both knowing and being. Stephanie's relationship with participants was already figured as a co-participant and partner-in-the-making; thus, adopting a formal, institutional position and ready-made research methods was inconceivable. She was already concerned about the risks of adopting the mantle of "researcher" in these communities, which might create some awkwardness (which it did) or even cause harm to individual composers and/or the network itself (which it didn't). To reduce the potential for harm, Stephanie decided on a primary data collection method that would honor existing relationships, epistemologies, and ontologies by engaging participants in making, quite literally, both material and discursive meanings about their experiences in the networks. Thus, she asked research participants to craft origami fortune tellers, to label those fortune tellers with salient material elements—place, people, objects, and ratings of affective disorientation—of their experiences, and to engage in game play with the fortune tellers to create small stories of encounters grounded in the materiality of matter, including the body. This method took the same amount of time as a traditional focus group or set of interviews might, but the activity aligned methodologically with the playful, maker-based values inherent to the research site and allowed for many unexpected and unplanned stories to emerge.

As she developed her research design through coursework in seminars and the comprehensive examination process, Stephanie was reminded by faculty advisors that she should use methodological triangulation to uncover a more comprehensive understanding of participant experiences and attend to concerns of validity in the study. As a good Ph.D. candidate, or at least one who wanted to finish and be PhDone (which is its own kind of good), Stephanie heeded that advice and integrated two other data sets: transcripts of semi-structured interviews conducted by the National Writing Project program assessment team and social media posts produced by participants in each network. Because Stephanie wasn't involved in the NWP-sponsored interviews, and the participants knew the data would be anonymized, controlling logics held that the transcription data would have a higher degree of objectivity, or at least offer a differently subjective story to compare to the other data Stephanie was more immediately involved in collecting. Similarly, because the social media artifacts were posted as part of everyday participation in the grant-sponsored program, not in response to researcher prompting, those artifacts were framed as a more reliable data source. The advice Stephanie was given at this stage of the research design was meant to help her establish the credibility of her study as well as her credibility as researcher, but at the time it was also frustrating. It felt as though she were being told that validity could be delivered from above instead of crafted collaboratively from within the research network. Something about that movement felt wrong to her at the time, but a dissertation is almost unavoidably a gaslighting project: you're told you don't know something or understand something about a field or method or methodology you are, in fact, somewhat new to, so you assume these other folks are right, that you're just somehow missing something.

Once Stephanie and Will began to analyze the data, however, interesting differences among the data sets began to emerge. Even a cursory read showed a marked contrast between the kinds of experience-based narratives that were produced via semi-structured interviews (NWP) and the fortune-teller game play (Stephanie). While both data sets were laden with expressed emotion and its affective valences, the semi-structured interview data skewed toward positive affective valences while the fortune-teller data was rich with both positive and negative affective valences. On the whole, during their interviews with the NWP researchers, participants expressed more emotions related to feeling "good" such as admiration, aesthetic appreciation, amusement, excitement, and satisfaction while the origami fortune teller game produced narratives that spanned from excitement and exuberance to anxiety, awkwardness, and empathic pain. The stories that were produced in response to interviews were what critical race theorists might call stock stories, those that reproduce dominant narratives, which, in this case, are narratives of success (Martinez; Bell). The fortune teller data then revealed a host of counter-narratives that upended that monolith of success, an ideology that is firmly entrenched in educational settings. For example, spoken word poets participating in the science literacy programming shared stories with NWP program evaluators such as the following about positive experiences with teaching and collaborating via Google Hangouts: "We did a Google Hangout and the kids got online and they did their poems and they were really excited about it and that to me was the best part because I got to see how they felt about it and how excited they were and so I think that was the best part."

When narrativizing experience with Google Hangouts through the fortune-teller game, however, a more complex picture of material interactions and affective experience began to emerge:

> Me, being the youthful, seemingly tech savvy college student
> I knew I would be able to figure out Google Hangout fairly
> easily. While sitting there with my group I setup a Google
> hangout link to use during our make cycle. I thought it was
> that simple, just making a hangout and pressing play. Fast for-
> ward 3 months and the day of the hangout arrived. I walked
> out of class to my apartment to start the hangout, and when
> I attempted it failed. The wifi disconnected from my laptop
> so I made a hotspot with my phone to use the wifi. This
> idea failed also. Next I tried restarting my computer. After
> which the hangout failed again. I failed three times before
> calling any of my group mates. Luckily, they were geniuses.
> I called [teacher's name] and explained my problem starting
> the Google Hangout and [they] happily fixed it using [their]
> IT expert on hand at school. I was able to participate on my
> phone teaching the workshop in the palm of my hand. (West-
> Puckett, "Materializing" 110–111)

Through processes of qualitative coding, the differences that emerged created real problems for data set triangulation. If, under duress to adhere to conventional notions of validity, we were to focus only on the places where coding patterns converged around "happiness," other kinds of not-so-sunny feelings would fail to materialize and matter in the research. Yet we knew, from our lived experiences in the network, that these negatively perceived emotions did (and do) matter in answering questions of how things materialize. And of course, they matter significantly to research in writing and rhetoric, particularly if we want to ask questions about our work beyond "what works" or "what is successful" when we theorize and teach writing.

As important, we want to note that the playful method Stephanie created to collect these divergent stories also matters: the stock stories of success that Halberstam has critiqued in *The Queer Art of Failure* can become so powerful, so seductive in late capitalism, that we all struggle to understand our experiences outside of the success-failure binary. More traditional interviews and focus groups would most likely have yielded the very same success narratives that the NWP program assessment folks got from participants because those are the stories we're supposed to tell; those are the stories, in particular, that teachers need to tell publicly because they exist in a context where their jobs, professionalism, and competence are constantly questioned and devalued in public forums like school board meetings and media "hot takes" on the state of education. The teachers in the study were so accustomed to stock stories of success that they offered those up easily when researchers came along and asked them about their experiences, but the origami fortune tellers playfully disrupted that narrative arc when game play pushed the participants to connect people, places, objects, and affects that they might not have thought to connect otherwise. We have no sense that the participants didn't still tell "true" stories out of this game play, but the truths they shared came from different places, pursued different narrative arcs, and engaged with materialities that were less "ready-to-hand" (Ahmed 2). By being open to playful methods of data collection, Stephanie was able to archive a host of counter stories that themselves opened new and intriguing paths for inquiry. Our shared commitments to queer methodologies likewise allowed us spaces to analyze and engage with those counterstories without forcing them to straighten up or flatten out.

WHEN DATA WANTS TO WRINKLE AND RUMPLE

As such, another major conundrum we faced during the research process was how to work with qualitative coding schemes that were restricting our ability to trace the emotions across bodies in the network. To make sense of participant narratives, we worked through three levels of recursive practice: qualitative coding, reflecting through the co-production of coding memos, and creating visual representations of the coding schemes. First, we analyzed the interview transcripts and then moved on to the origami fortune teller sets, which included the fortune teller itself as an artifact, participant game logs, and the anecdotal experience narrative. We used open, axial, and selective coding processes to identify common themes, ideas, tools, technologies, objects, and texts that were shared on the fortune tellers themselves (Neff; Teston; Farkas and Haas). Then we used the same process to code the anecdotal experience narratives. We organized our codes into tables and boxed the data neatly into their respective cells. From this vantage point, we were able to determine salient material aspects of individual participants' experience and understand how those experiences made them feel. We were also able to determine how experiences differed for each research participant and track commonalities of shared experience. However, we weren't necessarily able to make meaning beyond those discrete boxes or to answer the looming research question, "How do maker networks materialize?" The two-dimensional *tables with labels* were holding the data hostage, flattening the four-dimensional narratives that wanted to wrinkle, rumple, and unflatten the method.

During one of our many conversations about the data, we stumbled upon the idea of making a three-dimensional data model that would allow us to trace connections (and disconnections) among networked nodes. This move, while wildly inefficient when compared to digital systems like Dedoose or spreadsheet charts of data, respected the context which was itself framed through making and craft literacies. "Making" a method, then, felt to us like we were embracing the same creative practices as the participants in the grant-funded study and in doing so, we were able to experience similar moves, resistances, frustrations, breakthroughs, etc. That deep connection between our messy method(s) and the experiences of the research participants ultimately inflected the meaning we made from the data set by allowing our analyses to be entangled with/in the network.

Serendipitously, Stephanie found, by a dumpster at ECU, a 4' x 3' framed painter's canvas, likely chucked by an art school student, and decided it could be the backdrop for a data analysis/installation project. Inspired by Nick Sousanis' work in *Unflattening*, Stephanie and Will worked to represent this data and our coding schemes for it three-dimensionally, erasing the boxes that can promote a notion of bodies in a research phenomenon as discrete, individual, and static. As Sousanis writes, "Every procedure is designed to ensure that proper results are achieved. This all takes place in boxes, within boxes . . . Not only space but time and experience, too, have been put in boxes. Divided up and neatly packaged into discrete units for efficient transmission" (9–10). To blur the boundaries between the boxes and erase the notion that nodes on the network are separate and unchanged by other nodes, we worked here to show the relationships among material bodies, people, places, tools, and practices. Using everyday crafting materials like foam board, yarn, safety pins, construction paper, and the makers' original origami fortune-tellers (including our own) we made three-dimensional representations of the two compositional networks.

Like the relationships and connections represented in this three-dimensional visualization, the visualizations-as-compositions emerged over time. The construction of each data board took approximately fifteen hours of collaborative labor shared between the two of us. Most of the time, Will knelt on the floor in his office where we made the board, tying loops of yarn around safety pins and slipping them over the bamboo skewers to which the origami fortune-tellers were fixed (see Figure 1.1). Stephanie sat at Will's desk reading and re-reading the coded data, directing him to string the yarn from this marker to that marker and telling him which yarns should be gathered up into an affective web, stapled together and banded with orange construction paper loops (see Figure 1.2).

Figure 1.1. Zoomed-in view of research objects pinned to a board and linked by affective labels. Image credit to the authors.

Figure 1.2. Will places research objects on the board and connects them with string.
Image credit to the authors.

This process of making an analytical tool has enabled us to make new kinds of knowledge about the ways that makers produce and are produced by the affective pulses and flows of their engagements with other material bodies. This kind of knowledge-making was unavailable in the flat space of the digital spreadsheet. Through both "flattening" (Delanda) and "unflattening" (Sousanis), we worked to enact a queer materialist "both/and" practice that has enabled us to identify and theorize patterns of emergence in academic adjacent composing spaces like the makerspace funded by our teacher development grant from the National Writing Project (see Figure 1.3).

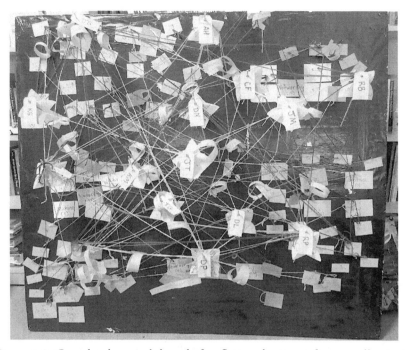

Figure 1.3. Completed research board of unflattened origami fortune teller stories. Image credit to the authors.

In the experience narratives, we found that emotions and affective currents were a driving force that materialized new nodes for both participants and researchers. In other words, as Sara Ahmed has pointed out, we noted how feelings are object-oriented, directed toward or away from others (human and non-human), and in these networks, these emotions created direction, movement, and connective threads that made a safety net to do the work of composing. In the end, queer theories of language and materiality helped us to walk away from the methodological expectations that we had started with. As such, we didn't attempt to "resolve" the conflicts between traditional positivist and post-positivst epistemologies and the more queer and new materialist epistemologies that framed our study; rather, we gave ourselves permission to keep those tensions there, to keep the lines taught between nodes, to become attuned to the music those strings offered us when plucked at in different ways rather that attend only to the objects themselves or to the nodes. Such a move recalls Dadas' point in her article on messy methods: "queerness as *techne* emphasizes process—the process of adapting previous approaches. When we attempt to use the same methods to address specific new research scenarios—because we have been taught that these are the "accepted" methods in our field—queer methodologies become degraded" (70).

DIVESTING IN TRADITIONAL NOTIONS OF VALIDITY

The experiences that we had as researcher and faculty mentor when working with Stephanie's dissertation project became a salient reminder of the ways that our work as researchers exists in spaces of tension between what has been valued and what might yet be valued. One way to think of this tension point is as *validity*. Whether we explicitly use the term or not, the specter of validity haunts our research designs, especially in cases where our theoretical grounding breaks with various intellectual traditions. Throughout most of the 20th century, validity was understood to exist in the research model itself (construct validity): does the research model or tool accurately or effectively measure what it claims to? As Yvonna Lincoln and Egon Guba have noted, researchers have often relied on concepts like internal and external validity to establish "trustworthiness" in their research (290). In this paradigm, internal validity focused on the ways that the instrument (test, method, study design) controlled for variations that might impact the findings, while external validity was concerned with creating sample sets that are generalizable across the broader range of possible participants in a study (Lincoln and Guba 290–91). In many ways, the languages and epistemologies that we learned in graduate school and have often repeated as graduate faculty grow out of these traditions and are difficult to silence when we want to imagine other possibilities.

More recently, however, some important critiques of validity have helped us to position our own emerging understandings, particularly those that have emerged in assessment scholarship, which has moved us away from frameworks built around correlation to ones centered on argumentation (Kane, "Validation"; Kane, "Explicating Validity"). As a normative practice, validation is "a process of constructing and evaluating arguments for and against the intended interpretation of test scores and their relevance to the proposed use" whereas validity "refers to the degree to which evidence and theory support the interpretations of test scores for proposed uses of tests" (AERA 11). In plain terms, validity is increasingly understood as an argument-making practice designed to justify truth-claims. Every time we generate a research question, construct a methodological framework, or outline methods that answer our question, we are building a logical argument for how we will arrive at answers and their meanings in a particular time and place. John W. Creswell and Dana L. Miller note that validity arguments must be able to address "how accurately the account represents participants' realities of the social phenomena and is credible to them" (124–25). These arguments, in their own way, build on the commonplace logics of the field, or borrow logics from adjacent fields, because doing so justifies the processes and products of our research. Validity arguments lay plain the claims, warrants, evidence, and counterclaims embedded in research design and allow others to decide for themselves if these are assembled in a way that is rhetorically sound and capable of producing trustworthy or credible results. In other words, validity inquiry is about justifying the use of particular instruments and processes in order to make meaning and take action in the world. Validation reassures us and our audiences that we are moving in the "right" (e.g., forward) direction. This linear directional pattern, however, comes to represent its own "truthiness": research, we believe, leads us from darkness to light, from unknowing to knowing, from ignorance to knowledge—and these trajectories become "right" directions when readers see our data collection methods as reasonable in the context of our theoretical/methodological paradigms.

As argument is traditionally thought of as a consensus-generating activity, familiar methods become familiar, in part, because they are used repeatedly. They become commonplace for researchers: the paths they lay out have actually already been laid out by previous researchers. Their validity comes to us as a set of sedimented practices, each deepening like the "coastal shelf" in Philip Larkin's poem "This Be the Verse." As such, familiar methods can become easier to argue for while less familiar or more contentious methods must stand up to greater scrutiny. In part, this is why Ellen Cushman has argued so persuasively against the colonialist imperative of traditional notions of validity: validity (and reliability), she has noted, "is used to claim, gather, and justify results with so many performance and survey tools, it has now more than ever been used to routinize inequities as naturalized parts of systems of educational access, predictions of success in school or on the job, psychological and intelligence measures, and as a foundation for knowledge creation in research studies" (n.p.). In this way, the onus of rhetorical persuasion falls disproportionately on those who stray from the well-worn paths of widely accepted methods. Those who choose queer paths that revel in messy research contexts and perhaps messier methods can experience a friction or drag as normative method/ologies work to restrict or restrain sideways knowledge-making movements.

Researchers looking for different ways to move with (rather than tidy up) the mess of methods, then, can benefit from queer approaches to framing validity. Queer approaches to validity are rooted in constructivism. Constructivist approaches to research position researchers as makers and crafters who must assemble their own representations of knowledge. Creswell and Miller note that constructivist research practices are "pluralistic, interpretive, open-ended, and contextualized (e.g., sensitive to place and situation) perspectives toward reality" (125–126). What "queer" brings to the constructivist sandbox or, to return to our magical metaphor, the conjuring circle, is permission to pick up the "wrong" wand or to use the right wand in the "wrong" ways. For example, in Stephanie's dissertation, we rejected sleek digital data models and instead crafted a way of knowing that was both monstrous and precarious. The board itself was a hideously beautiful sight (Figure 1.3), where one wrong move may lead to squished fortune tellers, unhinged safety pins, and unraveled yarn. Equally, there was no pre-made map/method that guaranteed us that the chaotic board would yield meaningful data. As researchers, we leaned into that contingency and risk, and those movements reoriented us to the data and the participants who generated it. Similarly, we argue (with our colleague Nicole Caswell) in *Failing Sideways: Queer Possibilities for Writing Assessment*, "Our interest in Queer Validity Inquiry (QVI), then, reflects a disinvestment in/disidentification with success and a willingness to follow the 'wrong' paths of validity inquiry, those that promise to disrupt" the more demure models of inquiry that permeate our practices (45). QVI unsettles normative notions of validity to introduce sideways paths and, we believe, offers a compass with an ever-shifting magnetic north wherein we navigate with intentionality that's rooted in continual reflection and re/consideration of the present rather than simply headed in one direction because of a predetermined outcomes we have established for a project. In thinking through disrupting normative logics of argument, whether they are related to assessment or research design (or the intersection of the two), we take our cue from Sara Ahmed's work on queer phenomenology and affectivity. Ahmed argues that bodies are shaped by their encounters with the material world and the paths they take to avoid or move closer to people, objects, and feelings. As bodies move, some objects recede from view, others come into view, and our movements put us in close proximity, close enough perhaps that we can grasp hold of them. Bodies that are attracted and repelled, confused, or confounded, become, through these serendipitous movements, queer bodies. The queer body no longer follows the normative and normativizing paths that have been laid out for it. Instead, it comes to delight in disorientation and dislocation, finding new spaces in which to dwell and new ways to occupy those spaces.

When we apply this idea of queer phenomenology to our research methods, we are prompted to dispense with the idea of the researcher as an *a priori* being operating out of a carefully constructed set of ideological and practical pathways, pathways that invariably lead to a precipice where knowing involves seeing from above, taking it all in, capturing a scene in its totality. Sure, aerial views might lead to different ways to see the research landscape, but those vantage points are no more trustworthy than any other. Similarly, we cannot think of concepts like positionality as static and unchanging. Movement necessitates quotidian repositioning and reorienting toward our methods, our processes, and our participants. We should also accept that researchers are, whether we acknowledge it or not, directed by our own desires and emotions, following interests and excitement, and perhaps avoiding or embracing risk, fear, and awkwardness. If we let them, these affective movements can queer preplanned research trajectories and prompt us to speed up, to slow down, and to change course in ways that allow alternative stories, patterns, practices, and experiences to emerge. This sort of move is about not settling for the stock stories and narrative archetypes we know, purposefully and intentionally resisting them through methods that resist traditional validity frameworks and their desire for "mastery" (Singh). We might spend more time collecting data, less time perseverating about fail-proof plans, and ultimately conjure different spells that unflatten and animate data in surprising ways.

WORKS CITED

AERA (American Educational Research Association), APA (American Psychological Association), NCME (National Council on Measurement in Education), and Joint Committee on Standards for Educational and Psychological Testing. *Standards for Educational and Psychological Testing*, American Educational Research Association, 2014.

Ahmed, Sara. *Queer Phenomenology: Orientations, Objects, Others*. Duke UP, 2006.

Banks, William P., Matthew B. Cox, and Caroline Dadas. *Re/Orienting Writing Studies: Queer Methods, Queer Projects*. Utah State UP, 2019.

Barad, Karen. *Meeting the Universe Halfway: Quantum Physics and the Entanglement of Matter and Meaning*, Duke UP, 2007.

Barnett, Scott, and Casey Boyle, eds. *Rhetoric, Through Everyday Things*. U of Alabama P, 2016.

Bell, Lee Anne. *Storytelling for Social Justice*. Routledge, 2010.

Bennett, Jane. *Vibrant Matter: A Political Ecology of Things*. Duke UP, 2009.

Bratta, Phil, and Malea Powell. "Introduction to the Special Issue: Entering the Cultural Rhetorics Conversations." *enculturation: a journal of rhetoric, writing, and culture, vol.* 21, 2016, http://enculturation.net/entering-the-cultural-rhetorics -conversations.

Chen, Mel. *Animacies: Biopolitics, Racial Mattering, and Queer Affect*. Duke UP, 2012.

Coole, Diana H., and Samantha Frost. *New Materialisms: Ontology, Agency, and Politics*, Duke UP, 2010.

Cooper, Marilyn. *The Animal Who Writes: A Posthumanist Composition*. U of Pittsburgh P, 2019.

Creswell, John W., and Dana L. Miller. "Determining Validity in Qualitative Inquiry." *Theory into Practice*, vol. 39, no. 3, 2000, pp. 124–130.

Cushman, Ellen. "Decolonizing Validity." *Journal of Writing Assessment*, vol. 9, no. 2, 2016, https://escholarship.org/uc/item/0xh7v6fb.

Cvetkovich, Ann. *An Archive of Feelings: Trauma, Sexuality, and Lesbian Public Cultures*. Duke UP, 2003.

Dadas, Caroline. "Messy Methods: Queer Methodological Approaches to Social

Media." *Computers and Composition*, vol. 40, 2016, pp. 60–72.

Edelman, Lee. *No Future: Queer Theory and the Death Drive*. Duke UP, 2004.

Farkas, Kerrie, and Christina Haas. "A Grounded Theory Approach for Studying Writing and Literacy." *Practicing Research in Writing Studies: Reflexive and Ethically Responsible Research*, edited by Kristina Powell and Pamela Takayoshi, Hampton Press, 2012, pp. 81–95.

Gruwell, Leigh. *Making Matters: Craft, Ethics, and New Materialist Rhetorics*. Utah State UP, 2022.

Halberstam, J. *The Queer Art of Failure*. Duke UP, 2011.

Holland, Dorothy, Debra Skinner, William LaChicotte, Jr., and Carole Cain. *Identity and Agency in Cultural Worlds*. Harvard UP, 2001.

Ito, Mizuko, Kris Gutiérrez, Sonia Livingstone, Bill Penuel, Jean Rhodes, Katie Salen, Juliet Schor, Julian Sefton-Green, S. Craig Watkins. *Connected Learning: An Agenda for Research and Design*, Digital Media and Learning Research Hub, 2013.

Kane, Michael T. "Validation." *Educational Measurement*, 4th ed., edited by Robert L. Brennan, American Council on Education and Praeger, 2006, pp. 17–64.

———. "Explicating Validity." *Assessment in Education: Principles, Policy & Practice*, vol. 23, no. 2, 2015, pp. 198–211.

Kirsch, Gesa. "Methodological Pluralism: Epistemological Issues." *Methods and Methodology in Composition Research*, edited by Patricia A. Sullivan and Gesa Kirsch, Southern Illinois UP, 1992, pp. 247–259.

Knoblauch, C. H. *Discursive Ideologies: Reading Western Rhetoric*. Utah State UP, 2014.

Larkin, Philip. "This Be the Verse." *Collected Poems*, Faber and Faber, 1974, p. 188.

Law, John. *After Method: Messiness in Social Science Research*. Routledge, 2004.

Lincoln, Yvonna S., and Egon G. Guba. *Naturalistic Inquiry*. Sage, 1985.

Martinez, Aja Y. *Counterstory: The Rhetoric and Writing of Critical Race Theory*. National Council of Teachers of English, 2020.

Neff, Joyce Magnotto. "Grounded Theory: A Critical Research Methodology." *Under Construction: Working at the Intersections of Composition Theory, Research, and Practice*, edited by Chris Anson and Christine Farris, Utah State UP, 1998, pp. 124–135.

Payne, Robert. *The Promiscuity of Network Culture: Queer Theory and Digital Media*. Routledge, 2014.

Powell, Malea, Daisy Levy, Andrea Riley-Mukavetz, Marilee Brooks-Gillies, Maria Novotny, and Jennifer Fisch-Ferguson. "Our Story Begins Here: Constellating Cultural Rhetorics." *Enculturation*, vol. 18, 2014, http://enculturation.net/our-story-begins-here.

Prins, Kristin. "Crafting New Approaches to Composition." *Composing (Media) = Composing (Embodiment): Bodies, Technologies, Writing, the Teaching of Writing*, edited by Kristin L. Arola and Anne Frances Wysocki, Utah State UP, 2012, pp. 145–161.

Prins, Kristin, Amber Buck, Megan Condis, Marilee Brooks-Gillies, and Martha Webber, eds. "Craft & DIY Rhetorics." *Harlot*, vol. 14, 2015, http://harlotofthearts.org/index.php/harlot/issue/view/14.

Rickert, Thomas. *Ambient Rhetoric: The Attunements of Rhetorical Being.* U of Pittsburgh P, 2013.

Singh, Julietta. *Unthinking Mastery: Humanism and Decolonial Entanglements.* Duke UP, 2018.

Smith, Linda Tuhiwai. *Decolonizing Methodologies: Research and Indigenous Peoples*, 2nd ed. Zed Books, 2012.

Stewart, Kathleen. *Ordinary Affects.* Duke UP, 2007.

Teston, Christa. "Considering Confidentiality in Research Design: Developing Heuristics to Chart the Unchartable." *Practicing Research in Writing Studies: Reflections on Ethically Responsible Research*, edited by Katrina Powell and Pamela Takayoshi, Hampton P, 2012, pp. 303–326.

West-Puckett, Stephanie J. "Remaking Education: Designing Classroom Makerspaces for Transformative Learning." *Edutopia.* 1 Oct. 2014. http://www.edutopia.org/blog/classroom-Makerspace-transformative-learning-stephanie-west-puckett.

West-Puckett, Stephanie J. "Crash Encounters: Negotiating Science Literacy and Its Sponsorship in a Cross-Disciplinary, Cross-Generational MOOC." *Community Literacy Journal*, vol. 16, no. 2, 2022.

West-Puckett, Stephanie J. 2017. "Materializing Makerspaces: Queerly Composing Space, Time, and (What) Matters." (Doctoral Dissertation, East Carolina University).

West-Puckett, Stephanie J., Nicole I. Caswell, and William P. Banks. *Failing Sideways: Queer Possibilities for Writing Assessment.* Utah State UP, 2023.

CHAPTER 2.

DELIBERATIVE DRIFTING OVER TIME: A CRITICAL REFLECTION ON DESIGNING SOCIAL MEDIA METHODS FOR LONGEVITY

Sarah Riddick

Worcester Polytechnic Institute

Paired reading:

- Riddick, Sarah A. "Deliberative Drifting: A Rhetorical Field Method for Audience Studies on Social Media." *Computers and Composition*, vol. 54, 2019, pp. 1–27.

This chapter addresses the ongoing methodological challenges of social media research in rhetoric and writing studies, including developing method/ologies suitable for this work. To do so, I reevaluate a method I introduced in 2019 called deliberative drifting, which I designed for researching spontaneous, ephemeral rhetorical activity on social media (e.g., audience engagement with livestreams). I begin with a brief overview of deliberative drifting's development. Next, I reflect on the institutional, disciplinary, and cultural conditions that informed its initial design, as well as three underlying methodological themes: engagement, positionality, and feasibility. To explore these themes, I examine deliberative drifting alongside current scholarship and research guidelines related to digital rhetoric, writing, and social media studies. I explain that although deliberative drifting is founded on an ethic of care and on careful considerations of the aforementioned themes, it—like any other method—is a product of its time and may benefit from updates. Rather than offer firm conclusions and solutions, I conclude by advocating for reflection (methodological and self) as part of responsible research, and I offer guiding questions to help rhetoric and writing researchers develop social media method/ologies today.

DOI: https://doi.org/10.37514/PER-B.2024.2241.2.02

Social media is an ever-moving methodological target. As platforms update, so does users' communication with/in them. Accordingly, researchers must continually endeavor to develop methods and methodologies suited to social media, rather than "try to shove their projects into" existing approaches whose designs don't align with the task at-hand (Banks et al. 20). In 2019 I joined others (e.g., McKee and DeVoss; McKee and Porter) in advocating for this kind of methodological flexibility when I introduced a method called *deliberative drifting*, which is designed for researching spontaneous, ephemeral rhetorical activity on social media, such as audience engagement with livestreams.

Yet, methods—like media—are emergent. Even after introducing and implementing a method, it may require updates. Although deliberative drifting has helped my research, I continue to navigate complex methodological questions with each new project—questions that highlight the ongoing methodological challenges of social media research. This chapter explores some of the challenges of social media research today by critically reflecting on and reevaluating deliberative drifting.

Following a brief overview of deliberative drifting's development, I reflect on themes I have been exploring since then: engagement, positionality, and feasibility. These themes have emerged over time as I have reflected on the institutional, disciplinary, and cultural conditions that informed deliberative drifting's initial design. To explore these themes in this chapter, I juxtapose and critically examine deliberative drifting alongside current scholarship and research guidelines related to digital rhetoric, writing, and social media studies. Although deliberative drifting is founded on an ethic of care and on careful considerations of the aforementioned themes, it—like any other method—is a product of its time. Rather than offer firm conclusions and solutions, I join methods researchers in arguing that reflection (methodological and self) can "foreground responsible research and model how to gracefully manage the gift of hindsight as a tool and not a weapon" (Rohan 27).

DELIBERATIVE DRIFTING'S DEVELOPMENT

I designed deliberative drifting as a method for rhetorically analyzing live, ephemeral digital fields. Broadly, "Deliberative drifting allows the researcher to freely follow the flows of thing-power and to later analyze how and why those flows carried others and themselves" (Riddick 5). Combining screen-recording with field notes, deliberative drifting is intended to help researchers archive more kinetic, non-verbal, and ephemeral elements of social media communication and events, such as livestreams and social media feeds, and to account more for researchers' subjective influence in these spaces.

Deliberative drifting arose from mid-2010s methodological need. For rhetorical analyses of more static content like tweets, approaches to data collection and processing were already fairly established by then (e.g., use apps to "scrape" and, to some extent, process tweets; take screenshots of image- and word-based content). In the mid-2010s, Facebook introduced two features: reaction buttons and Facebook Live. As I began to research these emergent parts of Facebook and their broader influence, I struggled to find ready-made method/ologies. Specifically, collecting data was challenging because of these features' distinctly kinetic and ephemeral qualities (e.g., reaction buttons that float across a livestream).

At first, one solution seemed relatively simple: *screenshots* are to *static content* as *screen-recordings* are to *moving content*. Although I could have efficiently collected and processed data by screen-recording it, I wanted to do so ethically. My thought process here can be broadly summarized through three questions that Mary P. Sheridan and Lee Nickoson pose in *Writing Studies Research in Practice*: "What practical, theoretical, and ethical problematics confront writing researchers today? What does one gain and lose from adopting a particular methodology? And, finally, what might researchers be overlooking, excluding, silencing?" (5).

Deliberative drifting was one way in which I worked through the first question in a particular context: "What practical, theoretical, and ethical problematics confront" me as I research these emergent forms of social media communication? As I pursued this question, I was mindful of potential consequences of "adopting a particular methodology," not just because of the novel challenges I was facing, but also because I wanted to uphold a larger commitment to researching without "overlooking, excluding, silencing" (5). Put differently, I was striving to cultivate what Jacqueline Jones Royster and Gesa E. Kirsch describe in *Feminist Rhetorical Practices* as "an ethos of humility, respect, and care" and to account for the ways in which this ethos "shape[s] our research" (21, 22). Royster and Kirsch elaborate, "[M]odern researchers and scholars are fully challenged to learn how to listen more carefully to the voices (and texts) that they study, to critique our analytical assumptions and frames, to critique guiding questions reflectively and reflexively" (14).

I also wanted to challenge a broader, problematic assumption that underpins scholarship writ large: the assumption that research can be absolutely neutral, objective, and unbiased. Research influences what is perceived, valued, circulated, and preserved as knowledge and truth. Thus, researchers must consider their subjective influence on knowledge production, among other areas, and they mustn't take for granted the potentially harmful ideologies and assumptions that their method/ologies may uphold. Fortunately, rhetoric and writing studies supports this work. As Sonja Foss summarizes, rhetorical criticism proceeds from "two primary assumptions": "that objective reality does not exist" and that researchers "can know an artifact only through personal interpretation of it" (24).

Along these lines, deliberative drifting may not get everything "right," but it stems from a sincere effort to research ethically. By combining screen-recording with detailed, first-person reporting about my research process, I was striving to let others speak directly for themselves—a complex point that I will return to shortly—and to communicate how my personal experiences and choices with/in these spaces might influence the research, including whom and what I am (re)presenting. Research is messy; that mess is meaningful. I carefully construct and conduct all of my research, and mess inevitably emerges within it, particularly given the ongoing need I face to experiment with social media method/ologies. By presenting this mess as valuable, I hope to help others embrace mess in their own research of emergent media and communication.

ENGAGEMENT

Deliberative drifting was designed to support research of emergent aspects of social media rhetoric and writing, drawing methodological inspiration from an also-emergent area of study called rhetorical field studies (MacKinnon et al.; Middleton et al.; Rai and Druschke). With deliberative drifting, I aimed to offer a method that would accommodate rhetorical fieldwork on social media, in which the researcher would approach a live event on social media as a digital field. This includes acknowledging the researcher's embodied presence and engagement in the field. While providing an overview for the article's case study, I elaborate on my rationale for this acknowledgment:

> . . . I remained logged into my personal accounts. By using my personal accounts—which minimally, if at all, would have affected my experience in these public fields—I wanted to explicitly position myself as an identifiable person and to honor my privileged role and responsibilities as a researcher. While deliberative drifting, I could participate at any time via a tweet, a comment, a reaction, or a share, and I would have to do so with my real name, as researchers often must do in traditional fields. Although there may be risks involved with identifying oneself, such as being harassed, threatened, or doxxed . . . , staying logged into personal accounts can be a feasible means of demonstrating an ethical commitment to and awareness of a researcher's presence and influence in the field. (Riddick 8)

I remain committed to parts of the above passage, namely those that speak to acknowledging "my privileged role and responsibilities as a researcher" and "demonstrating an ethical commitment to and awareness of a researcher's presence and influence in the field." That said, I would like to push back on other parts that are potentially problematic.

My suggestion invites researchers to "participate at any time via a tweet, a comment, a reaction, or a share." To be clear—as I hope I am in "Deliberative Drifting"—I believe that researchers should share how they engaged in digital fields, including but not limited to the aforementioned ways. In hindsight, however, I wish I had offered clearer parameters and better addressed conflicts this engagement could create, such as with institutional review boards (IRB).

Currently, IRB distinguishes between using the internet as a "research tool" and as an "object of study" as follows:

> Generally, when researchers actively engage and interact with individuals online to collect data, it is likely they are using the internet as a research tool. Conversely, if researchers collect data from individuals by merely observing the way people interact or behave online, it is likely they are using the internet as the object of study. (Martinez)

We might say that rhetorical analyses of social media communication with/in live digital fields and events align with using the internet as an object of study. I designed deliberative drifting specifically to facilitate such rhetorical analyses. A more useful framing for rhetoric and writing studies, however, may be Amber M. Buck and Devon F. Ralston's definition for studying online "discourse," or "studying how ideas and concepts are discussed in public online forums and social media platforms, including word choice and rhetorical framing" (8). Studying discourse in this way is precisely what I intended for deliberative drifting. However, I realize now that a small part of my 2019 article could complicate these categorizations, possibly shifting such analyses *technically* into the categories of using the internet as a research tool (Martinez) or studying people (Buck and Ralston 8). This shift seems to depend on how "human subjects research" is defined.

Generally, for IRB, human subjects research is determined by how (much) a researcher "interacts" with human subjects in their study. As Heidi A. McKee and James E. Porter explain, "*Interaction* is one of the determinants in the United States for institutional review boards (IRBs) to determine if someone is conducting person-based or text-based research" (250). The above IRB passage suggests that interaction leans toward more direct and explicit interaction between researchers and subjects (e.g., surveys, interviews). Yet, this boundary blurs if we compare interaction with engagement, particularly on social media.

It is worth noting that *engagement* as a term and concept is central to social media, and it is not necessarily synonymous with *interaction*. Social media companies consider engagement to include more than the verbal interactions that typify academic definitions of "interaction with human subjects." For instance, Twitter tracks more explicit, publicly visible engagement metrics like retweets, comments, and "likes," but also more subtle forms of engagement like "Impressions," "Detail Expands," "New Followers," "Profile Visits," and "Link Clicks" ("About"). Metrics like these illustrate how even passing glances in digital fields qualify and quantify as engagement, with high rhetorical stakes and rewards (e.g., algorithmic, financial). In pointing out these engagement metrics, I am not suggesting researchers follow social media companies' lead in determining what constitutes either human subjects or engagement, particularly given these companies' demonstrable prioritization of their profit over others' protection. Rather, I am advocating for critical considerations of what constitutes engagement so that researchers can sufficiently account for it.

When considering researchers' engagement in live digital fields, complicated questions arise: To what extent could engaging in an event's digital field disqualify researchers from later rhetorically analyzing it? Let's say they engaged *as a community member* in a digital field, then later—*as a researcher*—they want to analyze content they archived from that field; in this scenario, they did not engage with this content or the people who posted it beyond observing and archiving content. Does the fact that they engaged at all in the field mean that they shouldn't be able to analyze the aforementioned content? What if they had interacted as a community member in more explicit, publicly identifiable ways (e.g., retweeting, liking, sharing, commenting)? How would this affect their ability to research this field and their archived data? How might IRB approval and/or informed consent come into play?

Further, how many researchers are ever truly, completely offline these days, particularly those who research social media? Many researchers may rarely or never post their own content, but they routinely engage as lurkers in their everyday lives. In social media parlance, a lurker is someone who observes social media spaces and communication without explicitly and/or identifiably engaging. Importantly, lurking counts as engagement in social media, although it is labeled differently (e.g., "About"). By following someone's account or viewing their content, researchers are giving those accounts attention—attention that social media platforms' algorithms track and reward. Even if researchers don't comment, "like," share, or otherwise explicitly interact with users' content, their attention toward other accounts can nevertheless be measured and can impact users' public reach and influence. Questions and concerns like these are further complicated when we consider the ongoing eventfulness of rhetoric and writing, including on social media (Gallagher).

Regarding which account(s) a researcher uses: this decision can impact the digital field that the researcher encounters. To limit potential issues, perhaps researchers could use only professional accounts to collect data and do digital fieldwork. That said, I hesitate to suggest such uniform approaches, and I wonder what we really gain from that kind of approach beyond the illusion of neutrality. If a researcher, as a community member in their everyday life, has ever liked a post from an organization on their personal account, does logging into a different account *really* render them neutral when analyzing the organization's account? Rather than pretend to be completely "objective, impartial, and removed from the data," I continue to agree that researchers should instead be upfront about their influence on their research (Foss 24).

Overall, with open considerations of engagement, I believe deliberative drifting remains viable. One of the fundamental premises from which deliberative drifting proceeds is that researchers enact power through participation in their research. Deliberative drifting asks researchers to account for and acknowledge how they enact power in situ and otherwise in research, including subtler forms of engagement, such as navigational choices. In this sense, deliberative drifting requires researchers to recognize their "privileged role and responsibilities" as someone who is trusted with (re)presenting events, discourse, and people and with shaping knowledge production and public memory. Researchers should share information regarding their engagement, including honest insights about their possible influence with/in the field and on their findings. Because deliberative drifting requires the researcher to archive their field as they are navigating it, this step is quite feasible. Still, the responsibility remains—as it always does—on the researcher to disclose as needed. Regarding interaction and engagement, researchers could consult with IRB in advance about what their social-media-based rhetorical analysis would entail, which could help them determine across similar digital fields and events which steps are needed that involve other people (e.g., IRB, social media users). The point is that researchers should carefully make methodological choices like these to suit each specific case, rather than apply uniform approaches.

POSITIONALITY

Deliberative drifting's design is also informed by positionality—of social media *users* and *researchers*. These are not mutually exclusive categories. For instance, part of the methodological challenge I face as a social media researcher is that I am *also* a social media user, and it is increasingly difficult to separate those two positions. Deliberative drifting encourages researchers to reflect on and report out about their positionality, including in ways that acknowledge positionality's relationship to power. This process should include careful considerations of risks that users and researchers face.

Social media carries specific risks of harm to those who communicate and/or are circulated within it, "such as being harassed, threatened, or doxxed" (Riddick 8). These risks are amplified for members of historically marginalized communities. As Derek M. Sparby explains, "Not only is power unevenly distributed, but traditionally privileged people also maintain their social advantage in digital spaces while traditionally marginalized people continue to be disparaged" (88). Social media researchers should be aware of these risks, including how their method/ologies factor into them. For instance, in their article "I Didn't Sign Up for Your Research Study," Buck and Ralston discuss how BIPOC individuals and communities have been harmed by social media research. Accordingly, Buck and Ralston recommend "asking how researching the digital lives of BIPOC might contribute to the cumulative gaze and in what ways do research studies surveil rather than enrich? In what ways are communities spoken for rather than amplified?" (7). Additionally, researchers should be aware of the risks that researchers themselves face, including identity-based risks (franzke et al.; Gelms; Gelms et al.; Reyman and Sparby). Overall, ethical social media method/ologies must include efforts to minimize risks of harm to social media users and researchers.

Despite my efforts to account for positionality and to minimize risks, deliberative drifting's initial design may still fall short. At the time, I chose to quote users' content because I wanted to let people speak for themselves; however, I omitted (user)names and profile pictures to protect anonymity. Although these are two common methodological choices, they are *choices*, and these choices may introduce problems. First, it can be difficult to determine best practices for quoting social media communication without informed consent (Buck and Ralston; McKee and Porter). One reason this consent may be deemed appropriate is because the quoted content could be traced to an identifiable person, despite efforts to anonymize it; this could present risks for quoted rhetors, and these risks may be heightened for some people, "especially BIPOC and other multiple-marginalized communities" (Buck and Ralston 10). On the other hand, anonymizing quoted content is not necessarily the most ethical methodological choice. Alexandria L. Lockett et al. argue that "researchers must not separate issues of race and technology when deciding to study 'public' writing and communication"; one way in which researchers can avoid this is by "always credit[ing] the source" (26).

Given social media's emergent qualities and nuanced contexts, mixed methods approaches may be best for social media research. Deliberative drifting is no exception. Deliberative drifting is designed for archiving and analyzing more ephemeral, spontaneous, and difficult-to-scrape-and-screenshot social media communication, and I encourage researchers to combine it as needed with other method/ologies so that their overall approach is both ethical and effective.

For instance, before entering a digital field, researchers might consider frameworks like Buck and Ralston's. As Buck and Ralston note, "Writing researchers' concerns . . . move beyond ethical considerations spelled out by university IRB's in research protocols," thus they offer detailed guidelines for online writing research that address data collection and storage, terms of use, informed consent, community and individual impacts, researcher engagement, data privacy, and more (8–10). In these guidelines and throughout their article, Buck and Ralston discuss the ethical and logistical challenges of studying online writing, including topics that correlate with deliberative drifting (e.g., ephemerality). I would highly recommend researchers consult Buck and Ralston's guidelines while determining methodological approaches to studies of social media rhetoric and writing. A researcher could update or adapt parts of deliberative drifting to align with Buck and Ralston's suggested approaches so that their method is customized for their specific, contemporary research context and aims.

Likewise, researchers might pair deliberative drifting with McKee and Porter's heuristic for online writing research. In this heuristic, researchers evaluate five categories: "Public vs. Private," "Data ID," "Degree of Interaction," "Topic Sensitivity," and "Subject Vulnerability" (254). Using this heuristic helps a researcher determine, "Is consent necessary?" For a study in which the ratings are generally toward the "public" and "low" ends, it is less likely that consent is necessary; it becomes more difficult to make this call depending on which and/ or how many categories rank as "private" or "high." To demonstrate, I offer a brief evaluation of these events using McKee and Porter's heuristic.

In "Deliberative Drifting," I analyzed livestreams on Facebook Live and YouTube Live from public news media sources, as well as my Twitter feed during a public, hybrid (i.e., online and offline) protest. The most obvious potential problem is *degree of interaction*, as discussed earlier. Another concern is *privacy*. Technically, any Facebook content might qualify as private because Facebook requires users to log-in to view content. Yet, Facebook may be an exception to this general "rule," given Facebook's international influence as a source of social, cultural, and political communication. The boundaries of public and private also depend on context. For instance, we would likely consider communication within a private group on Facebook to be more private than comments on a public account's live-streaming event. McKee and Porter offer a useful comparison: is the content "like placards at a march (completely public and available to be quoted), or are they more like park-bench conversations (somewhat public but carrying expectations of privacy)?" (248). Deliberative drifting is intended for rhetorically analyzing discourse with/in public accounts in public digital fields on well-established, well-understood social media platforms, which is more "like placards at a march." *Data ID* is possible on Facebook Live because many users include real names and profile pictures, and comments remain visible after the livestream ends. However, it is difficult to find these comments quickly, unless one locates the original video and scrolls through all visible comments. Twitter also faces a Data ID issue, given that tweets often show up in search engines. Of the three spaces, YouTube Live seems the most ephemeral; comments disappear after two minutes, and many usernames are not personally identifiable. *Topic sensitivity* and *subject vulnerability* are also challenging considerations. For example, I researched in situ communication involving the high school student-led-and-focused "March for Our Lives" protest; it is possible that I observed, archived, and analyzed communication from such students. I strove to protect peoples' identities and to treat these categories with care by anonymizing quoted content (e.g., removing usernames and profile pictures), but screenshots and quotes could possibly be traced.

Overall, heuristics and frameworks like these are helpful for evaluating issues related to informed consent, but it is important to note that they are not flow charts. In "a problematic case," answers may vary across the high-low continuum in McKee and Porter's heuristic. In such cases, McKee and Porter do not insist on informed consent, but rather say that "a researcher would need to weigh carefully" these answers individually and together, "consulting with multiple audiences and comparing to other studies of similar contexts" to make their best judgment about informed consent (256).

FEASIBILITY

Alongside the ethics of social media method/ologies, researchers must also consider feasibility. A challenge I continue to confront in my research is establishing and implementing ethical and feasible method/ologies for researching spontaneous and/or ephemeral online events, venues, and discourse.

As noted earlier, deliberative drifting can potentially blur the line between using the internet as a research tool and an object of study. Accordingly, an "easy solution" could be to not interact in live digital fields while researching them if the researcher does not have prior IRB approval. That said, the more we really think about this line of demarcation, the more difficult it becomes to draw (i.e., interaction vs. engagement), and the more complicated feasibility becomes. For instance, the IRB process can take a long time, whereas social media events can develop immediately. Besides the challenge of anticipating a spontaneous digital field and/or event in order to seek IRB approval, there is the challenge of obtaining approval in time. One concern regarding feasibility is that there might come a day in which scholars who engaged in situ as community members in a live digital field—particularly spontaneously formed fields—might not be able to rhetorically analyze the event later because they did not receive prior approval for it and/or because they engaged in the field in ways that might be considered to be interaction.

A related feasibility challenge is informed consent. It may not be possible to obtain this consent—at all or in advance. How could researchers solicit consent in advance from users in spontaneous and/or ephemeral live-streaming public events? Even if prior consent is possible, it is worth noting the "chilling effect" that could occur (McKee and Porter 252). It may be more feasible to request consent to quote those users afterwards, which may help researchers engage better in ethical, antiracist research practices (Buck and Ralston 4; Lockett et al. 26). Yet, another complicated issue is the potential risks that obtaining consent and naming sources can introduce for the researcher. I am thinking here of the personal experiences with identity-based digital aggression that researchers have experienced (e.g., Gelms et al.), as well as the ways in which research like theirs (e.g., case studies of 4chan) might be hindered if prior informed consent is universally required for analyzing and/or quoting publicly available social media communication.

Important as logistical considerations are for deliberative drifting, so are more personal aspects of feasibility. Along these lines, I'd like to return to and further reflect on an earlier passage from "Deliberative Drifting." To engage in deliberative drifting, I described how "I remained logged into my personal accounts . . . to explicitly position myself as an identifiable person and to honor my privileged role and responsibilities as a researcher" (8). Although I still agree with the latter part of this statement, I am more reluctant now to recommend the first. I reasoned then that despite "risks involved with identifying oneself, such as being harassed, threatened, or doxxed . . . , staying logged into personal accounts can be a feasible means of demonstrating an ethical commitment to and awareness of a research-er's presence and influence in the field" (8). Again, although my commitment to others hasn't changed here, I want to challenge my former statement, particularly when I described this choice as "feasible." Something feasible is something that can be done, accomplished, achieved—but at what cost?

Before we are researchers, we are people—people with multifaceted identities and complex, ongoing lived experiences. We are subjects. Chanon Adsanatham "calls upon rhetoric scholars to continually cultivate reflexivity by situating and resituating ourselves, by heeding how our ever-shifting subjectivities, habitus, and standpoints (SHS) are intersubjective, fluid, and contingent" (79). Importantly, Adsanatham notes, "our SHS are never disinterested or constant. They change. They shift. They reform. . . . we must continually resituate ourselves along the way and heed the multiple facets of our subjectivities in the research process" (79–80). In foregrounding but also largely eliding this element of subjectivity in the aforementioned passage, I am concerned I fell too short. I am grateful for the opportunity to approach that moment differently now. To do so, I want to share some of how my own "ever-shifting subjectivities, habitus, and standpoints" inform deliberative drifting.

Part of my SHS that has notably shifted is my professional status. I designed deliberative drifting as a graduate student; now, I am an associate professor at a private polytechnic institute. Over the past few years, my knowledge, experience, and training in my discipline have continued to grow, and my professional position has changed. A complicated aspect of this shift is that, admittedly, I found myself more confused and conflicted as a graduate student about what to honor and to protect in my research regarding myself. As a woman, I face specific, identity-based risks of harm, including with/in social media; these risks extend into my research. By positioning myself in an identifiable way, I insufficiently protected myself from this potential. I recognize that I am describing one historically marginalized identity here: woman. Although I face certain risks because of this part of my identity, I also recognize my identity as a white cisgender woman and the privileges accompanying that identity.

Admittedly, I felt uneasy in 2018–2019 about engaging on the internet as myself, particularly given the layered risks it poses to all users, to researchers, and to people with certain identities. However, I felt a sense of cultural pressure to turn away from that concern and to pursue research as *researcher first, person second*. I had internalized an expectation that in order for my research to be valued by others, I had to subordinate concerns I had about protecting myself as a person so I could (appear to) participate confidently as a researcher first and foremost. Along these lines, I am indebted to the methodological work in our field that I am continuing to discover—work that challenges this kind of thinking and advocates for more inclusive methodological approaches, including in ways that consider the intersectional identities and positionalities of researchers (e.g., Adsanatham; Buck and Ralston; Gelms et al.; Lockett et al.).

Rhetoric and writing studies of social media need to be customized to suit the emergent spaces *of* social media and the people engaging *with/in* it. Just as rhetoric and writing studies generally requires actively and inclusively "[r]econstituting who 'counts' as authors" (Rohan 28), rhetoric and writing studies of social media requires actively and inclusively reconstituting who counts as human subjects. IRB says that research should not harm human subjects. Agreed, wholeheartedly. But even if we aren't the subjects of our own research, we are nevertheless subjects. Selecting and enacting our method/ologies requires ongoing, critical reflection about our subjectivity. Reporting out about my influence in data collection and data processing via deliberative drifting is one way in which I strove sincerely to hold myself accountable as a biased, subjective person who researches. But that effort is an act of ethical care for others. As we care for others, we must also care for ourselves.

DELIBERATIVE DRIFTING TODAY

Since introducing deliberative drifting in 2019, I have been critically reflecting on questions regarding engagement, positionality, and feasibility, and I have been wrestling with how method/ologies can responsibly and effectively attend to them. I would consider for future uses of deliberative drifting the following questions:

1. How will data be collected? Which technologies are required? What are the terms and conditions associated with the platform housing a digital field and/or event? How and where will the data be archived?

2. Will the researcher be logged into a professional account? A personal account? None? How will this choice impact the field's size, composition, and activity as observed and accounted for by the researcher?

3. Is this a study of people or discourse (Buck and Ralston 8)? Is IRB approval or review required? Is informed consent required? For whom? To what extent? Can consent be obtained after the event (e.g., for content the researcher wants to quote)?

4. To what extent can the digital field be considered public or private? How accessible will the field and/or event be after its "live" form ends?

5. What constitutes interaction and engagement in a digital field and/or live-streaming event? (How) will the researcher interact directly with others? How else will the researcher engage in the field, in the event, and/or with others? How will they account for their interaction and engagement?

6. How will data be (re)presented (e.g., quoted and/or paraphrased; anonymized and/or pseudonymized)? How will this (re)presentation affect understandings of the field? Of the event? Of people and communities involved in either?

7. How can the researcher acknowledge their influence on the field and/or event and those within it? How can they acknowledge that their (re)presentation to some extent produces limited, subjective knowledge?

8. How can the researcher acknowledge the potential impacts of their research on "the subject(s) and communities that they study" (Lockett et al. 26)? How can they enact ethical care for others (Adsanatham

83–84; Royster and Kirsch)? How can they minimize risks of harm? How sensitive is the communication within the field and/or event, and how vulnerable are the rhetors (McKee and Porter 254)?

9. How can researchers acknowledge their positionality and subjectivity as a researcher and as a person in a way that cares for others and for the self? How can they acknowledge their privileged position as researchers in fields while also protecting themselves as people?

These questions may seem like dwelling on minutiae, to which I'd say: yes. Researchers need to dwell on seemingly insignificant details to responsibly account for them. For the last several years, I have been ruminating on these questions, and I am reluctant to offer answers. I agree with McKee and Porter when they advise, "Be deeply suspicious of blanket pronouncements. . . . specific circumstances matter" (256). Accordingly, I encourage researchers to continually and critically question their methodological choices, accepting that this process may not provide perfect or prompt answers. We need to allow room for this methodological mess, so that we may carefully and rigorously work through the theory, praxis, and ethics of our work. Like social media itself, the methodological boundaries for social media research are emergent. In this way, deliberative drifting is a methodological product of its time, but with ongoing reflection and updates as needed, I hope its core aims and approaches will continue to support current and future research in this area.

WORKS CITED

"About Your Activity Dashboard." *Twitter*, https://help.twitter.com/en/managing-your-account/using-the-tweet-activity-dashboard. Accessed 13 May 2022.

Adsanatham, Chanon. "REDRES[ing] Rhetorica: A Methodological Proposal for Queering Cross-Cultural Rhetorical Studies." *Re/orienting Writing Studies: Queer Methods, Queer Projects*, edited by William P. Banks, Matthew B. Cox, and Caroline Dadas. Utah State UP, 2019, pp. 75–94.

Banks, William P., Matthew B. Cox, and Caroline Dadas. "Re/Orienting Writing Studies: Thoughts on In(Queer)y." *Re/Orienting Writing Studies: Queer Methods, Queer Projects*, edited by William P. Banks, Matthew B. Cox, and Caroline Dadas, Utah State UP, 2019, pp. 3–23.

Buck, Amber M., and Devon F. Ralston. "I Didn't Sign Up for Your Research Study: The Ethics of Using 'Public' Data." *Computers and Composition*, vol. 61, 2021, pp. 1–13.

Foss, Sonja K. *Rhetorical Criticism: Exploration and Practice*. Waveland P, 5th ed., 2018.

franzke, aline shakti, Anja Bechmann, Michael Zimmer, Charles M. Ess, and the Association of Internet Researchers. *Internet Research: Ethical Guidelines 3.0*, 2019. https://aoir.org/reports/ethics3.pdf.

Gallagher, John R. *Update Culture and the Afterlife of Digital Writing*. Utah State UP, 2019.

Gelms, Bridget. "Social Media Research and the Methodological Problem of Harassment: Foregrounding Researcher Safety." *Computers and Composition*, vol. 59, 2021, pp. 1–12.

Gelms, Bridget, Leigh Gruwell, Vyshali Manivannan, and Derek M. Sparby. "Intersectional Feminism & Digital Aggression: Research Experiences and Approaches." *Coalition of Feminist Scholars in the History of Rhetoric & Composition*, 9 Dec. 2020, https://cfshrc.org/event-intersectional-feminism-digital-aggression-research -experiences-and-approaches/.

Lockett, Alexandria L., Iris D. Ruiz, James Chase Sanchez, and Christopher Carter. "Introduction: Antiracism as an Ethical Framework for Researching Race and Racism." *Race, Rhetoric, and Research Methods*. WAC Clearinghouse, 2021, pp. 3–37. https://doi.org/10.37514/PER-B.2021.1206.

Mackinnon, Sara L., Robert Asen, Karma R. Chavez, and Robert Glenn Howard, editors. *Text + Field: Innovations in Rhetorical Method*. Penn State UP, 2016.

Martinez, Alejandro. "Internet-Based Research—SBE." *Worcester Polytechnic Institute— Human Subjects in Social & Behavioral Research—Basic/Refresher*. Citi Program, Jan. 2004. Online Course. Last updated Jan. 2019.

McKee, Heidi A., and Dànielle Nicole DeVoss, editors. *Digital Writing Research: Technologies, Methodologies, and Ethical Issues*. Hampton P, 2007.

McKee, Heidi A., and James E. Porter. "The Ethics of Conducting Writing Research on the Internet: How Heuristics Help." *Writing Studies Research in Practice*, edited by Lee Nickoson and Mary P. Sheridan, Southern Illinois UP, 2012, pp. 245–260.

Middleton, Michael K., Aaron Hess, Danielle Endres, and Samantha Senda-Cook, Samantha. *Participatory Critical Rhetoric: Theoretical and Methodological Foundations for Studying Rhetoric In Situ*. Lexington Books, 2015.

Rai, Candice, and Caroline Gottschalk Druschke, editors. *Field Rhetoric: Ethnography, Ecology, and Engagement in the Places of Persuasion*. U of Alabama P, 2018.

Reyman, Jessica, and Derek Sparby, editors. *Digital Ethics: Rhetoric and Responsibility in Online Aggression*. Routledge, 2019.

Riddick, Sarah A. "Deliberative Drifting: A Rhetorical Field Method for Audience Studies on Social Media." *Computers and Composition*, vol. 54, 2019, pp. 1–27.

Rohan, Liz. "Reseeing and Redoing: Making Historical Research at the Turn of the Millenium." *Writing Studies Research in Practice*, edited by Lee Nickoson and Mary P. Sheridan, Southern Illinois UP, 2012, pp. 25–35.

Royster, Jacqueline Jones, and Gesa E. Kirsch. *Feminist Rhetorical Practices: New Horizons for Rhetoric, Composition, and Literacy Studies*, Southern Illinois UP, 2012.

Sheridan, Mary P., and Lee Nickoson. "Current Conversations on Writing Research." *Writing Studies Research in Practice: Methods and Methodologies*, edited by Mary P. Sheridan and Lee Nickoson, Southern Illinois UP, 2021, pp. 1–12.

Sparby, Derek M. "Digital Social Media and Aggression: Memetic Rhetoric in 4chan's Collective Identity," *Computers and Composition*, vol. 45, 2017, pp. 85–97.

CHAPTER 3.

VOICING TRANSFER: EXAMINING RACE, IDENTITY, AND STUDENT LEARNING

Crystal VanKooten

Michigan State University

Paired readings:

- VanKooten, Crystal. "A Research Methodology of Interdependence through Video as Method." *Computers and Composition*, vol. 54, Dec. 2019, pp. 1–17.

- VanKooten, Crystal. *Transfer across Media: Using Digital Video in the Teaching of Writing*. Computers and Composition Digital Press/Utah State University Press, 2020, https://ccdigitalpress.org/book/transfer -across-media/index.html.

In this chapter, I reflect on how the decision to ignore race in writing research potentially upholds white, oppressive ways of writing, knowing, and being. To start to identify the importance of race within my research, I look back to video interview data I collected about two student participants of color, and I explore intersections between my white-researcher identity, their identities as Black students, and the conclusions I might draw about their learning in first-year writing. I interrogate the voice and voices within my research as they are connected to race and identities, and I question the ways that transfer becomes voiced in my work: whose voices are the focus, and why? How do I construct and represent these voices through video? In particular, how do I ethically represent the voices, bodies, and experiences of students of color on video? Through exposing my own omissions, failures, and questions related to the intersections of identity, race, student learning, and video in research, I call other (white) researchers in writing studies to likewise begin or continue a process of learning to pay careful attention to the role of race as we design and conduct new research.

"But my research isn't really about race…" I thought to myself. "It's about student learning, and transfer, and video technologies, but not directly about race. I shouldn't go there. I can't go there—I don't even know where to start."

I had these thoughts as I was working through the analysis of student interview data that I had collected on video for the first-year writing study, a qualitative research project. The student interviewee, Travon, completed a video project in his first-year writing course, and I interviewed him several times across the semester about his learning experiences. Travon was a Black student with a white writing instructor, and I was a white researcher. While this was rather obvious to all of us as I conducted the study, we never explicitly talked about race with one another. Travon didn't mention race or Blackness during his interviews with me, and I didn't ask. But Travon was a Black student, and I was a white researcher, and race and Black experiences were at the center of Travon's video, which featured images and voices from an array of Black students at the university speaking about the school's summer bridge program, as well as Travon as the narrator throughout the video.

Travon turned in an eight-minute first draft of this video, and his instructor then asked him to revise by drastically cutting down the video's length (the suggested length was two minutes). Travon talked with me about his dissatisfaction as he revised in response to the feedback. He didn't want to cut content, and he didn't want to reduce his own role as narrator. "I don't put nothing in a paper or in my video for no reason," he told me. He felt as if something was missing after cutting out his role as narrator to save time: "I'm missing in my video. So that's why I feel like, mmmm . . . it's lacking something."

As I thought through how to interpret Travon's comments about his composing experiences and his sense of a missing self in his video, I talked with a mentor who advised me to pay attention to how race—Travon's, that of his peers and teacher, and mine—were an important factor within this learning situation. And that's when I started making the excuses listed above as to why race didn't really belong in the study. I was overwhelmed with the thought of theorizing Travon's learning experiences through race, and I was unsure (and a bit afraid) of how to proceed in that direction. I wanted to protect the instructor participant (and myself) from negative scrutiny. I wanted to arrive at simple answers instead of complex questions that involved the intersections of learning, video, identity, and race.

A METHODOLOGY OF INTERDEPENDENCE— WITHOUT RACE?

The first-year writing study that Travon was a part of focused on student learning in writing courses, particularly what and how students learn when they compose with various modes and media. I looked and listened for *transfer across media* within Travon's and other students' experiences, and to do so, I used qualitative and digital research methods. I call the methodological approach to this work a methodology of interdependence through video as method, and I write about this methodology in detail in the companion texts to this chapter, "A Research Methodology of Interdependence through Video as Method," and my digital book, *Transfer across Media*. Drawing on the work of Kristie Fleckenstein, Clay Spinuzzi, Rebecca J. Rickly, and Carole Clark Papper, I approach classroom and interview research scenes as *interdependent*, with elements—participants, environment, technologies, and me—all interacting and influencing one another across "multiple linkages of the research web" and often in "wet, messy, rowdy" ways (Fleckenstein et al. 396). Video, then, is a key method within this research web in that I collect data on video, and then analyze that data and present findings on video, along with more traditional processes of analysis and presentation based in alphabetic writing. As I've written about in the two companion texts, this methodology and these methods often feel (and are) risky, experimental, messy, and chaotic. But they are also generative, freeing, helpfully disruptive, multimodal, and multi-sensory.

In *Transfer across Media*, I ultimately argue that video provides useful opportunities for transfer across media for students in writing courses through multimodal production. I work toward this thesis using an in-depth look at the digital video composing experiences of eighteen students in six different writing classrooms at two universities. For many students in the study, video composition was a productive site for transfer across media. While working with video, students transferred compositional knowledge via various pathways: by envisioning connections between assignments in their courses (*Transfer across Media* chapter 2); by applying functional and rhetorical literacies to a new context (*Transfer across Media* chapter 3), by developing critical literacies through multimodal production (*Transfer across Media* chapter 3), and by developing different kinds of meta-awareness about composition that opened pathways for future transfer (*Transfer across Media* chapter 4). In the book, I describe and analyze these moments of transfer via prose and via video, exploring recorded excerpts from classroom observations and interviews, as well as documents such as student-authored videos.

Much about the methodology of interdependence and the corresponding methods for *Transfer across Media* was developed and theorized along the way as I enacted the first-year writing study. Through collecting and analyzing video data in many classrooms at two universities across a several-year period, I learned to plan, make methodological choices, reflect, and adapt methods accordingly. The study, for example, was IRB-approved at two different institutions, and I was allowed to record students in class. If and how to discuss and share recordings and aspects of student identities and experiences, though, was still up to me as the researcher. As part of the informed consent process, I developed forms that asked participants to choose to be identified using a real name or a pseudonym and whether or not to give permission for the use of their recorded images and voices. In this chapter and in other work, I discuss student experiences—like Travon's—using real names with permission, and I share images and sounds from recordings also with permission.

In "A Research Methodology of Interdependence," I offer detailed description of the messy process of designing, conducting, and retooling the methodology of the first-year writing study as I came to understand the interdependent research scene and my own role within it with more complexity. In the article, I discuss how I made decisions like those described above around participant identification and video; how and why I chose to use video for data collection, analysis, and presentation; how I learned to consider and revise my approach to camera placement in classrooms and interviews; and how I experimented with new-to-me ways of data analysis using a video editor that included designing visual and aural juxtapositions, composing multimodal quotations, and using captions and narration for various effects.

I used video in these ways to analyze and present multimodal data about Travon's learning experiences in *Transfer across Media*, along with the experiences of other students who participated in the study. Through videos within the book, readers can see recordings of Travon and hear his speech patterns—and it's obvious from these videos that Travon is Black. But what I now notice when re-watching the videos about Travon is the omission of any *explicit* mention of race in my analysis. I also don't mention my own race, nor do I appear in any of the footage where Travon appears. Even as video renders Travon's race immediately visible, my other choices as a researcher render race nearly invisible. But race, and other elements of participant and researcher identities, are indeed a part of the interdependent, messy research ecology. Leaving race mostly out of the analysis was taking the easy road, a road that I went down willingly and quickly.

In this chapter, I reflect on how the decision to ignore race in writing research, and for me, within my own research on writing transfer, potentially upholds white, oppressive ways of writing, knowing, and being, and at the very least, assumes a neglectful "color blind" stance communicating that race is not so very relevant to writing or learning. Responding to Alexandria L. Lockett, Iris D. Ruiz, James Chase Sanchez, and Christopher Carter, I seek to start to identify the importance of race within my research. To do so, I look back to the video interview data I collected about two student participants of color—Travon and Daijah—and I explore intersections between my white-researcher identity, their identities as Black students, and the conclusions I might draw about their learning in first-year writing. Following Bump Halbritter and Julie Lindquist, I interrogate the voice and voices within my research as they are connected to race and identities, and I question the ways that transfer becomes voiced in my work: whose voices are the focus, and why? How do I construct and represent these voices through video? In particular, how do I ethically represent the voices, bodies, and experiences of students of color on video? Through exposing my own omissions, failures, and questions related to the intersections of identity, race, student learning, and video in research, I call other (white) researchers in writing studies to likewise begin or continue a process of learning to pay careful attention to the role of race as we design and conduct new research.

THE CONSEQUENCES OF IGNORING RACE, AND WHAT TO DO ABOUT THEM

Lockett, Ruiz, Sanchez, and Carter critique writing studies as a field, pointing to a lack of consistent, critical engagement with—and even a complete neglect of—race and racism in our histories, pedagogies, and methods and methodologies for research (10, 17). They point to a pattern in writing research that mirrors my own decision to ignore race when it came to Travon: "too many rhetoric, composition, and writing studies (RCWS) teacher-scholars-administrators select and execute forms of investigation that inadvertently, or perhaps all too knowingly, sidestep race in favor of less troubled territory" (11). This neglect, they warn, has dire consequences: "knowledge-making reifies colonial perspectives that privilege white hegemony" (17). Lockett et al.'s critique of the field is aimed directly at me and other white researchers like me who are complicit in these actions. To ignore race and racism in research is to promote white ways of knowing and to perpetuate white privilege and white supremacy.

In the past, rhetoric and composition's methodologies and methods for studying student learning—and particularly for studying writing transfer—have been overwhelmingly white. Not only are most of the published writing transfer researchers white (as, too, am I), but so are many of the participants that we have highlighted in published studies. While this whiteness does not invalidate the work on transfer in our field, we are in need of methodologies and methods that look beyond white-student and white-researcher experiences and positionalities and that engage the complexities of identity as it interacts with transfer. As white researchers, we need to look for and acknowledge the role of race and racism in the ecologies we study, and we must discuss our own identities, positionalities, and privileges in relation to the knowledge we seek to make.

Additionally, Lockett et al. encourage white researchers to go beyond simple acknowledgement of race and racism:

> Too often, predominantly White rhetoric and composition researchers carefully acknowledge the importance of taking race and racism into account when teaching and researching while concealing their specific relationship to racial identification. From a decolonial antiracist perspective, their self-image illustrates normative whiteness. They are almost always strategically naive, appearing before their audiences as benevolent, well-meaning colonizers who generously utilize their social status and privilege to study subaltern populations such as our composition students, or other downtrodden "barely literate" or "aspiring-to-become-literate" populations—including their historically marginalized colleagues (Heath; Sternglass). However, such posturing raises questions about how racial dynamics affect exchanges of power between researcher and the researched. (24)

To better illuminate these exchanges of power, Lockett et al. call white researchers to much action: to disclose what is at stake when writing about race, to take risks as they do so, to explicitly identify a relationship to race and racism, to acknowledge identity and privilege, to articulate how historical practices of exclusion are related to current practices, and to concede the limitations of their cultural knowledge as an outsider (25–26).

Below, I further discuss the first-year composition experiences of Travon, and of a second Black student from the first-year writing study, Daijah. As I do so, I take a few small steps toward responding to Lockett et al.'s call to identify, acknowledge, disclose, articulate, and concede when it comes to the role of race in research. I grapple with my own white researcher identities in relation to the data relating to Travon's and Daijah's writing experiences, and I ask questions that I hope will push me and other researchers toward more just and equitable research outcomes, for the field and for our students.

"ABOUT TO LOSE MY VOICE": TRAVON

Bump Halbritter and Julie Lindquist usefully trace the history of *voice* in writing studies, citing lively conversations about the metaphor of voice in student writing in the 1990s (see Kathleen Blake Yancey's 1994 collection *Voices on Voice*), followed by a waning interest in voice into the 2000s. Halbritter and Lindquist suggest we now "make an enthusiastic return to consideration of voice" through digital composition, where "qualitative researchers have ever-increasing capacities to make and manipulate audiovisual materials" (section 2, "The Idea of Voice"). "What does it mean to have—that is, to be in possession of—an audible voice?" they ask, demonstrating how editing audible voices can transform how we consider, share, and speak through research data (section 2). In section 4 of their webtext, Halbritter and Lindquist ask another set of questions about soundwriting that lead me to engage differently with the data I collected about Travon, especially as I think through Lockett et al.'s call for white researchers to pay more attention to race. Halbritter and Lindquist ask, "What are the roles of the researcher(s), who (all) emerges as the authors, who (all) speaks, who (all) hears, who (all) has the final say, and to what ends?" (section 4, "Listening Ahead").

Through research videos like those in *Transfer across Media*, Travon and other students speak: we hear their voices and see their bodies move. But I as researcher make methodological choices that control when, how, and how much they speak through selection and editing of interview clips. Halbritter and Lindquist's questions remind me that I all too often have "the final say" about what happened with a student's learning experiences. For example, you can read about, watch, and listen to Travon discuss his learning experiences in first-year writing in section 4.3 of *Transfer across Media* (https://ccdigitalpress.org/book/transfer-across-media/4-3-meta-awareness-of-process.html), where I include a research video featuring Travon speaking along with my own multimodal and written analysis of his experiences. The narrative I construct and present in this section, through both the video and written paragraphs, presents Travon as beginning his writing course disliking revision, but through the process of revising his papers and his video (and cutting out his narrator role), he develops a "meta-awareness of how revision might be one not-so-terrible tool he could use as a writer" (*Transfer across Media*, 4.3).

It may be that my tidy conclusions that Travon learned how to *really* revise through his writing course, and that video served as a site for transfer of this knowledge across media, serve my own ends as an eager, optimistic researcher. I return to the accounts of Travon's experiences now to explore how race and racial dynamics may have played a part in his learning. "Who (all) has the final say, and to what ends?"—Halbritter and Lindquist's question reminds me that the research conclusions I reach and if and how I choose grapple with the complexities of identity factors such as race, all of this makes a difference for the outcomes the research might achieve.

Looking back to my first interview with Travon near the beginning of the writing course, Travon talked about composing the first paper, a literacy narrative. He drafted the paper in one sitting and turned it in, and then met with his instructor to discuss the draft. She asked him to revise a lot of the content, according to Travon: "she tore it down paragraph by paragraph, sentence by sentence, kind of like, 'Okay, this don't need to be here. You'd be better on this one. You need to examine this more, more clarity.'" Travon described the process of receiving this feedback and considering how to revise the paper as "painful," continuing, "I'm about to lose my voice trying to basically, you know, critique my paper how she is, so I basically just did it over. I added some of her stuff, but instead of just adding what she wanted, I elaborated more on what she wanted so it could be more of my own." Travon was concerned that he was about to *lose his voice* by writing his paper using too much of his instructor's feedback and desires, and thus he compromised by elaborating on her requests in what he considered his own way. It seems important to me now to consider Travon's voice as tied closely to his identity—and to his race—and I note how much value Travon placed on having a clear, unique voice in his writing.

Travon experienced a similar feeling of losing his voice when it came to his video project later in the term. His video was about the summer bridge program at the university, of which he had taken part as a student a few months before, and of which many of his classmates of color had also been involved. Travon's section of first-year writing was a part of the school's Comprehensive Studies Program (CSP), which provided classes tailored to students from underrepresented communities, and his instructor had taught in that program for several years. Thus, Travon composed his video about the summer bridge program for an audience of his instructor and classmates, many of whom were Black students or students from other minority groups underrepresented in the academy, who had also completed the summer bridge program. As I write this, I realize that I never included such a detailed description of his writing course section in *Transfer across Media* or in my doctoral dissertation, where I discussed Travon's and his classmates' learning in depth. As a part of the CSP, Travon's section was filled with students of color (out of eighteen students in the class, twelve—66 percent—were Black, Hispanic, or Asian, and six students were white), which was in stark contrast to other sections at the same school that I observed for the study that had a much smaller minority student representation (in another non-CSP section with eighteen students, four—22 percent—were Black, Hispanic, or Asian, and fourteen were white).

Thinking back to my classroom observations, I noticed the racial makeup of Travon's first-year writing section right away as a white person used to classrooms mostly filled with other white faces and bodies. The white instructor and I were racial minorities in the class, which was filled with students of color. At the start of data collection, I remember being excited because of the racial makeup of the course and its designation as a CSP course, and I was glad that varying student perspectives would be included in the study. Somewhere along the way, however, I chose not to highlight or even to mention the racial makeup of the class in my descriptions in *Transfer across Media*, and likewise to ignore this element of the research scene in my analysis of the students' work and learning. The demographic statistics listed above make clear that racial dynamics were likely often relevant in such a course, as students of color interacted often with each other and with a professor and a researcher of a different race. To ignore race as a factor that may have had influence on student learning in such a situation seems, at the very least, foolish and irresponsible.

So, Travon composed his long video draft for his classmates—many of whom were Black—and the draft included interview clips with other Black students from across campus about their experiences in the summer bridge program. When Travon's writing instructor asked him to cut down his video, he went to the in-class peer editing workshop (see Figure 3.1) asking for advice on how to cut the video down, and his classmates suggested he cut out himself as narrator: "They were leaning towards, *well, maybe if you cut yourself out and keep the interviews*, and I was like, *well, fine* [shrugs shoulders]." Travon's classmates gave advice that attempted to align with the instructor's feedback, and thus the instructor's suggestion and the assignment's length requirement dictated Travon's compositional choices. In the moment, Travon shrugs, seemingly ambivalent, feeling forced to make cuts that he didn't want to make and to remove himself from the video. In the end, Travon was not happy with the result: "it didn't turn out how I wanted it to turn out. [. . .] I had to cut a lot of the themes out that made the video more creative how I wanted it."

Figure 3.1. Travon (left) workshops his video in class with two peers.

Travon's earlier statement again comes to mind: "I'm about to lose my voice . . ." Reflecting on his statement now causes me to wonder, what is at stake when we (instructors) ask students, and especially students of color, to heavily revise their work with our (white) input? What standards or conventions (here, the length of the video) are important to uphold, and what do we trade when we uphold these conventions over other concerns, such as voice? What do we *lose* when we ask students to write and revise in ways that *we* stipulate? For Travon, we may have lost some of what he interpreted as his own voice. We may have lost footage highlighting other Black experiences at the university. We may have lost perspectives of students of color at a predominantly white institution. And as a researcher, I originally decided not to dig into the potential role of race in this situation.

Halbritter and Lindquist question: "Who speaks? Who has the final say? And to what ends?" Revisiting this data about Travon's composing experiences with explicit attention to race highlights that Travon did not speak in ways he valued highly nor have the final say in this compositional moment—and he felt it. The instructor's pull and power were strong, and her values as to what was needed in the composition were different than Travon's. Even so, Travon took the feedback, revised his video, and by the end of the course, he spoke about the importance of learning to revise his work overall, something he rarely did before the course. In *Transfer across Media*, I focused on Travon's learning about revision, which may have been the "end" that the instructor valued. An alternate "end" would perhaps simultaneously value and encourage the development of the writer's own voice in ways that the writer envisions, a voice that may be closely tied to race and other identity factors.

LEAVING OUT A VOICE: DAIJAH

Halbritter and Lindquist state that "sometimes, it is the conspicuous absence of voice that speaks most loudly" (section 6, "No Words, Guys. No Words."). In their project, they discuss the ethics of representing Jovanna's voice on video, the sister of their research participant Liberty. Jovanna "has no spoken language," due to severe cerebral palsy, and Liberty introduces the audience to Jovanna on video in a dark bedroom, where Jovanna is barely visible. Halbritter and Lindquist describe for us what decisions they made when deciding how to edit—or not to edit—the footage and audio where Jovanna appears. In the transcript for their videos, they chose not to transcribe Jovanna's nonverbal sounds, rendering her voice "conspicuously absent" from the transcript. They explain, "we do not mean to silence Jovanna's voice, but to help you *see* the conspicuous absence of her audible voice and offer to you our shared challenge: How do we transcribe what we may be only beginning to hear, let alone understand?" In combination with the transcript, the audiovisual video footage of Liberty and Jovanna thus "allows viewers/auditors to sort through, negotiate, position, and reposition the action in this scene" for themselves and to evaluate Halbritter and Lindquist's interpretations (section 6, "No Words, Guys. No Words."). Halbritter and Lindquist's careful discussion of how they negotiated (and omitted) visual and aural representations of Jovanna leads me to return to my experiences with student participant Daijah, and my omission of much of her voice from my study.

I didn't write very much about Daijah or compose any videos about her experiences in *Transfer across Media*. I may even say now that her voice was left out of the book in many places, or that there is a "conspicuous absence" of her voice in my work. In part, this absence occurred because the coding and analytical methods I used did not lead me to write much about her. I also shied away from in-depth analysis of Daijah's experiences because she did not complete the multimodal composition assignment that was at the heart of the study. In Daijah's course, this assignment was the Career Investigation Project, where students were asked to select a future career of interest, research the career using primary and secondary methods, and report on their research through a one-minute video, a Prezi, and an in-class oral presentation. Daijah talked with me during an interview about working on her video and Prezi, but she never turned in the final draft.

Looking back, I now question what was going on in my coding process that Daijah's experiences rarely came up in my coding scheme. I coded the interview data with a grounded theory approach to analysis (Corbin and Strauss; Merriam). I read and re-read through interview transcripts, placing codes on meaningful excerpts, and then I grouped these codes into categories. Themes emerged as I looked across and further grouped the categories. I then used these emergent themes and the coded segments of data within them to select and arrange video clips within a video editor. I further analyzed selected clips through video editing, cutting down the clips, moving them around, and placing them into juxtaposition with other clips. After working with the data in this way, I selected some student participants to feature in research videos or sections of the book. Travon was one such student who I featured in his own research video, linked in the previous section. But excerpts from Daijah's interview did not appear often across the analytical categories. In the end, because her material rarely appeared in my coding scheme, I did not feature Daijah in her own research video in the book, and during the analysis process, I didn't consciously reflect over why.

My choice to leave out Daijah's voice from many parts of the book was surely influenced by a web of complex factors. But unlike Halbritter and Lindquist, I made no careful, informed decision to omit or edit her voice. In light of Lockett et al.'s urging to acknowledge and think more often about race as a factor that influences research and student experiences, I return to my interviews with Daijah to ask questions about the potential role of race and other identity factors in her learning and our interactions, and perhaps in my analysis of the data. I was a white female researcher in a position of power, looking for insight into how multimodal composition may or may not have contributed to moments of transfer for first-year writing students. Daijah was a Black female student who didn't have a great experience with the multimodal project in her course, and ultimately didn't turn it in for a grade.

Daijah chose to do her Career Investigation Project on becoming a dentist. As part of the project, students had to research the role of writing and communication in their chosen career. However, Daijah hit an early roadblock when she interviewed an orthodontist who told her that they didn't use writing and communication outside of referrals. Daijah told me that with this information, she would have preferred having to write a more traditional essay instead of a multimodal project. She stated, "I would have rather wrote a paper on it. [. . .] Because I think it depends on the career you have. Like mine, it's not really much I could—not much I can say. It's not a lot to talk about, 'cause we don't—as an orthodontist, you don't really use writing in your daily job. I would have rather just had a regular writing assignment." Daijah seemed stymied by the unexpected information she collected from her interview, and this combined with the video and Prezi format of the project, made it difficult for her to know how to proceed.

At the end of class, Daijah told me that the video/Prezi project was the project she could see having least application to her future writing. Prezi, she reported, made it harder to organize her thinking:

> *Daijah*: It was just like with the Prezi, … It was like you
> need to know exactly where you want to put things or it can
> get confusing to have to take it out and put it back and makes
> it like it was just—I'd rather be able to erase it or backspace
> delete and then type it again.
>
> *Crystal:* It wasn't easy to put—to organize your ideas?
>
> *Daijah:* Yeah, to organize my thoughts.

A few seconds later, Daijah added, "I mean it [the multimodal project] did teach me one thing, that I don't want to be a dentist anymore." Due to her struggles with the assignment, along with what she learned as she talked with and observed a professional in the field, Daijah seemingly altered her career aspirations.

There is much here that would be useful to dig into for a researcher interested in how multimodal composition might facilitate transfer across media, or why transfer might not occur in a given learning situation. Daijah did not experience transfer as I was defining it in my study, but she did begin to articulate why Prezi in particular was a difficult composing environment for her, especially when faced with unexpected information about her research topic. In looking back to my codes from when I open-coded Daijah's interview transcripts, I did mark Daijah's comments about the multimodal project as a negative instance of transfer across media. I did not follow up on this code in my later analysis or selection of data to use and feature, though, and Daijah's narrative of struggling to compose with unexpected information and with Prezi did not make it into any publications nor my book—until now. This omission is not necessarily rooted in race. However, had I been more open to exploring the many factors—including race—that were influencing Daijah's learning, I might have been more curious about her narrative, and more willing to dig into what I may have considered "disconfirming evidence," evidence that I thought didn't further my thesis of video as an apt site for transfer.

Daijah also mentioned that she missed the peer review session for the Career Investigation project, and we did talk a little bit about why:

> *Crystal:* Okay. You just missed it [the peer review]? *[Pause]*
>
> *Daijah:* It was. It was online. I think it was a homework, but your Prezi had to be done, and mine wasn't done in time for it to put the link up.
>
> *Crystal:* Okay, so you didn't put it up?
>
> *Daijah:* No.
>
> *Crystal:* Do you want to talk about what was going on with it and why you couldn't finish it on time?
>
> *Daijah:* It just wasn't ready in time. *[Laughs a bit while speaking]*
>
> *Crystal:* That's all you want to say? *[Laughter]*
>
> *Daijah:* Yeah.
>
> *Crystal:* Okay. That's fine.

Why was Daijah reluctant to talk with me about her missing work, and why did the fact that she did not turn in the assignment for a grade not come up in our conversations? We both laugh in the exchange above in part because the interaction was a little bit forced and awkward. (To view a recording of this interaction between Daijah and me, please visit https://youtu.be/nAk8a6icSe8). She didn't want to elaborate, and I wanted more information.

Figure 3.2. Daijah and I talk during an interview.

Perhaps Daijah did not want to share her shortcomings with me, a researcher of a different race that she didn't know well. Perhaps there was a personal situation in her life preventing her from finishing the assignment that she did not feel comfortable sharing. Perhaps she thought I might judge her negatively for not completing the work, or she knew that I was a fan of digital composition and she was not. Asking these questions about our interaction and identities, though, was something I did not do as part of my initial analysis of Daijah's interview material.

While Daijah was not a fan of the multimodal assignment, she talked at length about another assignment from the writing class that she *did* enjoy, the ad analysis essay. Students were tasked with selecting an advertisement, analyzing the rhetorical situation and appeals within the ad, and then redesigning the ad for a new audience. Daijah's selected ad was a print ad for leave-in conditioner from the magazine *Ebony*, a magazine tailored to a Black audience. This assignment was one of Daijah's favorite assignments from the class because "it wasn't something I had to research. . . . I'd rather talk about something that I could possibly make up than actually help to have the facts from or about." Here, Daijah begins to articulate the value that she placed on writing about something she had personal knowledge and connection to, instead of writing about a disconnected topic that required outside research. Indeed, she told me during our first interview that "I'm more of a better freestyle writer. Like I'm not good on specific topics. . . . Freestyle writing as a—like you have to write about maybe something that happened to me personally, or I can just write about anything I want."

Daijah's comments here bring me back to questions of voice in our teaching and research, and of choosing to omit, or even to edit a voice. Whose voice is edited or omitted in the classroom through assignments that ask students to write about topics they can't (or don't) invest in? Whose voices are edited or omitted from our research when we code and categorize data with stated (or unstated) priorities? Halbritter and Lindquist explain that for video and sound editing, "the voice of the editors is characterized not by way of sound as much as by way of choice" (section 7, "Audible Voice as Synecdochic Identity"). What choices did I make as a researcher that then ultimately silenced Daijah's voice?

For Daijah, the answers to Halbritter and Lindquist's questions of "who speaks? Who has the final say? And to what ends?" are complex. Personal factors that included race and racial dynamics between her and I may have influenced Daijah's willingness to speak in interviews. Then, my analytical choices as the researcher, some deliberate and others less so, also influenced her ability to speak within the study. Revisiting Daijah's experiences now makes clear that paying closer attention to how race and identity influence who speaks, how they speak, and who does not speak is an important and often overlooked aspect of research methodology and reflection.

TOWARD ANTIRACIST METHODOLOGIES AND METHODS

Lockett, Ruiz, Sanchez, and Carter note that "racial dynamics affect exchanges of power between researcher and the researched" (24), and this is indeed true in the first-year writing study, as this chapter begins to reveal. As a white researcher, I am someone who benefits from white privilege, a relatively able body, a tenured faculty position at a university, and many other support systems. In revisiting and asking questions about Travon's and Daijah's learning experiences and my choices as the researcher, I expose some ways I was careless with or even misused my power and privilege, ignoring or directing attention away from race as a contributing factor in the interdependent research scene. While it might seem that the use of video for data analysis and presentation automatically brings race and other identity factors to the forefront of research, my reflections and remaining questions make clear that it is indeed possible to virtually ignore race and race's influence on research findings even while viewing, listening to, selecting, and editing images and sounds of Black bodies and Black voices. Such a color blind researcher stance does no favors to participants from traditionally marginalized groups, and in fact perpetuates a white, seemingly-raceless learning environment where race and other identity factors are not relevant.

At stake in the revisiting within this chapter is the need to disrupt comfortable whiteness, where white researchers get to dismiss questions of race and identity as irrelevant to inquiry, or as too complex or enmeshed to consider. At stake is a need to strive for greater equity and justice for BIPOC students and research participants, even if that equity means admitting carelessness or fault on the part of the researcher. At stake is the ability to design and conduct research that is not simply aware of race, but overtly antiracist.

In this chapter, I look and listen more carefully to Travon and to Daijah with these high stakes in mind, and I conclude now with several takeaways gleaned from this revisiting that I hope might be useful to other researchers. First, researchers might more often consider the role of identity factors such as race *from the start* in writing research, even if the study at hand isn't explicitly about identity or race. I may have paid closer attention, for example, to particular moments in Travon's and Daijah's narratives had I been looking and listening specifically for ways their identities intersected with their learning, or I may have noticed additional information had my researcher senses been better attuned to race and identity as they intersected with learning from the beginning.

Second, it is likely normal and probable for a researcher to feel resistance and even fear when beginning to analyze data relating to race and identities, especially if the researcher is white. Digging into the role of race might be unfamiliar or intimidating, and findings might be uncomfortable or even disturbing. These emotions, however, can be productive and may signal a need to pay close attention to the interaction of elements within the research scene. In response to the fear and apprehension I felt when I was first prompted to consider the role of race in my study, I initially rejected the idea that I might find new insights if I did consider race, and I chose not to pursue the topic, which for a time resulted in the silencing of participant voices and experiences. Instead, the negative emotions I felt may have been an indication that my white privilege was being revealed and that race—my own, the students' and the instructor's—warranted more investigation.

Finally, when race or other identity factors emerge *during* a research study, as they did during mine, it is likely important to explore those avenues, even when doing so requires more work. There may be more reading to do, or different reading, and more time needed. A focus on identity may require at-times uncomfortable self-reflection about race and privilege. It may require asking new questions, or different questions, or learning to be comfortable with difficult, complex answers. These actions are small steps for researchers to prioritize so that more voices can speak freely, so that more voices can have a final say, and so that these voices can help us discover more just and equitable ends.

WORKS CITED

Corbin, Juliet, and Anselm Strauss. *Basics of Qualitative Research: Techniques and Procedures for Developing Grounded Theory.* 3rd edition, SAGE Publications, 2008.

Fleckenstein, Kristie S., et al. "The Importance of Harmony: An Ecological Metaphor for Writing Research." *College Composition and Communication*, vol. 60, no. 2, Dec. 2008, pp. 388–419.

Halbritter, Bump, and Julie Lindquist. "Sleight of Ear: Voice, Voices, and Ethics of Voicing." *Soundwriting Pedagogies*, edited by Courtney S. Danforth et al., Computers and Composition Digital Press/Utah State University Press, 2018, https://ccdig italpress.org/book/soundwriting/halbritter-lindquist/index.html.

Lockett, Alexandria L., et al. *Race, Rhetoric, and Research Methods.* The WAC Clearinghouse, 2021. https://doi.org/10.37514/PER-B.2021.1206. https://doi.org/10 .37514/PER-B.2021.1206.

Merriam, Sharan B. *Qualitative Research: A Guide to Design and Implementation.* Jossey-Bass, 2009.

VanKooten, Crystal. "A Research Methodology of Interdependence through Video as Method." *Computers and Composition*, vol. 54, Dec. 2019, pp. 1–17, https://doi.org /10.1016/j.compcom.2019.102514.

———. *Transfer across Media: Using Digital Video in the Teaching of Writing.* Computers and Composition Digital Press/Utah State UP, 2020. https://ccdigitalpress.org /book/transfer-across-media/index.html.

PART 2.

RESISTING METHOD/OLOGICAL DEFINITIONS AND NORMS

CHAPTER 4.

REVISING TEXTILE PUBLICATIONS: CHALLENGES AND CONSIDERATIONS IN TACTILE METHODS

Sonia C. Arellano

Independent Scholar

Paired readings:

- Arellano, Sonia C. "Quilting as Qualitative Feminist Research Method: Expanding Understandings of Migrant Experiences." *Rhetoric Review*, vol. 41, no. 1, 2022, pp. 17–30.

- Arellano, Sonia C. "Sexual Violences Traveling to El Norte: An Example of Quilting as Method." *College Composition and Communication*, vol. 72, no. 4, 2021, pp. 500–515.

When employing new methods of research in rhetoric and writing studies, researchers can face challenges aligning their methods with publication and university expectations. The reality for many scholars is that we must publish to maintain relevancy in the field and to ensure security in university positions. Therefore, this chapter discusses challenges of the composing and revising process employing a new tactile method of research, Quilting as Method (Arellano). Drawing from the experience of completing a tactile research publication (a research quilt), this chapter discusses the messy process employing Quilting as Method. This chapter details the complex revising/recomposing/restitching process of a material publication— incorporating new information, expanding the piece with new materials, and learning new skills to revise the piece. Additionally, this chapter considers the collaborative nature of such research methods involving animals and humans when working from home with physical materials. Lastly, this chapter suggests the field consider how mentoring, timelines and cost, and tenure and publishing requirements can facilitate or hinder innovative research methods. Overall,

DOI: https://doi.org/10.37514/PER-B.2024.2241.2.04

this chapter illuminates the challenges researchers face and the labor necessary when employing innovative research methods in hopes that publication venues and universities consider how to better support faculty using such research methods.

As many researchers agree, our methods and methodologies are inarguably connected to what we value as research and as knowledge making. Therefore, the methods of research we are taught, often in graduate school, are methods deemed important by others. When starting my academic work in a Ph.D. program, my mentors and teachers presented research methods that prompted me to reconsider what methods researchers should value and why. Additionally, methods and methodologies are inarguably connected to how we choose to revise according to feedback. Giving thoughtful and thorough productive feedback for revision is hard and time consuming and receiving such feedback is dependent upon a community of colleagues. Often, scholars are left with anonymous reviewer feedback, which isn't always structured in a dialectical way. Considering how we choose methods for our research and how we learn to revise according to feedback, it is apparent that mentorship significantly influences these important parts of the research and publication process.

Therefore, in this chapter I consider the relationship between the research methods we employ and our revision processes through a lens of mentorship. While many challenges arise when employing new research methods, here I focus on the challenges of the composing and revision process employing a new tactile method of research, quilting as method ("Quilting as Method" 85). First, I situate myself and my research to provide context about how this method came about and why I decided to take the tough route of employing a tactile method. Next, I briefly discuss two publications referenced throughout this chapter. One article explains QAM (quilting as method) in practice, and the other is a research quilt demonstrating the product of QAM. Throughout this chapter, I draw from the experience of completing these two publications (focusing on the quilt publication). Then I discuss the incredibly messy process of revising a tactile research publication, pointing to two distinct ways this method challenges Western notions of research: the complex revision process, which meant expanding and recomposing in this case, and the collaborative revision process, involving animals and humans when working from home with physical materials. Lastly, I suggest ways that readers can prepare for such challenges, and I suggest ways for publications and institutions to better support faculty using nontraditional research methods.

SITUATING THE RESEARCH AND RESEARCHER

The CFP of this collection claimed to be a "call not only for more inclusive and diverse frames to guide our research, but one that is also driven by an ethical imperative." In order to articulate how and why the QAM approach disrupts and diverges from traditional methods, I felt it necessary to begin with the origin story of my quilt project and this research method because as Gesa Kirsch previously stated, "[f]eminist researchers start with the premise that research methods are never neutral, impartial, or disinterested" (257). Although the impetus for my research may seem to be happenstance, it is part of my familial histories and my ways of knowing and being in the world.

As I was completing graduate coursework many years ago, I was emotionally affected by two seemingly disparate experiences: (1) losing my stepmother to a brief and nasty battle with lung cancer and (2) working with undocumented migrants in the Tucson, Arizona community. To cope with my stepmother's death, I devoured as many readings, podcasts, and movies as I could to learn about death, grief, and memorializing and to learn from others who experienced a parent's death at a young age. To channel the deep sadness and empathy I felt for the migrants I worked with regularly (both volunteer teaching English and working at a migrant shelter), I consumed as many readings, documentaries, and government documents that I could to better understand the plight of migrants entering the US during that time.

As I was deciding on a dissertation topic, my mentor Adela C. Licona pointed me to a quilt project that memorialized migrant deaths. The Migrant Quilt Project makes quilts from migrant clothing left behind in the desert, and each quilt names migrants (or lists them as unknown) per year who die in the Sonoran Desert crossing into the US. When I first saw the quilts, immense emotion came over me, as they are incredibly evocative. This was the starting point of my research that brought together the rhetorical power of memorializing textiles and the incredible travesty of migrant deaths at the southern US border. Without realizing it, this research was influenced by familial knowledge of sewing; I come from a family of feminist seamstresses.[1] Additionally, I come from a family of migrant farmworkers who traveled to the northern US each summer to work the fields. Therefore, the creative capacities and the knowledge base necessary for sewing projects, as well as the knowledge of working the land and the difficulties of migration within the US, are a familiar part of my family history. The ability to engage in these areas and learn these skills came from a place of necessity in my family history.

---

1   See "Heart, Mind, and Body in Quilting Research" for a guest blog about this.

By the time I came to my research with the Migrant Quilt Project, I knew more about the complicated story of migrant deaths expressed in the quilts as well as the rhetorical prowess necessary to create such quilts. As I embarked on my dissertation research, I chose safe, established methods: visual rhetorical analysis of the quilts and feminist semi-structured interviews of the quilters. Although my Ph.D. program discussed accepting nontraditional genres and methods for a dissertation, the college would only allow a written dissertation, which of course dictated how I would conduct and present my research. However, a chance encounter changed the trajectory of my research significantly. While interviewing a quilter, she asked if I would like to contribute a quilt to the project because they needed someone to complete the 2003–2004 quilt. I said yes without much thinking that I was also completing a dissertation. I knew how to sew but did not know how to quilt. With a grant from my university, I was able to take a beginner's quilting class and purchase materials for the quilt (along with the clothing given to me from the Migrant Quilt Project). As I completed this quilt, I gained experiential knowledge of just how difficult completing a quilt was, not just theoretical. I realized the process of completing this quilt had to be a part of my dissertation research because it was too much work and there were too many composing parallels to simply leave the quilt as a "side project" to the dissertation. The dissertation chapter I wrote discussing quilting as method was underdeveloped because, although I knew there was something there, I couldn't thoroughly articulate it. However, the more I learned about migrant deaths, the more I knew this method was an ideal method to study a phenomenon that is complex to understand and lacking the type of data other areas of study may provide.

The point of this background story is to inspire others and situate myself by explaining the context I was working within, including university expectations and norms of our discipline. I did not initially intend to disrupt or challenge traditional Western notions of research when I took on this work. However, as I dove into the research and attempted to convey it through the quilt, I knew traditional methods would leave the data, the story, and the exigency underdeveloped and incomplete. As I've stated elsewhere referencing a powerful quote by Malea Powell, "I believe that QAM—as a method that produces a visual and verbal material object—provides the potential to facilitate flowering meanings, particularly about complex and traumatic stories" ("Quilting as Method" 24).

Although I was challenged—a committee member told me, "This isn't a thing"—and not everyone I've encountered has been supportive of QAM, thankfully my dissertation chair was. She mentored me through the challenges and doubts because she believed in this work, and for that I am thankful. The importance of mentorship is paramount, especially for graduate students and junior scholars who are using nontraditional methods in their research. In completing my research with the Migrant Quilt Project, I knew that the lives and experiences of migrants was only partially conveyed through alphabetic writing. Our field is logocentric, but my life and my family history are not. I knew I had to draw from those embodied knowledges to figure out a method that would try to provide dignity and voice to the dead. I kept asking myself, how do you tell the story of those who leave behind no written record, of those who you cannot interview, of those whose bodies disappear in the desert without a trace? These questions informed the ethical imperative calling me to think beyond established methods in rhetoric and composition.

QUILTING AS METHOD, EXPLANATION AND EXAMPLE

Years after writing the dissertation chapter that discussed quilting as method (QAM), I took a very long revision journey (expanded into a book chapter that didn't work out, then majorly revised and cut down to a journal article, then revised and resubmitted, and then revised one last time and submitted), before publishing it in *Rhetoric Review* in early 2022. "Quilting as a Qualitative, Feminist Research Method: Expanding Understandings of Migrant Deaths" is a thorough explanation of quilting as method with examples of how the method functions in my own research with the Migrant Quilt Project. In the article, I support the claim that quilting is a qualitative, feminist research method: qualitative as it fills the gaps that quantitative research leaves; feminist as it values experience, equity, and risk-taking; an arts based research method as a non-discursive knowledge creation to better understand phenomena. Drawing from arts based research (Barone and Eisner) and feminist rhetorical practices (Royster and Kirsch), I explain how QAM functions as a three-fold scaffold in practice: employing critical imagination through tacking in and tacking out, crafting a narrative, and gaining a better understanding of the phenomenon at hand. The "Quilting as Method" article draws from my experience making a quilt for the Migrant Quilt Project to provide examples of how the method functions using Royster and Kirsch's concept of critical imagination through tacking in and tacking out.

As I was in that long revision process with the "Quilting as Method" article, I decided to take on the task of demonstrating QAM with another quilt project. My goal this time was to intentionally use QAM and publish the quilt as the final research product. The quilt piece was initially created in response to a special issue CFP that didn't work out, but I found a home for it with *College Composition and Communication*. I never imagined a flagship journal would publish a textile research project. However, the editor had seen the beginning stages of the quilt and asked me to consider *CCC*. Published in 2021, "Sexual Violences Traveling to El Norte: An Example of Quilting as Method" is a quilt publication with a short, written piece to accompany it. While the quilt is the research publication, the written piece is akin to a footnote providing a bit more context. The quilt publication chronicles the state-sanctioned violences migrant women experience crossing from Central America, through Mexico, and into the US, mostly based on Oscar Martinez's book *The Beast*.

Fortunately, these two research publications came out within a few months of one another because they work together. While one explains the method, the other is an example of the method, which reifies the argument that the quilt is the completed research product (not a written paper). Although the argument is a hard one to make in our logocentric field, and despite the limitations of printed publications with material research products (even photos of the quilt), I was fortunate to be mentored through the process of these publications so they could significantly contribute to the field of rhetoric and composition. Although these two publications inform one another, for this chapter I will focus mostly on the process of composing and revising the published "Sexual Violences" quilt. Lastly, I'll mention because it supports many points of this book chapter, both publications were awarded for being the best publication in that journal in that year—"Sexual Violences" was awarded the 2022 *CCCC*'s Richard Braddock Award and "Quilting as Method" was awarded the 2022 Theresa J. Enos Anniversary Award for Best Publication.

COMPLEX AND COLLABORATIVE REVISION EXPERIENCES

Through the process of completing the "Sexual Violences" quilt, it became more apparent that completing textile projects with tactile methods challenge some salient Western notions of research in our field. For example, the idea that the research process is completed and written by one person, with a singular, clear answer in the form of an article or book, could not be more different than the process of completing this quilt publication, which was incredibly messy to say the least. Although the ways that this tactile approach to research about sexual violences is multifaceted in challenging Western notions, I will focus on two ways here: the complexity of revising a textile project and the collaborative nature of such work.

COMPLEX REVISING/RECOMPOSING/RESTITCHING

As scholars in rhetoric and writing studies continue to expand the field putting forth research methods and methodologies to consider, a complication that scholars face is aligning their research methods with expectations of publication venues and universities because the expectations of publication venues and universities tend to value and understand traditional and established methods. The reality for many scholars is that we must publish research to maintain relevancy in the field and to ensure security in university positions. Additionally, because publication expectations are often on set timelines, like tenure, such expectations may discourage or even hinder the work of new methods.

What follows is a discussion of the challenges I faced during the revision process of "Sexual Violences" because of external expectations that did not necessarily understand or align with this textile project. Importantly, I must mention that my university, flagship journals in our field, and colleagues were supportive of my research using this new method, but I'm sure that is not the case for many scholars. My tenure guidelines did not require a monograph, and they clearly articulated the value of collaborative research. Additionally, both *Rhetoric Review* and *College Composition and Communication* editors and reviewers were encouraging and provided productive feedback. Lastly, colleagues who were skeptical of this work still took the time to thoughtfully engage with it to help me improve my argument and demonstrate the value of this research. My point is that even in ideal situations with lots of support, employing messy and nontraditional methods still bring challenges.

The initial submission of the "Sexual Violences" research quilt to *CCC* consisted of four written pages along with photos of the drafted quilt (Figure 4.1). The first draft of the quilt top was about 24 by 16 inches and consisted of four small blocks and two large ones. As a draft that needed to remain malleable, the top was mostly complete, but the backing, binding, or quilting of the layers was not. I was unsure how the reviewers[2] would understand and interpret the quilt, which was not so different from how I felt about the QAM written article. I was unsure if readers (especially those who do not quilt) would understand the argument. I was pleased to receive an "accept with revisions" decision from *CCC*, with generous reviewer feedback.

As I read through the reviewer feedback, I realized a lot of the comments were about how to better articulate the value of this work to *CCC* readers in the written portion, which was helpful. However, I did not receive much feedback on the quilt itself, which was the research product. The response from the reviewers is common in our field; although we say we value multimodal work, what counts and how it is assessed has not expanded to accommodate that multimodal work. Conversations concerning this conundrum have been ongoing concerning grading within composition classrooms, concerning nontraditional

---

2   It's important for me to mention that the reviewers were sent photos of the quilt, not the actual quilt. Without starting a discussion about material genres that is beyond the scope of this chapter, I will simply state that a photo of the quilt is not the same as seeing the quilt in person nor feeling the quilt in person.

genres of dissertations in graduate programs, and concerning digital, community, and creative research and other types of labor within tenure and promotion requirements. I am thankful that *CCC* gave the research quilt a chance, but I also hope the journals in our field continue to expand the parameters for effective feedback on multimodal publications.

*Figure 4.1. First Draft of "Sexual Violences" Quilt Publication;
Photo by Author Sonia C. Arellano.*

I started my revision process by reading the scholarship reviewers suggested, which further informed the written portion, but not the quilt piece itself. At the time, the *CCC* journal asked if the author would like to be mentored through the revision process, and I was fortunate to work with a senior colleague Raúl Sánchez, who was supportive of this research quilt. As he was generously mentoring me through the revision process, he said that if my point is to provide an example of QAM, maybe I didn't need more writing, but I needed more quilt. This set off a lightbulb for revision. At this same time, a news story came out about a nurse whistleblower who claimed that undocumented migrant women in detention centers were being forced to have hysterectomies. Her claims reinforced and extended the argument of the quilt: state-sanctioned sexual violence that migrant women experience does not stop at the border but continues long after they enter the US. My mentor's comment and this news story were central to my revisions.

After reading more scholarship suggested by reviewers as well as government documents and news stories about migrant hysterectomies, I began to revise the research quilt by recomposing the quilt top from scratch. While I kept the story of the four main blocks, as well as the top and bottom flags, I decided to add a block to reflect the recent news story and to add a centerpiece of Mexico. I sketched a visual draft and now had the opportunity to add more details because the quilt would be bigger. With the blocks that maintained their stories, I added more maps and more details so that the flow of the journey and the argument could be understood through the movement within and between the blocks. Maps have been incredibly important in this work because the geography tells stories and histories. The central map of the US, Mexico, Guatemala, and Belize reflected important additions, as I stated previously:

> I chose the color purple because it has been used world-wide
> in marches, movements, and protests against femicide and
> gender-based violence . . . The United States, Belize, and
> Guatemala are in an iridescent light purple to represent the
> beautiful home country of a migrant's past and the idealized
> potential future in the United States. ("Sexual Violences" 512)

None of the fabric from the original first draft was reused. I had to recompose the quilt top because the organization and the content were both expanded. The final revised draft research quilt (Figure 4.2) is about 60 by 48 inches, and the written portion is about 15 pages.[3]

---

3   See "Sexual Violences" in *College Composition and Communication* for the final draft version. The final version is not included here to reify that it is research already published elsewhere.

*Figure 4.2. Revised Draft of "Sexual Violences" Quilt Publication;
Photo by Author Sonia C. Arellano.*

This long and arduous revision process supports my argument that the quilt is the research product because similar to completing major revisions with a written article, the revision process for the quilt maintained the same argument and basic support, just refined and revised to be clearer and more impactful.

However, one aspect that is entirely different from more traditional research methods and products are the difficulties brought about because of the material nature of a tactile method. As I mention in "Quilting as Method," time and particular skills are necessary to employ this method, but it's also important to consider the time and money it costs. During fall 2020 while revising "Sexual Violences," I was teaching one online course, so thankfully, I had the time to engage in thoroughly revising the quilt. I did not ask for funding to help facilitate the revisions (for more material and other needs) from my department, because our funding is clearly marked for travel, technology, and books. However, if I had the chance again, I would have advocated for funding for this textile project.

With a textile revision (really recomposing and restitching), I needed new and more material. As with many things during this time,[4] there was a shortage

---

4   In fall of 2020 COVID-19 was still new, and we did not have a vaccine available in the

of pre-cut fabric squares, and I tried to take selective trips to the store because the pandemic was new with still so much unknown about it. Such difficult access to resources is quite different from a written piece. If you need a specific scholarly source, there are ways to access it with interlibrary loan and libraries able to scan sources. If you need a certain amount of purple fabric and the store is sold out, good luck trying to get it elsewhere or in small amounts. This is rhetoric though, identifying and working with the available means.

The available skills to draw from can present challenges as well. I intended to quilt this project myself with my sewing machine. Often quilters outsource the quilting part (sewing through the top, batting, and backing layers) of their quilt to someone with a large quilt machine. With smaller quilts, a regular sized machine will suffice. The quilt I made for the Migrant Quilt Project was too large to fit in my machine, so I quilted the layers through another method—adding buttons at key parts of the quilt to hold the layers together. For the "Sexual Violences" research quilt I wanted to incorporate free motion quilting because the quilt was small enough to do so on my machine. However, I did not know how to free motion sew, so I watched a lot of YouTube videos and practiced enough to incorporate this design aspect into the quilt, which was a rhetorical design element. Again, this is different from a traditional method because scholars do not usually need to learn new skills in the middle of revising a research product.

Parts of the revision process with QAM parallel the process of revising more traditional products with more traditional methods. However, scholars can face many difficulties revising when using tactile methods such as this one, and they can end up recomposing in order to address reviewer feedback and clarify their argument. Just a few challenges (to which I offer suggestions at the end of this chapter) researchers may face when employing such methods and revising include time and space for revising, reviewer expertise, cost and availability of materials, and knowledge of all skills needed for revisions.

COLLABORATIVE NATURE OF COMPOSING AND REVISING

In addition to the complex process of revising with tactile methods, the "Sexual Violences" research quilt also confronts Western notions of research by demonstrating the collaborative nature of revising with tactile methods. Although most revision processes are collaborative, the collaboration with quilting as method may look different because the relational human component is more apparent. Personally, I never send out any piece of important

---

US. Many jobs and classes were still fully remote. Many materials and types of labor were unavailable for various reasons.

writing without having someone look at it first. Although we may not always cite our collaborators (who provide feedback and inspiration throughout our writing process), we often thank them in our acknowledgements or a footnote.[5] However, in the final product itself, academics typically only include citations, not daily inspirations.

When using tactile methods, the human relational component is much more apparent and spans far outside of my immediate academic circle. During the fall of 2020 as I revised the "Sexual Violences" quilt, I turned my dining room into my quilt workshop. The dining table was the only place I could have the quilt fully laid out with my sewing machine at the end of the table. My setup faced the living room TV, with the iron and ironing board situated between the dining table and the dog bed. I needed the space and time to work in my home, so my work involved everyone and everything in my home.

I often had to use the tile floor to draft pieces and see how they looked before sewing them together. Anyone who lives with cats knows it is impossible to put something new on the floor, especially a square piece of fabric, without them jumping on it. The dog and cats were collaborators in that my workspace was their daily living space. The cats joined me on their window perches right behind where my sewing machine was set up and on the dining chairs, always nearby while I worked, often messing up my materials. My docile and lazy dog (he's a puggle) stayed sleeping in his bed nearby as well, with constant snoring providing a soothing sound along with the sewing machine.

As Laura Micciche claims in her book about writing partners, "[c]ompanion animals are most certainly not objects but subjects who contribute in significant ways to writerly identity and persistence" (93). Her study showed that many scholars thank their pets for facilitating sustained periods of writing or much needed breaks. Micciche also cites her Facebook feed full of pictures of people writing (mostly at a computer) with their animal companion nearby (86–88). My Facebook feed is similar with other academics posting photos of their animal writing companions nearby with books spread across the floor or sleeping near a laptop keyboard. However, one aspect is different when using tactile methods: the remains of this collaboration are apparent in the cat hair left behind on the research project. The cats rolling on fabric drafts literally leave their mark on the final product, the quilt.

---

5   For example, Laura Gonzales' book *Sites of Translation* has a beautiful acknowledgements section that thanks many people in her life and includes her dog. And *Rhetoric Review* has an established practice of acknowledging the two reviewers in a footnote within the first sentence of the article.

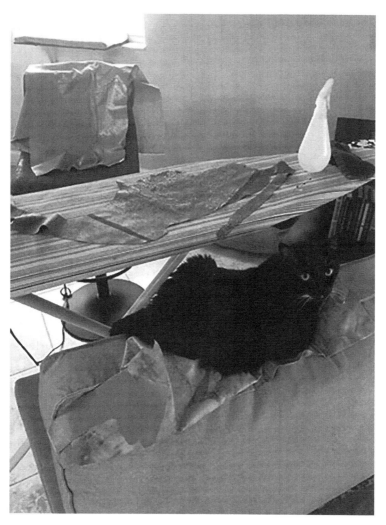

Figure 4.3. Carlos overseeing the composing of "Sexual Violences" while also lying on part of the quilt publication; Photo by Author Sonia C. Arellano.]

In addition to the non-human actors who take part in this messy method, human actors in my household did as well. First, my non-academic partner was a big part of the process as he was working from home and watching the daily progress. He offered input when asked and even when not, often about visual design choices.[6] He is in IT, so it's always refreshing to gain perspective from

6   Similarly, my mom often reads my writing intended for people outside our field. I ask her to highlight the parts she doesn't understand because if she can't understand it, then I'm not writing well.

an average viewer about design choices. Additionally, various visitors would ask about the quilt piece on our dining table including neighbors who were appalled by the content of the quilt. Once while visiting, my mother-in-law asked about the quilt, and when hearing the stories of migrant women, she referenced her knowledge about women experiencing sexual violence back in her home country of Venezuela. She drew from her own background and knowledge about the subject to engage in conversation about my research. Normally when I'm at a social gathering and someone asks about my research, my answer tends to shock them into awkward silence. However, in these instances, visitors offered insight, knowledge, and thoughtful engagement, perhaps because they were in my house, or perhaps because they had a visual and tactile method of understanding my research. These conversations and responses were undoubtedly a part of the collaborative revision process for this quilt. The humans in my life helped me to articulate the argument clearly and thoughtfully, repeatedly. The input and imprint of others, particularly non academics, involved in the physical space of research was even more pronounced than in other types of research products that employ other research methods.

SUGGESTIONS FOR ENGAGING THE MESSINESS OF QAM

Overall, this chapter intends to illuminate the challenges (even in the most supportive environments) researchers face and the labor necessary when employing innovative, messy methods of research. I hope that this information helps other scholars consider how to prepare for these challenges, and I hope that publications and institutions consider how to better support faculty using nontraditional research methods. I leave readers with a few suggestions for both researchers and institutions (universities, departments, journals, and university presses) to promote employing complex, messy, and innovative methods.

CONSIDER MENTORING TO FACILITATE MESSY METHODS AND METHODOLOGIES

My first suggestion is to consider what type of mentoring you can provide as a mentor and what types of mentoring you need as a mentee to facilitate successful completion of courses, degrees, and publications, because successful completion can depend on the methods and methodologies we learn and put forward. Scholars in our field often reference their own mentors when discussing their own experiences as mentors. We can learn from some of these instances to be contentious of how we mentor students and junior colleagues and how we can ask important questions of ourselves as mentors. Additionally, we can consider how we need to be mentored whether it's through a graduate program or to meet tenure requirements. For example, in an interview about her own writing practices, Jessica Enoch mentions that she teaches students about genre to pull "back the veil a little bit"; she works on a calendar basis with her students; And she claims, "the biggest thing I think I do helpfully, I hope, is to teach graduate students how to revise from comments" (69). She references learning a lot from her mentor, Cheryl Glenn, such as asking students to revise multiple times. Enoch discusses where her mentoring practices come from, and she also explains how to help students tangibly and specifically in their writing and revision process. Although she doesn't mention method here, undoubtedly that is part of the conversation when she's helping them through revisions and feedback.

Considering how to help students with their writing is just as important as helping them with bigger picture questions that also are related to their methods and methodology, like how or where do they fit in an academic conversation? Fatima Chrifi Alaoui and Bernadette M. Calafell discuss how their mentor/mentee relationship developed as Calafell helped Alaoui embrace a methodological "homeplace." As Alaoui claims that "[t]raditional research methodologies have always left out the expressions and stories that make up the whole meaning of the text I write and the experience I live" (70). Calafell not only demonstrated the practice of mentoring through love and care, but also helped Alaoui find a method that worked to give meaning to her struggles and embodied experiences (70–71). Additionally, Calafell writes elsewhere about mentors who helped her find her own homeplace in academia (Calafell).

Another instance of a mentoring relationship is a story about indigenous rhetorical practices with Andrea Riley-Mukavetz and Malea D. Powell. Not only do they discuss the relationship between one another, but also to their students as they collaboratively taught a graduate seminar. The layering of practice in this piece is important as they make visible "how stories function methodologically and theoretically" because they piece together their own stories as well as stories about the course in order to demonstrate "story as methodology is one of the common features of indigenous rhetorical practice" (146). They recount the challenges faced putting into practice the approaches they were teaching as well as the difficult decisions they had to make based on restricting parameters such as time and money. Their chapter provides some important questions and challenges of putting into practice the methods, methodologies, and theories that guide our research, our teaching, and our lives.

It's important to remember as scholars that the approaches we teach, we write about, and we practice will be the approaches that our students take forward with them. As Barone and Eisner argue, graduate students need support from faculty because:

> [i]t is demanding enough to do a dissertation well using conventional forms of research method, let alone a research method that is at the edge of inquiry. Yet it seems to us to be particularly important to encourage students to explore the less well explored than simply to replicate tried and true research methods that break no new methodological grounds. (4)

Therefore, I suggest that faculty consider how they can mentor students and junior colleagues to support diverse methods in research and to ensure that we welcome scholars with diverse methods into the field. Additionally, I suggest that (of course if they are comfortable) students and junior faculty find and ask senior faculty for support when they are engaging in messy and not well-established methods. For example, while working on the QAM article for *Rhetoric Review*, I was on a national grant committee with Dylan Dryer, a senior scholar with expertise in research methods and design. I casually asked if he would look at my article, and he agreed. He provided the most thorough feedback I've ever received on my writing. Although his research has to do with writing programs, he was able to provide incredibly useful feedback to refine my argument to better reach the readers. This key mentor was a random encounter and he owed me nothing. However, he took the time to provide this crucial feedback to develop my work, and his honest and kind feedback gave me confidence with my seemingly risky argument in the article. I only hope to pay it forward (Ribero) in the future to junior colleagues who are trying to innovate with nontraditional methods.

Lastly, I suggest that publishers (journal editors and university press editors) make room to consider innovative methods and work with scholars to make their research legible for the audience. For example, the journal *constellations: a cultural rhetorics publishing space* has a practice of asking the reviewers if they'd be willing to mentor the author through revisions and asking the author if they'd like a mentor to help with the revision process. Additionally, when I worked with *CCC*, they practiced the same process under their editor Malea Powell, who was also the founding editor of *constellations*. When journals encourage these types of mentoring practices during revision, the idea of journals shifts from a selective, gate keeping space (which can discourage risky, innovative research) to a space that facilitates a dialectical process of revision and ensures that important research is shared with the discipline.

CONSIDER TIMELINES AND COST OF MESSY METHODS

As explained here, the timeline for messy, tactile methods can look very different from traditional research methods. Time and space can seriously affect the ability to compose and revise. Additionally, there are many aspects beyond the researcher's control—availability of materials, cost of materials, and access to those materials—that can affect the timeline of employing such methods. Just as community-based research must work on the timeline of the community and their needs, not the scholar and the scholar's needs, tactile methods can present such challenges that pay no mind to our institutionally imposed deadlines. Therefore, scholars and their institutions need to consider this when working with messy methods. Although I've seen scholars unreasonably pressured to adhere to institutional timelines when completing longitudinal human subject research, I believe that institutions should consider the timelines they impose and whether it facilitates innovative methods. A university cannot simultaneously claim to value innovative methods, while maintaining incredibly high teaching loads, high publishing expectations, and a universal timeline for tenure regardless of the research or field.

Additionally, what counts for funding should be considered. A previous department chair once asked a question about what kind of technology I would need, assuming I didn't do any work with technology based on the understanding of technology as only digital. I responded very confused because, of course, sewing machines, needles, and thread, are all technologies to me. Maureen Goggin has thoroughly articulated the argument for the needle as pen (Goggin). Therefore, I suggest university departments consider how and when they allocate funding to scholars who are using messy methods.

CONSIDER TENURE PUBLISHING REQUIREMENTS

One last and large suggestion is for both scholars and institutions to consider their tenure publishing requirements. Scholars should consider how to make the argument for their work with messy and innovative methods and consider how can we expand what we see as "publishing." The composing process of quilting is parallel to other more traditional research methods and products in our field, so I've been able to at least make the argument. However, as I recently submitted my tenure dossier, I realized that meeting the requirements was dependent upon journal editors being open and supportive to my research.

It's worth mentioning that the current editors of *College Composition and Communication* and *Rhetoric Review*, two incredibly important journals in our field, are BIPOC scholars who saw the potential contribution of my work with quilting as method.[7] Without their support and encouragement, I would not have published such nontraditional research in these venues. I depended on

---

7   Malea Powell and Elise Verzosa Hurley

journals being open to publishing this research instead of my tenure requirements accepting a quilt publication. In other words, the venue validates the research and argument, not the tenure definitions. I suggest that departments evaluate how their current requirements (I know many still require a monograph) do not facilitate innovative and messy research.

In considering the relationship between the research methods we employ and our revision processes, I hope that academics think about how we've learned both of these processes and what values are reflected in those processes. As Gesa Kirsch asked previously, "[t]he question, then, is whether scholars are willing to break from a relatively rigid adherence to their disciplinary orientation in order to entertain alternative methodologies" (256), and I believe we continue to grapple with this question in our field. In response to my work, I've been asked "when does the expanding of our field lead us to something that is no longer a field?" And I've been told, "if everything is rhetoric, then nothing is rhetoric." However, the more important points in my work consider who established norms for fields, methods, and research? Who gets to say those established norms are best, right, or accurate? I believe good research should lead to more questions or a more nuanced understanding, not singular answers. And that, I hope, leaves you reader with a snapshot of my research process in between design and publication: Revision.

WORKS CITED

Alaoui, Fatima Chrifi, and Bernadette M. Calafell. "FOUR: A Story of Mentoring: From Praxis to Theory." *Women of Color Navigating Mentoring Relationships: Critical Examinations*, edited by Keisha Edwards Tassie and Sonja M. Brown Givens, Lexington Books, 2016, pp. 61–81

Arellano, Sonia C. "Heart, Mind, and Body in Quilting Research." *Academia de Cruz Media*, 26 Sept. 2016, http://www.academiadecruz.com/2016/09/sonia-arellano.html.

———. "Quilting as Qualitative Feminist Research Method: Expanding Understandings of Migrant Experiences." *Rhetoric Review*, vol. 41, no. 1, 2022, pp. 17–30.

———. "Sexual Violences Traveling to El Norte: An Example of Quilting as Method." *College Composition and Communication*, vol. 72, no. 4, 2021, pp. 500–515.

Barone, Tom, and Elliot W. Eisner. *Arts Based Research*. SAGE, 2011.

Calafell, Bernadette M. "Rhetorics of Possibility: Challenging the Textual Bias of Rhetoric through the Theory of the Flesh." *Rhetorica in Motion: Feminist Rhetorical Methods and Methodologies*, edited by Eileen E. Schell and K.J. Rawson, U Pittsburgh P, 2010, pp.104–117.

Enoch, Jessica. "5 Jessica Enoch." *How Writing Faculty Write: Strategies for Process, Product, and Productivity*, edited by Christine E. Tulley, Utah State UP, 2018, pp. 63–71.

Goggin, Maureen Daly. "Visual Rhetoric in Pens of Steel and Inks of Silk: Challenging the Great Visual/Verbal Divide." *Defining Visual Rhetorics*, edited by Charles A. Hill and Marguerite Helmers, Lawrence Erlbaum, 2004, pp. 87–110

Gonzales, Laura. *Sites of Translation: What Multilinguals Can Teach Us about Digital Writing and Rhetoric*. U Michigan P, 2018.

Kirsch, Gesa. "Methodological Pluralism: Epistemological Issues." *Methods and Methodology in Composition Research*, edited by Gesa Kirsch and Patricia A. Sullivan, Southern Illinois UP, 1992, pp. 247–269

Micciche, Laura R. *Acknowledging Writing Partners*. UP of Colorado, 2017.

Ribero, Ana Milena, and Sonia C. Arellano. "Advocating Comadrismo: A Feminist Mentoring Practice in Rhetoric and Composition." *Peitho: The Journal of the Coalition of Feminist Scholars in the History or Rhetoric and Composition*, vol. 21, no. 2, 2019, pp. 334–356.

Riley-Mukavetz, Andrea, and Malea D. Powell. "Making Native Space for Graduate Students: A Story of Indigenous Rhetorical Practice." *Survivance, Sovereignty, and Story: Teaching American Indian Rhetorics*, edited by Lisa King, Rose Gubele, and Joyce Rain Anderson, Utah State UP, 2015, pp.139–159.

Royster, Jacqueline Jones, and Gesa Kirsch. *Feminist Rhetorical Practices: New Horizons for Rhetoric, Composition, and Literacy Studies*. Southern Illinois UP, 2012.

CHAPTER 5.

MESSY LANGUAGE, MESSY METHODS: BEYOND A TRANSLINGUAL "NORM"

Jerry Won Lee

University of California Irvine

Paired readings:

- Dziuba, Allison, and Jerry Won Lee. "Post-Aristotelianism and the Specters of Monolingualism." *Rhetoric Review*, vol. 40, no. 3, 2021, pp. 257–269.

- Lee, Jerry Won and Christopher J. Jenks. "Doing Translingual Dispositions." *College Composition and Communication*, vol. 68, no. 2, 2016, pp. 317–344.

This chapter argues for the need to adopt methodological decisions in a manner that are in alignment with translingual realities. If translingual practice, as the scholarship suggests, is inherently "messy," then we need to seek out a way of adopting "messy" methods that can help us make sense of the chaotic and unpredictable ways in which we encounter and engage with language in its varied forms in the context of globalization, characterized by what Blommaert describes as "a messy new marketplace." I respond to recent calls in scholarship to pluralize primary and secondary source citational practices and reflect on my experiences publishing in the field to consider what is to be gained by attending to diverse epistemologies, specifically with attention to the uneven geopolitics of knowledge production (Canagarajah, Geopolitics) and the need for a "disinvention" (Makoni and Pennycook) of normative epistemological stances. Afterwards, I describe how the methodological priority for understanding the realities of language in this messy new marketplace is an anticipation and indeed embrace of "messy" research methods.

In their 2011 *College, Composition, and Communication* article, Bruce Horner, Samantha NeCamp, and Christiane Donahue argue for the need to move composition scholarship away from "English only" toward a translingual "norm" (269). At first glance, their argument is convincing because we do live in, to borrow the words of the late Jan Blommaert, a "messy new marketplace," in which language practice is increasingly chaotic and unpredictable (28). English is obviously not the only language in the world, and it can indeed be argued that the "norm" is not the isolated use of English or any other language for that matter, but the hybridized use of multiple languages and registers to communicate across linguistic and cultural difference in an increasingly globalized world. In addition, in an effort to capture the realities of such "messy" languaging in a messy new marketplace, it has become important to pay attention to the ways in which communication occurs not simply through "language" alone but through other communicative resources (Pennycook and Otsuji). Yet, from a methodological perspective, Pennycook argues that "we cannot merely add more semiotic items to our translinguistic inventories, but need instead to seek out a way of grasping the relationships among a range of forms of semiosis" ("Translanguaging," 270–271).

Following an analogous line of reasoning, this chapter argues that, in this messy new marketplace, we should focus not only on adding more languages to our primary and secondary source inventories, but need instead to adopt methodological decisions in a manner that is in alignment with the dynamics of translingual practice. Put differently, if translingual practice is inherently "messy," then we need to seek out a way of adopting "messy" methods that can help us make sense of the chaotic and unpredictable ways in which we encounter and engage with language in its varied forms. In this chapter, I first return to Horner, NeCamp, and Donahue to describe some affordances but also limitations to their proposed approach to establishing a translingual "norm." I afterwards return to some of my previous publications and reflect on my experiences publishing in the field to consider what is to be gained by attending to diverse epistemologies, in line with Horner, NeCamp, and Donahue's point, but specifically with attention to the uneven geopolitics of knowledge production (Canagarajah, *Geopolitics*) and the need for a "disinvention" (Makoni and Pennycook) of normative epistemological stances. Afterwards, I describe how the methodological priority for understanding the realities of language in this messy new marketplace is perhaps not the establishment of a translingual "norm" but, more generally, an anticipation and indeed embrace of "messy" research methods.

TOWARD A TRANSLINGUAL "NORM"?

It is no secret now that the field of US composition studies has in many ways been a "monolingual" discipline. As Horner and John Trimbur problematize, composition curricula in institutions of higher education in the US are guided by a tacit policy of English-only monolingualism ("English"). Paul Kei Matsuda argues that the field is guided by a "myth of linguistic homogeneity" in which it "assumes the state of English-only, in which students are native English speakers by default" (Matsuda 637). The issue, of course, has not been limited to multilingual students who speak a language other than English. Vershawn Ashanti Young, noting that the practice of insisting that African American students "switch" to standardized academic English in formal writing contexts reinforces a racialized stratification of "academic" English over African American English, argued for an alternative paradigm of "code-meshing," or "allowing Black students to mix a Black English style with an academic register," which is "more in line with how people actually speak and write anyway" (713). Suresh Canagarajah would later develop Young's concept of code-meshing, exploring how such a practice could be beneficial to users of World Englishes as well ("Place").

And while a wealth of scholarship had problematized, and continues to problematize, the monolithic curricular assumptions shaping the teaching of writing in US postsecondary contexts, Horner, NeCamp, and Donahue's 2011 article was unique in that it shifted the attention to ideologies of monolingualism guiding research and scholarship in the field as well. As they rightly point out, composition studies "operates on the tacit assumption that scholarship in composition is located—produced, found, and circulated—in English-medium, US-centric publications only" (271–72). They further note that the issue is not only the fact that composition scholarship is published only in English but also the fact that secondary scholarship cited in the field is overwhelmingly English-language sources. The corrective that Horner, NeCamp, and Donahue propose is what they describe as a "'translingual' model of multilingualism" (270), which is guided by a series of assumptions including the fact that "languages and language boundaries are fluctuating and in constant revision" and that "mutual intelligibility" is prioritized over "fluency" as a static concept (287).

While Horner, NeCamp, and Donahue are correct to identify the epistemological limitations of the tacit practice, if not policy, of monolingual ideology in composition, it would be productive to revisit some of their suggestions. To begin, though they emphasize the need to engage with non-English sources, it is important to think through what constitutes an "English" source to begin with. By raising this question, I do not mean to reiterate Canagarajah's point that English has always been translingual (*Translingual*) or Pennycook's point that English is a language "always in translation" ("Always"). I am instead alluding to my work with Allison Dziuba, "Post-Aristotelianism and the Specters of Monolingualism," in which we explore the extent to which rhetorical studies can imagine itself as moving "beyond" Aristotle. Though I need not rehearse the entirety of the project here, relevant to our present inquiry is the fact that, by comparing 15 different

English-language translations of Aristotle, Dziuba and I show how one's conceptualization of Aristotelian thought can differ markedly depending on which English-language translation is referenced. It also became clear that identifying and acknowledging the translator of a given text, whether in the bibliography and to a lesser extent within the main text of the article itself, was not common practice. This reflects, on the one hand, the "translator's invisibility" as described by Lawrence Venuti, the paradoxical condition by which "[t]he more fluent the translation, the more invisible the translator, and, presumably, the more visible the writer or meaning of the foreign text" (1) but also, on the other, the reality that it is difficult to assume whether a text that has been translated into "English" is a reliable or accurate representation of the text to begin with, which in turn raises the question of whether the text can be categorically "English."

An intriguing account of the challenges of delineating language according to conventional "codes" is found in Jan Blommaert's landmark work, *The Sociolinguistics of Globalization*, which presented sociolinguists and other scholars in language-oriented fields a framework for making sense of the complexities of language in the era of globalization. One of the more memorable examples from Blommaert is the unusual case of a sign for a chocolate shop in Tokyo called "Nina's Derrière." Though "derrière" for a chocolate shop is at first glance "a rather unhappy choice," Blommaert argues that its function in this context is not "linguistic" but rather "semiotic" (29). More specifically, it indexes "a complex of associative meanings" that can be "captured under the term French *chic*" (29). Such dynamics can be conceptualized through the heuristic of spatiotemporal scales offered in the book. As Blommaert argues, given the multilingual realities of globalization, many individuals practice multilingual competence not through what Monica Heller has called "parallel monolingualism" (5) but rather through what might be called "truncated" multilingualism, by which speakers use not "languages" but rather "repertoires" (103). This is perhaps best explained in Ofelia García's conceptualization of translanguaging, which calls attention to the fact that many individuals who speak multiple languages do not necessary view them as static and separate entities but as existing and accessible through a "continuum" (47). Languages, in other words, are not merely "codes" but better understood as a "mobile complex of concrete resources" (Blommaert 47). Critically, as Blommaert argues, the extent to which such mobile resources are (or are not) attributed value can be understood in relation to scales of time and space by which they are invoked and circulate:

	Lower Scale	**Higher Scale**
Time	Momentary	Timeless
Space	Local, situated	Translocal, widespread (34)

Importantly, such scalar ordering is a dynamic process and increasingly unpredictable in the era of globalization. Simultaneously, the manner by which certain language resources come to be distributed and mapped according to scalar logics has a tendency to reinforce extant intercultural and interlingual power dynamics.

The case of the mobility of French-origin language resources, "derrière" or other choices, in particular, whether in Asia or another part of the world, is a reminder that the distribution of language resources and their spatial or temporal upscaling capacities is an inherently uneven process. In the case of French, one needs to acknowledge that French, like English, is a dominant language in the contemporary geopolitical order. Not dissimilar to the case of English, the dominant status of French did not occur automatically: it was colonially imposed in many parts of the world, including Africa, Asia, and Latin America and is a direct beneficiary of whiteness and European cultural hegemony. If this seems like an obvious point, I must confess that it was not for me, at least when I first read the piece by Horner, NeCamp, and Donahue. I realized this when I received a reviewer report for a manuscript on Korean/American translingual practice I had submitted to a high-profile journal in composition studies. I was struck by one reader report in particular, which recommended that I reference a series of French-language texts, including the same ones that were referenced in the Horner, NeCamp, and Donahue article. I couldn't help but wonder, why did a paper on translingualism in the global Korean context need to be accountable for and situate its theoretical premises in French before it could earn a readership in US college composition studies? Imagine, for instance, the uproar if an author of a piece of French-English translingualism was told that they needed to engage Korean-language references to the complicated history of Korean as a translingual language.

This is, of course, not to suggest that Horner, NeCamp, and Donahue's suggestions should be dismissed outright. For instance, in my 2016 article, "Doing Translingual Dispositions," co-authored with Christopher J. Jenks and published in *College Composition and Communication*, we included a Chinese language abstract in addition to the English version. Based on a global classroom partnership between a US and a Hong Kong university, one of the main takeaways of the article was to promote a "disposition" of "openness to language plurality and difference" (318) while also acknowledging that such dispositions can be articulated in unpredictable ways, and in some cases in ways that reflect an ideological commitment to standard language ideology. Though this is a common practice in journal publications in other fields such as applied linguistics and sociolinguistics, it was not and still is not common practice in composition studies. For many scholars in composition studies, encountering Chinese in an article in a major journal in the field might lead to some cognitive dissonance and, dare I say, be a "messy" experience. What is an Asian language doing being featured in a scholarly resource targeted toward teacher-scholars of *English* composition in *US* postsecondary institutions? Should we focus on the fact that it is illegible and inaccessible to a majority of its primary readership? Or should we focus on the fact that it is legible and accessible to a new potential readership, who can in turn be invited to learn from, engage with, and eventually contribute to the knowledge being produced in this emergent translingual space?

BEYOND A TRANSLINGUAL NORM

At this juncture, I think it would be difficult to debate the reality that US college composition is a space of linguistic plurality, serving and supporting the literacy needs and aspirations of students from a wide range of backgrounds, whether multilingual or monolingual but otherwise language minoritized. Given this reality, adopting a translingual "norm," in the words of Horner, NeCamp, and Donahue, would seem sensible. However, I would like to try and take their argument a step further and explore the affordances of adopting a translingual orientation to composition research methodology more generally. At the more obvious level, any time we invoke the possibility of a linguistic "norm," even translingual, we run the risk of ritualizing behaviors and practices while deviating from the intended purpose of establishing the norm in the first place. Consider, for instance, standard English ideology. Its adherents will argue that establishing, promoting, and teaching a norm helps to ensure communicative efficacy among users. The reality, of course, is that even if the norms were established through well-intended action, the very question of who gets to decide on the norm is a power-laden process which in turn exacerbates all kinds of social and educational inequalities. To clarify, I don't think there is anything inherently suspect or problematic in advocating for a translingual norm in methodological approaches to US college composition research. Instead, I simply want to suggest that we be open to actively revisiting what such a norm looks like and to avoid a situation in which the new norm, even if translingual, inadvertently creates new inequalities, for instance, demanding scholars to establish reading proficiency in (one more) colonial language in order to earn a seat at the table.

As a way forward, we may need to attend more carefully to what Canagarajah has called the "geopolitics of academic writing," which encompasses the numerous barriers that academics from the Global South have to face on a daily basis, including biases against non-mainstream varieties of English and discourse styles and reliable access to recent scholarly literature. Particularly memorable is Canagarajah's description of trying to obtain print copies of relevant research articles via post in the midst of an ongoing civil war in Sri Lanka. He also describes not having reliable access to things like stationary and electricity, things many academics in the US and other privileged parts of the world take for granted. He even describes ethnographic interviews needing to be canceled because of a bombardment happening nearby. Today, Canagarajah is globally renowned as a leading scholar of translingualism (see, for instance, Canagarajah's award-winning 2013 book, *Translingual Practice: Global Englishes and Cosmopolitan Relations*). However, I can't help but wonder if translingualism were as influential today as it were in the early 1990s and an emerging early career scholar in the Global South were to receive a "revise and resubmit" notice requiring them to read numerous French-language resources before their work *might* be considered for publication.

One of the most important, but also frequently overlooked realities of the translingual orientation to language is that its theoretical premises can be traced to metadiscursive philosophies of language in the Global South. Notably, scholars have pointed out that communities in the Global South, including those in Africa, Latin America, South Asia, and Southeast Asia have always managed intercultural communication with little to no regard to language demarcated along clear boundaries or "codes" (see Canagarajah, *Translingual*; Khubchandani; Makoni, "African," "Misinvention;" Silva and Lopes). Among the most influential attempts to desediment the dominance of Global North logics of language is found in Sinfree Makoni and Alastair Pennycook's 2005 article, "Disinventing and Reconstituting Languages," in which they historicize how the very idea of "language" is an invention of European epistemology and stress the importance of working toward a "disinvention" of language (137). Disinvention, I believe, can take many forms, and in the remaining pages of this contribution I will explore how it can apply to the question of research methods.

In order to do this, I revisit some points I made in an article, "Translanguaging Research Methodologies," published in the inaugural issue of the journal *Research Methods in Applied Linguistics* in 2022. I argue for the importance of not only "drawing on appropriate research methodologies to make sense of translanguaging but also how to translanguage research methodologies themselves in our pursuit of understanding language practices that have historically been marginalized in various realms of society and education and overlooked or dismissed by researchers in applied linguistics" (2). Although the article was geared toward a readership of researchers in applied linguistics, I have always maintained that there are considerable overlaps between the fields of applied linguistics and composition studies, not only through the venerable tradition of research in second language writing that by necessity moves between but also beyond. Applied linguistics, after all, is a multidisciplinary field of research focused on investigating real-world problems and implications associated with language, broadly conceived, and composition is very much a language-oriented practice and institution. My point, therefore, that we need not limit ourselves to mapping extant research methodological premises and approaches onto research data, including "progressive" theoretical frameworks such as translingualism, applies to research in composition studies as well. Consider, for instance, the approach of establishing a theoretical framework via an engagement with both English-language and French-language secondary material. On the one hand, this would be a step forward in composition studies scholarship, which, as Horner, NeCamp, and Donahue rightly point out, does not regularly feature engagement with non-English sources, and could thus conceivably be reflective of a translingual citational politics. On the other hand, it could be reflective of a translingual orientation to composition research that represents the reification of a translingual "norm" in which Global North epistemology once again prevails.

Returning to Blommaert's theorization of a "messy new marketplace" might be productive here because his inquiry into what it means for a language resource originally from French to be semiotically mobilized and rescaled in a different geographical context. The complexities of language in the era of globalization are indeed increasingly "messy." This is akin to Heller's observation of how it has become increasingly expected to encounter language in unexpected places: "As soon as we start looking closely at real people in real places, we see movement. We see languages turning up in unexpected places, and not turning up where we expect them to be. We also see them taking unexpected forms" (343). Pennycook takes up this issue in order to call into question the criteria by which we delineate differences between the expected and the unexpected: "this is not so much about being light on one's feet, ready for the new, as it is a question of asking why the unexpected is unexpected" (36). Relevant for our purposes is the opportunity to interrogate what gets categorized and treated as "unexpected" versus "expected," and more importantly, who gets to decide. I am referring here not only to language resources (French being proposed as a language resource in a new translingual "norm") but also methodological choices. More specifically, if we are to embrace the realities of this "messy new marketplace" of language, I would propose that the priority is not merely adding more languages to the field of secondary material we can draw on (though, to reiterate, I am not opposed to that proposition in principle) but to embrace "messy" research methods. I of course do not mean "messy" in a pejorative sense. Rather, I am referring to the process of following one's intellectual intuition in the pursuit of new knowledge about language in a manner that is analogous to the ingenious ways in which everyday people draw on language resources to achieve communicative success in globalizing contexts.

One of the most intriguing cases of adopting "messy" research methods is found in Finex Ndhlovu's article, "Omphile and His Soccer Ball: Colonialism, Methodology, Translanguaging Research." Ndhlovu describes his experience taking a break from an academic conference in Johannesburg, South Africa and meeting a young boy named Omphile outside the conference venue. He recalls them fluidly moving between words and expressions from isiZulu, Setswana, Sepedi, and English, contrary to the rigid and systematic use of multiple languages being promoted at the conference. Having learned more from this chance encounter outside the conference than in the conference itself, Ndhlovu uses this experience to argue for the importance of being open to research methods that are frequently treated as unscientific, in his case autoethnography. Ndhlovu's essay lays bare the impact of traditional (Western, colonial, English-only) academic publishing, citation, and linguistic practices on the methodological choices for global writing researchers. To return briefly to the Canagarajah anecdote above, we also need to take seriously the ways in which the review process constrains researchers, not only in terms of language choice but also the expectations and requirements to meet certain traditionally-defined methods, which in turn impact the questions researchers (are allowed to) ask, the methodological frameworks they can draw from, and/or the methods used to conduct research. In other words, by being open to "messy" methods, we are able to invite a more diverse range of voices and perspectives in the process of knowledge production.

In the case of composition studies, the field is already welcoming of a diverse range of methodological approaches, and it is difficult to provide a uniform set of guidelines on what is a "messy" approach to research versus, say, a "neat" one. Further, citational politics (i.e., making decisions about what secondary source material to cite and by extension what *not* to cite) is but one small part of the research process. I should also note that my call to be open to "messy" methods does not mean we should treat with caution or suspicion research that is the result of more conventional or systematic approaches. But I would also argue that conventional methods, approaches, and instruments cannot always capture the complexities of today's translingual realities. Imagine, for instance, a study that uses surveys with Likert scales to "measure" instructors' or students' "attitudes" toward translingual writing. Even from the outset, such a study would invariably compartmentalize language epistemology into rigid categories and the "findings" would likely reify extant possibilities of knowledge about language, reducing the complexities of translingualism to that which can be conceptualized in a survey instrument or via coding schemes. Embracing "messiness," then, challenges us as researchers to follow our intuition to continually rethink the givens of research and to take risks in order to push the boundaries of thought in language. Everyday users of translingual practice, after all, take risks in the ways they use language and as a result are able to think and communicate beyond the boundaries of language as such, and we should demand no less from researchers as well.

CONCLUSION: EMBRACING MESSINESS

Composing can frequently be an inherently messy process, and when it comes to translingual composition, things can get even more complicated. Therefore, when it comes to research methods, particularly when the subject of our inquiry is translingualism, it would behoove us to be open to "messy" research methods. The influential 2011 opinion piece in *College English* by Horner, Min-Zhan Lu, Jacqueline Joynes Royster, and John Trimbur, catalyzed the translingual turn in composition studies. In it, they emphasize that adopting a translingual orientation to writing does not mean that there are no "errors" or that we should dismiss all "standards" (310–11). Likewise, adopting a translingual orientation to research methods does not mean "anything goes." In other words, it does not mean accepting anything and everything that is "unexpected." Rather it simply means being open to that which is unexpected and not unilaterally rejecting it on the basis of its unexpectedness. Indeed, in the same way that it is becoming increasingly difficult to determine what is or is not an unexpected encounter with language nowadays, it will become increasingly "messy" to sift through what is an unexpected research method and an expected one. However, if we are to embrace the premises of translingualism, then we need to embrace "messiness" as the new "norm" but one that is anything but.

WORKS CITED

Blommaert, Jan. *The Sociolinguistics of Globalization*. Cambridge UP, 2010.

Canagarajah, Suresh. *A Geopolitics of Academic Writing*. U of Pittsburgh P, 2002.

———. "The Place of World Englishes in Composition: Pluralization Continued." *College Composition and Communication* vol. 57, no. 4, 2006), pp. 586–619.

———. *Translingual Practice: Global Englishes and Cosmopolitan Relations*. Routledge, 2013.

Dziuba, Allison, and Jerry Won Lee. "Post-Aristotelianism and the Specters of Monolingualism." *Rhetoric Review* 40.3, 2021, pp. 257–69.

García, Ofelia. *Bilingual Education in the 21st Century: A Global Perspective*. Oxford: Wiley-Blackwell, 2009.

Heller, Monica. *Linguistic Minorities and Modernity: A Sociolinguistic Ethnography*. Pearson Longman, 1999.

———. "The Future of 'Bilingualism'?" *Bilingualism: A Social Approach*, edited by Monica Heller. Palgrave Macmillan, 2007, 340–345.

Horner, Bruce. "'Students' Right,' English Only, and Re-Imagining the Politics of Language." *College English* vol. 63, no. 1, 2001, pp. 741–758.

Horner, Bruce, Min-Zhan Lu, Jacqueline Jones Royster, and John Trimbur. "Language Difference in Writing: Toward a Translingual Approach." *College English*, vol. 73, no. 3, 2011, pp. 303–321.

Horner, Bruce, Samantha NeCamp, and Cristiane Donahue. "Toward a Multilingual Composition Scholarship: From English Only to a Translingual Norm." *College Composition and Communication*, vol. 63, no. 2, 2011, pp. 269–300.

Horner, Bruce and John Trimbur. "English Only and US College Composition." *College Composition and Communication*, vol. 53, no. 4, 2002, pp. 594–630.

Khubchandani, Lachman. *Revisualizing Boundaries: A Plurilingual Ethos*. Sage, 1997.

Lee, Jerry Won. "Translanguaging Research Methodologies." *Research Methods in Applied Linguistics* vol. 1, 2022, pp. 1–6.

Lee, Jerry Won, and Christopher J. Jenks. "Doing Translingual Dispositions." *College Composition and Communication*, vol. 68, no. 2, 2016, pp. 317–344.

Makoni, Sinfree. "African Languages as European Scripts: The Shaping of Communal Memory." *Negotiating the Past: The Making of Memory in South Africa*, edited by Sarah Nuttall and Carli Coetzee. Oxford UP, 1998, pp. 242–248.

———. "From Misinvention to Disinvention: An Approach to Multilingualism." *Black Linguistics: Language, Society, and Politics in Africa and the Americas*, edited by Sinfree Makoni, Geneva Smitherman, Arnetha F. Ball, and Arthur K. Spears. Routledge, 2002, pp. 132–53.

Makoni, Sinfree, and Alastair Pennycook. "Disinventing and (Re)Constituting Languages." *Critical Inquiry in Language Studies*, vol. 2, 2005, pp. 137–56.

Matsuda, Paul Kei. "The Myth of Linguistic Homogeneity in US College Composition." *College English*, vol. 68, 2006, pp. 637–651.

Ndhlovu, Finex. "Omphile and His Soccer Ball: Colonialism, Methodology, Translanguaging Research." *Multilingual Margins*, vol. 5, 2018, pp. 2–19.

Pennycook, Alastair. "English as a Language Always in Translation." *European Journal of English* Studies, vol. 12, 2008, pp. 33–47.

———. *Language and Mobility: Unexpected Places*. Multilingual Matters, 2012.

———. "Translanguaging and Semiotic Assemblages." *International Journal of Multilingualism*, vol. 14, 2017, pp. 269–282.

Pennycook, Alastair, and Emi Otsuji. *Metrolingualism: Language in the City*. Routledge, 2015.

Silva, Daniel N. and Adriana Carvalho Lopes. "*Hablar portuñol é como respirar*: Translanguaging and the Descent into the Ordinary." *Translinguistics: Negotiating Innovation and Ordinariness*, edited by Jerry Won Lee and Sender Dovchin. Routledge, 2020, pp. 104–114.

Venuti, Lawrence. *The Translator's Invisibility*. Routledge, 1995.

Young, Vershawn Ashanti. "Your Average Nigga." *College Composition and Communication*, vol. 55, 2004, pp. 693–715.

PART 3.
RETHINKING
METHOD/OLOGICAL DISPOSITIONS

CHAPTER 6.

EMBRACING THE POTENTIALS AND NAVIGATING THE PITFALLS OF INTERDISCIPLINARY METHOD/OLOGIES

Meagan E. Malone

The University of Alabama at Birmingham

Paired reading:

- Malone, Meagan E. "Expression of the Embodiment Contradiction in Natalie Wynn's ContraPoints Video, Beauty." *Computers and Composition*, vol. 63, 2022.

This chapter reflects on the generative complexity of hybrid approaches to research, discussing their potentials and pitfalls. In writing about trans woman Natalie Wynn's YouTube channel, Contrapoints, *I combined feminist rhetorical method/ologies with those used in analytic feminist projects. My messy, nonlinear experience of researching, writing, revising, and publishing about Wynn's channel was shaped by the intersection of these approaches. At times, this dual approach came into conflict and led to impasses. I demonstrate, however, that it was the presence and influence of both these and other methodological dispositions within my toolkit that allowed me to challenge existing paradigms about queer rhetoric. The chapter suggests that when we take time to examine and shine a spotlight on our method/ological assumptions even as we conduct research, we can register which of our existing perspectives enable or preclude meaningful discoveries and can take advantage of all the tools at our disposal for achieving research goals.*

It was the fall of 2017, and I chose a seat at the single, long table that dominated the lecture room to begin my first class as a Ph.D. student at Georgia State University (GSU) in English rhetoric and composition. Despite my novice status, everything about my surroundings was completely familiar to me. While I was now on the 24th floor of 25 Park Place, the most towering of the buildings on GSU's campus, I sat in nearly identical classrooms just eight floors below in the philosophy department for the two years prior. Even the course I was preparing to take felt eerily the same as much of my philosophy master's degree curriculum. I was there for a graduate seminar on feminist rhetoric when, just a year before, I'd taken a course in feminist philosophy in the very same building.

Yet once the syllabus was in our hands and we began discussing what the semester promised, I was most excited by the differences rather than the similarities between these parallel experiences. The purposes of conducting philosophical and rhetorical feminist research often overlap; in many contexts, both disciplines aim to facilitate the flourishing of all people by, among other aims, expanding normative understandings of gender in order to attend to the needs of *all* people. While the aims of these two disciplines can converge, their research method/ologies sharply diverge in most cases. On that August day in 2017, I was eager to flee the constraints of analytic philosophical methodologies and capitalize on what I saw as the affordances of a more flexible approach in rhetoric and composition.

Three years later, I had defended my dissertation prospectus and was hard at work gathering, coding, and analyzing data from Natalie Wynn's popular YouTube Channel, *Contrapoints*. The theoretical lens with which I proposed to study Wynn's channel came out of important research in the field of rhetorical studies and computers and writing. Furthermore, it aligned with the kind of work I'd studied in that first seminar in feminist rhetoric. Despite my excitement for the project, however, frustration infused the early research process. As I worked through the data, I felt that the rhetorical framework I was using was unable to facilitate discovery of any clear or respectful conclusions.

I now recognize that, regardless of how carefully I had set up my study, defined my lenses, and placed my boundaries, analytic philosophical approaches were unconsciously operating within what Laurie Gries calls my "research dispositions" (85). My close work with certain methods in the feminist philosophical tradition, specifically a project called ameliorative inquiry, informed the *way* I looked and *what* I looked *for* within Wynn's work. Only when I unpacked and laid bare my specific methodological commitments did I uncover assumptions that were precluding me from making sense of Wynn's channel within a rhetorical framing.

In this chapter, I reflect on the generative complexity of hybrid approaches to research, discussing their potentials and pitfalls. My messy, nonlinear experience of researching, writing, revising, and publishing about Wynn's channel was shaped by the intersection of philosophical and rhetorical method/ologies. At times, these conflicted unproductively, impeding progress. Ultimately, however, it was the presence and influence of both these and other methodological dispositions within my toolkit that set the stage for me to challenge existing paradigms in my published work.

HABITUS OF METHOD AND UNCONSCIOUS METHOD/OLOGICAL ASSUMPTIONS

Using the concept of "habitus of method" to frame a conversation about methodology is helpful because it foregrounds the reality that research does not proceed along a singular theoretical or technical line but develops out of a set of intersecting traditions and means. For Gries, "habitus of method can be understood as a set of dispositions embodied in a shared tradition of inquiry that influences a community of scholars to conduct research in certain ways" (85). In other words, some project's methodology is complex, informed by multiple voices and sources. It is not a discrete variable one can plug into a research project that prescribes how to gather data, analyze that data, and draw conclusions. Instead of employing *a* methodology, researchers within a particular field develop methodological dispositions influenced by previous work in that and adjacent fields. These dispositions animate inquiries, providing scholars a point of entry for a research project but also placing limits on how scholars conduct their research. Thinking of methodology as part of a larger "habitus of a method" forces scholars to reflect on and lay bare the different "tradition[s] of inquiry" they bring to their projects.

As a new researcher in rhetorical studies, however, I did not engage in this kind of reflection. Without consideration of previous influences, I attempted to tightly construct and control my study by naming its exact variables and boundaries which I intentionally built from existing scholarship in computers and writing. Specifically, the study grew out of concerns on embodiment and digital technology that guest editors Phil Bratta and Scott Sundvall articulated in their special issue of *Computers and Composition*. In their introduction, they highlight the exigency for additional scholarly work that "continues discussions and practices on the entanglement of digital technology, bodies and embodiments with attention to power, oppression, and resistance" (6). Answering their "plea" for additional research on "how different embodiments address systems of domination differently with a vast array of digital technologies," I proposed a study that would look for if and how Wynn's digital compositions served to recompose bodies oppressed by harmful gender norms (4). In her videos, Wynn manages to parse thorny social and political issues, emphasizing concerns related to gender. Her work has been widely recognized by journalists for de-converting alt-right young men, leading them to hold less harmful positions about women and progressive politics (Cross; Faye; Marantz; Fleishman; Roose "The Making"; Roose "A Thorn"). As a trans woman composing on YouTube, Wynn's work represents the exact kind of work that Bratta and Sundvall urge scholars to study.

I assumed that I would need to run as far away as possible from older method/ologies and section off my study from any influences or processes that were not specifically sanctioned by my new discipline. I did not just use but *clung* to John R. Gallagher's "A Framework for Internet Case Study Methodology in Writing Studies" which offers "researchers…a practical framework about how they might go about crafting a case study" of online spaces (2). Intended to guide people to articulate the contours of some online space so as to study them more effectively, I naively took Gallagher's article as a blueprint for creating a concrete edifice around my research, believing that I could develop a controlled case study with perfectly transparent values, commitments, methods, and steps. Gallagher writes that "it is the job of any case study researcher—and especially an internet case study researcher—to be explicit about the methodology that one uses to create a case so that the case can be better understood on both its own terms as well as the reasons researchers present the case in the way they do" (2). I went into my research thinking that I had explicitly articulated the methodologies that guided my case study when in fact I had been explicit about how I *wanted* the research to proceed without reflecting on how my prior, disciplinary training unconsciously mixed in these thematic waters.

"FEMINISM/S" AND METHOD/OLOGIES

Perhaps what I did not immediately recognize was that, without naming their inquiry "feminist," Bratta and Sundvall's introduction turned around issues that various feminism/s purport to address; therefore, the method/ologies from my prior work in feminism/s were unconsciously activated in my thinking. I use *feminism/s* as opposed to feminism due to the slippery nature of the term. Ask anyone to define feminism, and the answers will vary wildly. This is not just a symptom of what many want to call misinformation but reflects the actual difficulty of capturing its meaning. For example, in her capacity as a UN Women Goodwill Ambassador, actress Emma Watson boldly proclaimed in a 2014 speech that "for the record, feminism by definition is: 'The belief that men and women should have equal rights and opportunities. It is the theory of the political, economic, and social equality of the sexes.'" Yet she gives neither a citation for that theory nor unpacks manifold, conflicting understandings of "rights" or "opportunities." Furthermore, nonbinary and gender nonconforming people remain unrepresented in her definition, creating distinct problems for this version of feminism. One can know this relatively standard and oft-mentioned definition by heart but still have relevant questions about what it means and whether it is a worthy project around which to rally.

The term feminism can be confusing academically, as well as colloquially, which can pose problems when engaging in research that claims to be feminist. In the academy, feminism encompasses a broad set of concerns and styles of inquiry that find their way into numerous disciplines. This makes feminism/s a worthy site from which to explore the concept of hybridity in method/ology. After having studied feminism/s from both an analytic philosophical perspective as well as a rhetorical one, my only deeply held conviction about the term is that it is not simple, despite what anyone—progressive, conservative, centrist, apolitical, or otherwise—might claim. In her *Stanford Encyclopedia of Philosophy* entry on "Feminist Philosophy," Noëlle McAfee writes that some scholars in this tradition locate the definition of feminism within the historical movements in the nineteenth, twentieth, and twenty-first centuries while others hope to identify a "set of ideas or beliefs" that characterize feminism/s within philosophy writ large. However, controversies abound when attempting to define those beliefs to the extent that McAfee asks, "Is there any point, then to asking what feminism is?" While she goes on to offer her own definition, her expression of frustration signals that this term is quite complicated.

Feminist work in rhetorical studies is similarly contested. In their *College Composition and Communication* article about feminist rhetoric, a precursor to their seminal 2012 work *Feminist Rhetorical Practices*, Gesa E. Kirsch and Jacqueline Jones Royster reflect on the difficulty of pinning down the meaning of feminism for their research. They find it impossible to think of "'feminism' as a singular concept." Rather, "[t]here are many views from which to choose, anchored by many perspectives and combinations of perspectives—theoretical, ideological, geopolitical, historical, social, biological, and more across multiple sectors of interest and engagement. All matter" (643).

Yet people from both scholarly traditions—analytic feminism and feminist rhetorical studies—have managed to broadly articulate the values and methodologies of each tradition. While the methodologies differ greatly, the values and goals have many points of overlap as both engage in scholarship hoping to counter unjust domination often attributed to patriarchy. According to social and political philosopher Ann Cudd, the aim of analytic feminism is to "counter sexism and androcentrism" (qtd. in Garry). In part, this happens through an examination, unpacking, and critique of traditional, male-dominated understandings of philosophical concepts. The lack of women's voices in philosophy has led to a distortion of "philosophers' pursuit of truth and objectivity," and analytic feminism hopes to expand traditional views to better reflect the capital-T Truth (Cudd 3). Similarly, feminist rhetorical studies begin from the notion that traditional rhetorical scholarship has been and is a patriarchal pursuit (Royster and Kirsch 30). The definition of rhetors and rhetoric often excludes those who are not men and therefore limits the meaning of these concepts (39). Royster and Kirsch suggest that the purpose of engaging in feminist rhetorical studies is, in part, "to deepen, broaden, and build rhetorical knowledge and to offer multiple mechanisms for enhancing our interpretive capacity with regard to the symphonic and polylogical ways in which rhetoric functions as a human asset" (132). Just as studying philosophy from a feminist perspective changes notions of what philosophy is, feminist rhetorical studies are meant to transform the discipline for the purposes of building a more inclusive understanding of what rhetoric is and how it functions.

As for *how* these disciplines go about achieving their aims, there is little overlap between the two. Before moving on to discuss feminist rhetorical method/ologies, I will spend some time discussing the specifics of analytic philosophical approaches to provide context for the research decisions I made later in my rhetorical work.

Analytic feminist philosophers work towards the goal of ending patriarchal domination "through forming a clear conception of and pursuing truth, logical consistency, objectivity, rationality, justice, and the good" (Cudd qtd. in Garry). Given analytic philosophy's commitment to truth and logic, any project within this discipline that hopes to make claims about and politically intervene in women's oppression must carefully define terms and craft clear propositions that precisely reflect the reality of patriarchy. As Ann Garry writes, analytic feminists "believe that feminist politics require that claims about oppression or denial of rights be true or false and able to be justified." Among the tools available to these scholars are "methodological approaches often used while training in analytic philosophy." These approaches are like an "ever-expanding toolkit that may include such instruments as conceptual and logical analysis, use of argumentation, thought experiments, counterexamples, and so forth" (Garavaso qtd. in Garry). In other words, these feminists work to articulate propositions about women's oppression, clearly define the terms within those propositions, then interrogate the extent to which these propositions are true. Scholars test the strength of the definitions and propositions through "thought experiments" and generating "counterexamples," looking for ways to enhance these statements by making them better reflect reality. If they find contradictions within their definitions or propositions, or if they find them to be over- or under-inclusive of some concept, scholars go back to the drawing board to find ways to amend their terms.

One specific tool that would eventually influence my research on Wynn in rhetorical studies is ameliorative inquiry, a type of "conceptual analysis" developed by Sally Haslanger. The purpose of an ameliorative inquiry is to generate definitions of terms we can use to craft logically verifiable statements capable of describing and intervening in oppression. These definitions are not the kind you might find in a dictionary as they do not describe "ordinary understandings of the concept." Rather, an ameliorative inquiry is a method by which one builds definitions "that a particular group should aim to get people to use, given a particular set of goals that the group holds" (Jenkins 395). Haslanger uses this analysis to build a definition of "woman" that does not rely on widespread beliefs about what a woman is but that includes all people who identify as such. I would later see in Wynn's work a similar attempt to define "trans woman." These definitions may lay the theoretical groundwork for the creation of social and political interventions capable of granting rights, protections, privileges, and material benefits to marginalized groups.

What makes ameliorative inquiry difficult—and what came to hinder my research in rhetorical studies—is the complexity involved in avoiding "the inclusion problem." Many definitions of some term end up leaving out relevant aspects of the concept under consideration such that the definition excludes things that we politically *need* to fall under the conceptual category. For example, Emma Watson's definition of feminism suffers from the inclusion problem when it claims that "men and women should have equal rights and opportunities." Because the definition only mentions "men and women," it excludes those who do not identify as men or women, eliminating consideration of equal rights for non-binary or gender non-conforming people. Given that these definitions are often meant to be used in political projects—that is, used in crafting policy and social movements—they must reflect the group of people these projects intend to support. Analytic feminist scholars continue to disagree about the best way to define "woman" because most competing definitions suffer from the inclusion problem. The project of crafting definitions of "woman" capable of recognizing "everyone who needs to be included for the purposes of feminism" is, indeed, fraught (Jenkins 421).

Method/ologies in feminist rhetorical studies are much more fluid than those in analytic feminism. Nevertheless, in their book, Royster and Kirsch offer some unifying "terms of engagement" that form the "terrain" of feminist rhetorical approaches to research (18–19). In their survey of and reflection on over three decades of feminist rhetorical scholarship, they detail robust and creative scholarly engagement and argue "that a feminist-informed operational framework has emerged organically from well-regarded work in the field." They outline four general practices that they see as belonging to that framework: critical imagination, strategic contemplation, social circulation, and globalization. These practices involve broad but consistent approaches to research that Royster and

Kirsch see as common to feminist rhetorical scholarship and that facilitate "gathering multiple viewpoints," "[balancing] multiple interpretations," "considering the intersections of internal and external effects," and "deliberatively unsettling observations and conclusions to resist coming to conclusions too quickly" (134).

Central to my own messy process of researching about Natalie Wynn, though I did not immediately notice it at the time, was what Royster and Kirsch call strategic contemplation, or the process of "taking the time, space, and resources to think about, through, and around our work" (21). While all research requires scholars to spend time thinking, Royster and Kirsch describe strategic contemplation as a more expansive, intentional process that includes a "meditative dimension" (21). Specifically, strategic contemplation:

> involves engaging in dialogue, in an exchange, with the women who are our rhetorical subjects, even if only imaginatively, to understand their words, their visions, their priorities whether and perhaps especially when they differ from our own....It entails creating a space where we can see and hold contradictions without rushing to immediate closure, to neat resolutions, or to cozy hierarchies and binaries. (21–22)

After a brief survey of the method/ologies of these two disciplinary approaches to feminism/s, it is clear that the approaches differ. The difference in the way the two treat the presence of "contradictions" is particularly stark. As I will discuss, this divergent attitude toward contradiction unconsciously impacted the way I analyzed data in my study of Wynn. In the analytic philosophical tradition, discovery of a contradiction is a red flag moment; it signals that there is an untenable glitch in some system that needs to be ironed out. When using strategic contemplation, however, the researcher intentionally lingers in the presence of contradiction and listens again and again to the voices of those speaking.

DISCOVERING LIMITATIONS OF PHILOSOPHICAL THOUGHT STYLES

As a student of both philosophical and rhetorical feminist traditions, Gries might say that I have appropriated a mix of feminist thought styles. Gries cites Ludwick Fleck who defines thought styles as "a historical-cultural conditioning that manifests when individuals are exposed to the exchange of scholarly ideas from a particular thought collective or closely related thought collectives" (87). Just as habitus of method best describes the reality that our method/ologies are always complexly plural, thought styles best describe the plurality of *any discipline's* approach to some area of inquiry. It is not the case that my work in philosophy or rhetorical studies resulted in a fixed set of ideas about feminism/s but instead "exposed" me to certain dispositions about how to do research and "conditioned" me to call upon those approaches when I undertake new studies.

Given the centrality of the concepts "oppression" and "domination" in feminist studies, Bratta and Sundvall's call for research (consciously and unconsciously) activated feminist thought styles that inevitably affected the way I went about gathering and analyzing data. In order to combat the tendency of scholarship to "decompose" marginalized bodies, Bratta and Sundvall ask scholars to question how online composing tools and environments might allow for "recomposing" the bodies and embodiments of oppressed persons. They write that "thinking in terms of having a body/embodiment . . . marks an inevitable decomposing of bodies," whereas "thinking in terms of being/becoming a body/embodiment . . . marks a necessary recomposing of bodies and embodiments" (5). Language and work that *decompose*, by this framing, focus on the static reality of "*having* a body/embodiment" and appear complicit with harmful gender norms whereas compositions that *recompose* attend to the experience of "*being/becoming* a body/embodiment" and offer possibilities for flourishing despite those norms. Having identified the significance of the decomposition/recomposition metaphor in their introduction, my aim was to understand how Wynn uses and treats language that *decomposes* and *recomposes*.

In the early stages of my research, I watched and took notes on all the 25 public-facing videos on Wynn's channel at the time, focusing on sonic, linguistic, and visual language around gender. Grounded theory broadly describes the method I used to analyze and draw conclusions about Wynn's work; I coded all my notes on Wynn's treatment of gender, allowing relevant categories to emerge as I worked through the data. However, I also used predetermined codes, categorizing some language as participating in either the decomposition or recomposition of trans women.

What I noticed after my first pass through all the videos was a thematic preoccupation with the question: What makes a person a trans? Just as analytic feminist philosophers engage in ameliorative inquiries to define woman, the characters on Wynn's channel debate how to define trans women in a public-facing way that will help them gain rights and freedoms in society. Wynn herself rarely offers answers to this question as a narrator or talking head; rather, she uses her characters as embodied manifestations of current competing definitions of what it means to be trans and of beliefs about how trans people ought to present themselves to win greater rights and freedoms. Through dialogue, the characters articulate the worldviews of various cultural groups engaging with this issue: trans women of a variety of presentations, nonbinary trans people, straight cis women, cis trans exclusive radical feminist (TERF) women, and more, all with conflicting beliefs about what it means to be "authentically" trans ("Autogynephilia"; "The Aesthetic"; "Gender Critical"; "The Left"; "Tiffany Tumbles"; "Transtrenders"). These portrayals are often highly sarcastic, drawing the audience's attention to the harmfulness and hypocrisy of some character's view. In other cases, these same transphobic, bigoted, or narrowminded characters make insightful objections to the arguments of their more reasonable interlocutors. One or another character may appear to win a debate; however, this is neither an indication of the superiority of their argument nor of Wynn's endorsement of the position.

Because Wynn presents ever shifting and often contradictory views of what it means to be trans, I struggled to apply Bratta and Sundvall's decompose/recompose distinction to her work. I suggest that my difficulty was the result of the unexamined operation of analytic feminist thought styles within my habitus of method. Specifically, I believe I was unconsciously applying the method of ameliorative inquiry to my reading of Wynn, looking for "clear conceptions" of what it means to be trans. From an analytic feminist perspective, the path to recomposing the bodies/embodiments of marginalized women requires establishing consistent, logical conceptions of what a trans woman is. Yet Wynn subverts the search for such clear conceptions at every turn. Given my unconscious search for inclusive, logical definitions, I assumed that any composition that works towards recomposing trans bodies ought to spell out and then build on such a definition. Wynn does not allow any of her characters to have a satisfying final word that neatly does the work of facilitating the flourishing of trans life. Furthermore, the analytic tradition primed me to see definitions that contained contradictions or that failed to satisfy a set of criteria as prima facie harmful; I assumed that laying bare and refusing to resolve the contradictions in the competing definitions was a move that necessarily, in the words of Bratta and Sundvall, decomposes the bodies/embodiments of trans people. The rhetorical framework I was using, as well as the unacknowledged method/ological dispositions in my habitus of method, led to the conclusion that Wynn's compositions are complicit with oppressive dominant discourse in their failure to avoid the inclusion problem.

CHANGING COURSE WITH STRATEGIC CONTEMPLATION

Yet feminist rhetorical thought styles also operated within my habitus of method, perhaps unconsciously inviting me to go back to the data and spend more time listening. Strategic contemplation occurs when researchers return to contradictions and impasses as sites of potential meaning and when they "pay attention" to both the "outward" and "inward journey" of research. For Royster and Kirsch, the "outward journey" of research involves the actual legwork of gathering data, whereas research's "inward journey" involves "researchers noticing how they process, imagine, and work with materials" (85). In response to my initial frustrations, I took that inward journey, stopping to recognize that Wynn's rhetorical moves were not conforming to my assumptions about them and reckoning with the reality that I needed to broaden my perspective to "process, imagine, and work" with Wynn's channel in a more inclusive way. Outwardly, I decided to take a step back from focusing on particular videos, dialogues, and issues, instead zooming out to reexamine the whole channel and listen more carefully to what Wynn was saying and doing. Within my habitus of method was Royster and Kirsch's work which "[highlights] the necessity of pausing in our work to question definitions…that we may have taken for granted but that have defined—perhaps limited—the boundaries of rhetorical inquiry" (139–40). This step is especially important as a cis-researcher looking at work by a trans composer.

Strategic contemplation first led me to code the data again and again in multiple rounds, tracking the presence of several visceral, embodied features through the oeuvre to see if they illuminated some way in which Wynn's work fit into a decomposition/recomposition lens. To do this, I first revisited my notes seeking out specific characteristics such as body language, costuming, and set decor, looking for ways in which these components fit with the various themes each video explored. In one round of coding, for example, I noted and categorized all instances in which Wynn or her characters ate or drank in the videos; beverage consumption is consistent feature of many of the videos, from milk to tea to vodka. While at times I felt hot on the trail of some interesting connection, the thread was inconsistent and ultimately unhelpful. Yet part of strategic contemplation is having that dialogue with the text: asking a question and listening for the answer. When I interrogated the text and its response was "This is not a relevant question," I listened.

My approach here is similar to Carol Gilligan's feminist Listening Guide (LG), a method by which to analyze interview data (Boehr). This approach requires "a minimum of four successive readings, called listenings," of some interview transcript in which the researcher pays attention to different aspects of the data: first, the "major themes" that arise in the conversation; next, the way the speakers present themselves in relation to others; third, "the rhythm, moves, and use of pronouns in women's voices"; and lastly, "potential tensions and contradictions between" the speakers. Christine Boehr, writing about her experience using Gilligan's LG, explains that this approach prompted "a change in [her] sensitivity to the words of others," leading her to "re-think [her] positionality, question preconceived notions, and double-check associations."

While I did not use the LG for my analysis, my approach was similar and led to the same changes in how I interpreted Wynn's work, much as they did in

Boehr's case. When I engaged in multiple listenings to Wynn and her different characters, I finally allowed their priorities and perspectives to supersede my own. This was not the result of any one specific question I asked or lens I used as I went back through my notes or rewatched videos; rather, the very act of returning again and again to the data allowed me to feel like I had stepped inside the world of the videos and that I knew and understood each of the characters' motivations on their own terms. I could finally see connections between character dialogues in one video and their changing views in another. I found that Wynn's *characters* may be preoccupied with finding a rational way of explaining what it means to be trans. However, if one pays attention to the progression of theorizing from video to video, one notices that Wynn *herself* ultimately rejects the project of defining "trans," instead advocating for trans people to have the right to simply accept themselves without explanation. It took several passes through the data, rewatching the videos, and listening again and again to each of Wynn's characters for me to disrupt my search for an inclusive definition of trans. I saw, then, that Wynn's channel as a whole—if not one particular video—argues that trans people ought to define themselves as they see fit regardless of how dominant ideologies may respond *and* regardless of the way those definitions might not be compatible with others' definitions. This embodied argument, unfolding over the entirety of Wynn's channel, is a force that affords trans people the agency to define their own existences: to recompose themselves.

I do not suggest that the analytic philosophical project of ameliorative inquiry is inherently disrespectful or harmful. I recognize the need, in certain contexts, to do definitional work that avoids contradiction as much as possible. These definitions have a place in social and political theorizing meant to secure rights and safeties for oppressed persons. Yet when it comes to looking at digital compositions by people from diverse bodies/embodiments, contradiction is a source of meaningful insights. When I notice the way Wynn both recognizes and accepts the problems with each of her characters' beliefs, I am then able to see that Wynn *herself* acknowledges problems with oppressive, dominant language around gender while also strategically affirming it in some contexts. Bratta and Sundvall might say that some language decomposes the bodies of trans people. Wynn, on the other hand, happily uses that language at one turn, critiques it at another, and condemns it in other contexts.

MAKING USE OF THE AFFORDANCES OF PHILOSOPHICAL THOUGHT STYLES

While feminist rhetorical method/ologies gave me the perspectives and tools to foreground Wynn's radical embrace of contradiction, analytic philosophical method/ologies nevertheless played a vital role in my research. Having inter-rupted my search for clear definitions and accepted Wynn on her own terms, the question remained: how does her work fit into Bratta and Sundvall's decomposi-tion/recomposition framework I started with? The article that finally grew out of this research asserts that Bratta and Sundvall's framing is not sufficient for cap-turing the unique rhetorical moves of trans rhetors. I suggest that the presence of philosophical thought styles within my habitus of method eventually led me to diverge from and add to the existing queer rhetorical project that underpins Bratta and Sundvall's approach.

In working to locate Wynn within the decomposition/recomposition frame-work, I kept coming back to the word "underinclusive," a word that got tossed around in a philosophy seminar like a badminton shuttlecock. Recall that part of the analytic philosophical method is engaging in thought experiments and posing counterexamples to expose weaknesses of a theory, concept, or definition. These methods are absolutely not unique to philosophy as they have a place in most all disciplines; nevertheless, they are central to philosophical research. Using such methods requires conceiving of scenarios and imagining whether the framework under consideration will fit the needs of the scenarios or will lead to unproductive or unintended consequences. Often, the outcome of a thought experiment or considering a counterexample is to pronounce that the theory, concept, or definition is either underinclusive or overinclusive: that the frame-work does not capture features central to its purpose or includes features that create unnecessary problems. The method of ameliorative inquiry uses thought experiments to determine whether some definition is underinclusive. Jenkins, for example, emphasizes that "an analysis of the concept of woman that respects gender identifications of trans women will need to provide space for a variety of articulations and interpretations of trans experiences." She, therefore, out-lines "four possible scenarios" in which Haslanger's definition of woman fails to include trans women" in order to demonstrate its shortcomings and advocate for a different definition (399).

In my analysis, I used Wynn's channel as a "scenario" by which to test Bratta and Sundvall's framework, looking for whether it was inclusive of embodied digital composing practices of trans rhetors. I began to model Wynn's rhetorical strategies as if on a spectrum represented by a horizontal line on which language used to decompose existed on the far left and language of recomposition existed on the right. Equipped with a tiny, portable white board, I went through sev-eral iterations of this model, plugging in different data points on the spectrum including video titles, specific pieces of dialogue, examples of costuming, and set design. What I saw was that, in the process of asserting each person's right to define trans for themselves, Wynn uses and affirms language and arguments that

Bratta and Sundvall might say is complicit with hegemonic structures: language that decomposes. Yet as my earlier analysis established, her work, on the whole, is liberating and freeing: a force that allows for recomposition of trans bodies/embodiments.

Inspired by analytic philosophical methods, the visualization tactic allowed me to test Bratta and Sundvall's framing and conclude that it was underinclusive of at least one kind of trans rhetorical practice. Their introduction implies that queer rhetorical theory is the default lens for studying works by rhetors with diverse embodiments. My reading of Wynn, however, demonstrates that the queer framing, while helpful in some ways, cannot capture all the rhetorical moves of trans rhetors. This suggests that scholars of computers and writing and of rhetorical studies more broadly cannot rely on queer framings alone when studying the work of trans rhetors. In my *Computers and Composition* article, I demonstrate this finding and propose a new analytic, the embodiment contradiction, that helps scholars foreground the embodied reality of the trans composing practice that is distinct from queer composing practices.

EMBRACING HYBRID METHOD/OLOGIES

My experience of researching and publishing a piece about Wynn's channel demonstrated the need to unpack our method/ological commitments and make sense of how and when to use the various tools we have as researchers. Without the feminist rhetorical practices in my habitus of method, I would not have taken the time nor done the work of deeply listening to Wynn in order to hear her on her own terms. In this phase of the research and writing process, my analytic philosophical tools were not just inappropriate but were a hindrance. Yet I needed to call upon those methods to enable me to test and then challenge existing approaches in rhetorical studies. It is necessary to ground a project in a shared set of disciplinary method/ological approaches and values, but it can be valuable to borrow perspectives from other disciplines. Royster and Kirsch echo this, noting that feminist rhetorical studies has "benefited from dynamic intersections . . . from more-traditional areas" including "philosophy" (40–41).

As individual researchers, we necessarily bring our prior knowledge, assumptions, and experiences to the studies we undertake. Just as we all bring *baggage* to our various personal relationships, we each carry around certain *disciplinary baggage* to our research subjects. Failure to deal with baggage in relationships can lead to frustration and damage while opening up to others about our past can help each person uncover potential pitfalls *and* identify common ground to enhance the connection. Similarly, when we take time to examine and shine a spotlight on our method/ological assumptions even as we conduct research, we can register which of our existing perspectives enable or preclude meaningful discoveries and can take advantage of all the tools at our disposal for achieving research goals.

WORKS CITED

Boehr, Chrstiane. "The Praxis of Listening in Feminist-Relational Research." *Peitho*, vol. 23, no. 3, 2021. https://cfshrc.org/article/recoveries-and-reconsiderations -the-praxis-of-listening-in-feminist-relational-research/.

Bratta, Phil and Scott Sundvall. "Introduction to the Special Issue: Digital Technologies, Bodies, and Embodiments." *Computers and Composition*, vol. 53, 2019, pp.1–8, https://doi.org/10.1016/j.compcom.2019.102526.

Cudd, Ann E. "Analytic Feminism: A Brief Introduction." *Hypatia*, vol. 10, no. 3, 1995, pp. 1–6.

Cross, Katherine. "The Oscar Wilde of YouTube Fights the Alt-Right with Decadence and Seduction." *The Verge*, 24 Aug. 2018, https://www.theverge.com/tech /2018/8/24/17689090/contrapoints-youtube-natalie-wynn.

Faye, Text Shon. "ContraPoints is the hilarious YouTuber delivering hardcore politics in drag." *Dazed*, 2 July 2019, https://www.dazeddigital.com/life-culture /article/45244/1/contrapoints-interview-youtube-trans-left-wing-politics-shon-faye.

Fleishman, Jeffrey. "Transgender YouTube star ContraPoints tries to change alt-right minds." *Los Angeles Times*, 12 June 2019 https://www.latimes.com/entertainment /la-et-st-transgender-youtuber-contrapoints-cultural-divide-20190612-story.html.

Gallagher, John R. "A Framework for Internet Case Study Methodology in Writing Studies." Computers and Composition, vol. 54, 2019, pp. 1–14. https://doi.org/10 .1016/j.compcom.2019.102509.

Garry, Ann. "Analytic Feminism." *The Stanford Encyclopedia of Philosophy*, edited by Edward N. Zalta, 2021. https://plato.stanford.edu/archives/spr2021/entries /femapproach-analytic/.

Gries, Laurie. *Still Life with Rhetoric: A New Materialist Approach for Visual Rhetorics.* Utah State UP, 2015.

Haslanger, Sally. "Gender and Race: What Are They? What Do We Want Them to Be?" in *Resisting Reality: Social Construction and Social Critique.* Oxford UP, 2012, pp. 221–247.

Jenkins, Katharine. "Amelioration and Inclusion: Gender Identity and the Concept of Woman*." *Ethics*, vol. 126, 2016, pp.394–421. https://doi.org/10.1086/683535.

Kirsch, Gesa E., and Jacqueline J. Royster. "Feminist Rhetorical Practices: In Search of Excellence." *College Composition and Communication*, vol. 61, no. 4, 2010, pp. 640–672. https://www.jstor.org/stable/i27917864.

Marantz, Andrew. "The Stylist Socialist Who is Trying to Save YouTube From Alt-Right Domination." *The New Yorker*, 19 Nov. 2018, https://www.newyorker.com /culture/persons-of-interest/the-stylish-socialist-who-is-trying-to-save-youtube -from-alt-right-domination.

McAfee, Noëlle. "Feminist Philosophy." *The Stanford Encyclopedia of Philosophy*, edited by Edward N. Zalta, 2018. https://plato.stanford.edu/archives/fall2018/entries /feminist-philosophy/.

Royster, Jacqueline Jones, and Gesa E. Kirsch. *Feminist Rhetorical Practices*, Southern Illinois UP, 2012.

Roose, Kevin. "The Making of a YouTube Radical." *The New York Times*, 9 June 2019 https://www.nytimes.com/interactive/2019/06/08/technology/youtube-radical .html.

———. "A Thorn in YouTube's Side Digs in Even Deeper." *The New York Times*, 12 Feb. 2020, https://www.nytimes.com/2020/02/12/technology/carlos-maza -youtube-vox.html.

Watson, Emma. "Gender equality is your issue too." 20 Sept. 2014. *UN Women*, https://www.unwomen.org/en/news/stories/2014/9/emma-watson-gender-equality -is-your-issue-too. Transcript.

Wynn, Natalie. "Autogynephilia." *YouTube*, 1 Feb. 2018, https://www.youtube.com /watch?v=6czRFLs5JQo&vl=en.

———. "The Aesthetic." *YouTube*, 19 Sept. 2018. https://www.youtube.com/watch ?v=z1afqR5QkDM.

———. "Gender Critical." *YouTube*, 30 Mar. 2019, https://www.youtube.com/watch ?v=1pTPuoGjQsI.

———. "The Left." *YouTube*, 24 Sept. 2017, https://www.youtube.com/watch?v =QuN6fUix7c.

———. "Tiffany Tumbles." *YouTube*, 2 June 2018, https://www.youtube.com/watch?v =j1dJ8whOM8E

———. "Transtrenders." *YouTube*, 1 July 2019, https://www.youtube.com/watch?v =EdvM_pRfuFM.

CHAPTER 7.

SHIFTING METHOD/OLOGIES: MY JOURNEY WITH COUNTERMAPPING

April O'Brien

Sam Houston State University

Paired reading:

- O'Brien, April. "Mapping and/as Remembering: Chora/graphy as a Critical Spatial Method-Methodology." *Enculturation*, no. 31, 2020, http://enculturation.net/mapping_as/and_remembering

This chapter tells a story about the evolution of my research method/ ologies and the aha moments (or what I'll call "punctum moments") that motivated this journey. While this is a chapter about counter- mapping, it is also about how I had to face some hard truths about the injustices in my own anti-racist work. I write about the impor- tance of critical spatial perspectives as a white, cis woman scholar, and I have done this work often alongside/about multiply marginalized people. As I define and analyze countermapping, I also explain how I came to this method/ology after spending three years focusing my efforts on chora/graphy. I frame the conversation within the context of the chapter's paired reading, "Mapping and/as Remembering." From there, I briefly identify the two characteristics of maps that are relevant to rhetoric and writing scholars and follow up with a work- ing definition of countermapping. After these grounding discussions, I return to my story to the three punctum moments that shifted my method/ology and demonstrate how I applied this knowledge to my research, teaching, and community work. To complete the chapter, I provide some practical ways that a rhetoric and writing scholar can apply countermapping to their research and teaching.

Google maps and any other kinds of maps, while they are helpful, are in English and Spanish, and so they completely leave off the meaning of the place. It is replacing our language and eclipsing our language and

DOI: https://doi.org/10.37514/PER-B.2024.2241.2.07

knowledge with something different, with something that is not really from here. This whole constellation of what makes up a map is far beyond a piece of paper.

—Jim Enote, A:shiwi farmer and director of the
A:shiwi A:wan Museum and Heritage Center

I've always been fascinated by maps. My favorite uncle (Uncle Mike), who lived across the country, would send me long hand-written letters each month when I was a child. Included in each letter were 2–3 detailed geography questions. These questions would send me to my atlases, my globe, and my encyclopedias (yes, this was before Google existed!) to find the answers to his questions. My early fascination with maps and mapping emerged many years later during my Ph.D. work. I was fortunate enough to be in a Ph.D. program that provided varied interdisciplinary connections, and I became aware of Geographic Information Systems (GIS), Existential Positioning System (EPS),[1] story mapping, virtual reality (VR) and augmented reality (AR). As I spoke to cultural geographers, sociologists, philosophers, and GIS experts, I began to compose a research method/ology called chora/graphy (see "Mapping and/as Remembering" and "(Digital) Objects with Thing-Power"). Chora/graphy can be best understood as writing place/place writing, and it works as a theory that guides research and informs analysis; yet it also functions as a fluid, loosely arranged set of research methods. My dissertation research centered around the town where I lived and the intersection of racism, public memory, and place. Chora/graphy provided a theoretical foundation and the means to answer my research questions: What is the source of this town's residential segregation? How has racism impacted the landscape? How are we remembering or forgetting narratives in this space? What is my relationship with these racialized landscapes? I wrote my dissertation based on chora/graphy as a method/ology, and I defended it a few months before I graduated.

I was finished, right?

To my surprise, the work had just begun. After I had the mental distance away from my dissertation, some questions began to haunt me. How am I ethically dealing with my positionality when I write about racism, place, and public memory? Whose voices do I highlight? What are my goals? At first, these questions scared me. I had expended so much time and energy on chora/graphy—how could I abandon this method/ology? I wondered what a methodological shift would mean for future publications or the monograph that was supposed to come from my dissertation. These questions were all valid, but I couldn't

---

1   Gregory Ulmer is the creator of both EPS and choragraphy. I am indebted to him for his support and mentorship, as well as his influential work about space/place.

shake the idea that I needed to redirect my research. And I learned some important lessons during this difficult liminal season of "PhDone-but-before-tenure-track-job-starts." Namely, I learned this: It's okay for method/ologies to shift. In fact, it could be a sign that you are open to self-examination if you ask yourself difficult questions about your method/ologies. In my case, the method/ology changed as my mindset shifted. The more I read the work of cultural rhetoricians, Indigenous scholars, and Black feminist geographers, the more I wanted my work to reflect these ways of knowing/thinking. So, I have continued to examine public memory, race, and place, but I now begin with scholars whose lived experience added a richness and nuance to my own positionality as a white, cis woman scholar. I hope my work disrupts the white male scholarship that has dominated these conversations, and so I moved from Plato, Roland Barthes, and Edward Soja to Katherine McKittrick, Natchee Blu Barnd, and Jim Enote. As I did so, I identified countermapping,[2] which began a new season for my research.

In this chapter, I want to tell a story about the evolution of my research method/ologies and the aha moments (or what I'll call "punctum moments") that motivated this journey. While this is a chapter about countermapping, it is also about how I had to face some hard truths about the injustices in my own anti-racist work. I write about the importance of critical spatial perspectives as a white, cis woman scholar, and I have done this work often alongside/about multiply marginalized people. As I define and analyze countermapping, I also explain how I came to this method/ology after spending three years focusing my efforts on chora/graphy (see O'Brien, "Mapping and/as Remembering). Toward that end, I have organized this chapter in the following manner: First, I frame the conversation within the context of the chapter's paired reading, "Mapping and/as Remembering." From there, I briefly identify the two characteristics of maps that are relevant to rhetoric and writing scholars and follow up with a working definition of countermapping. After these grounding discussions, I return to my story to the three punctum moments that shifted my method/ology and demonstrate how I applied this knowledge to my research, teaching, and community work. To complete the chapter, I provide some practical ways that a rhetoric and writing scholar can apply countermapping to their research and teaching.

This chapter is both reflective and instructive; it is also deeply honest. As I've learned from cultural rhetoricians Malea Powell and Andrea Riley-Mukavitz: I come with a good heart. And this is my story.

---

2   The term "counter-mapping," was recently used by cultural geographers Derek Alderman, Joshua Inwood, and Ethan Bottone, but it has also been used by Indigenous activists like Jim Enote. I apply the term as a countermemory method/ology as an act of resistance.

PAIRED READING: "MAPPING AND/AS REMEMBERING"

The paired reading for this chapter, "Mapping and/as Remembering: Chora/graphy as a Critical Spatial Method-Methodology," comes from parts of my dissertation and establishes my first attempts to reconcile a methodological shift from chora/graphy to countermapping. In the article, I first examined the potential for countermapping to promote disruptive spatial narratives. I positioned countermapping as one of the three elements of chora/graphy. As with many published articles—especially my own, as a junior scholar—substantial revisions are often required. The evolution from the first proposed article to the published version was quite dramatic, and while the amount of work was challenging, it also gave me the opportunity to add some of my new ideas in relation to Indigenous and Black feminist geographies. Around the same time that I was working on these revisions, I began a co-authored book project with James Chase Sanchez. Our book, *Countermemory*, stemmed from a co-authored article where we first introduced countermemory as a disruptive form of public memory. As a result, I began to move away from chora/graphy as my method/ology and towards countermemory—and countermapping, as a spatial method/ology that originates from countermemory. This shift occurred for two reasons: (1) I wanted to understand the potential for spatialized representations of countermemory to disrupt racist and colonial understandings of space and place; and (2) I wanted to highlight Black and Indigenous perspectives and experiences. From the beginning of my research as a graduate student, I kept coming back to the violent erasure of Black and Indigenous public memory. While the US's actions towards many other groups is likewise abhorrent, I concur with Tim Gruenewald, who writes, "Two racially defined groups were subject to longer-lasting and more systematic collective violence than any other: Native Americans and African Americans" (21). To compound the historical and contemporary injustices towards Black Americans and Indigenous people, systems of white supremacy continue to fight against truth-telling attempts in public memory. For these reasons, I began the movement away from chora/graphy and towards countermemory and countermapping. At face value, maps and mapping do not seem relevant to rhetoricians, but as I will explain, rhetoric scholars can provide an important perspective to cartography—what Nedra Reynolds calls geographic rhetorics (4).

WHAT DO RHETORICIANS NEED TO KNOW ABOUT MAPS?

Maps tell stories. In fact, they are the preface to a much larger story, and the way we set up the story defines how the story will be told. Cultural geographer Denis

Cosgrove argues that mapping is a "deceptively simple activity" because maps have been historically viewed as transparent or as a neutral informative transfer (1, 3). Like Cosgrove, though, many cultural geographers maintain that maps are also ideological and depict what a culture wants to remember (Barton and Barton; Cosgrove; Harley; McKittrick). As rhetorician Amy Propen articulates, maps are "always in flux" as they "respond to . . . shifting contexts and relations" (11). This interpretation of maps, illustrative of a critical spatial perspective, views maps as "opaque" artifacts that involve choices, submissions, uncertainties, and intentions and likewise change our perception of spaces and places (Cosgrove 3, 7). In Malea Powell's 2012 CCCC Chair's address, she centers the relationship between stories and place: "Stories take place. Stories practice place into space. Stories produce habitable space" (391). Thus, maps are place-based stories that have the capacity to alter the way we view ourselves and our relationship to the land.

Secondly, maps are rhetorical. They "allow [us] to see relationships between spaces and objects that [we] would not be able to see otherwise" (O'Brien, "(Digital) Objects"; Propen 6). Consequently, we recognize that maps are impacted by a variety of social, cultural, ideological, and rhetorical contexts—and, alternatively, maps also shape these same contexts (O'Brien, "Mapping"; Propen 6). Maps create meaning. They construct meaning through using specific cartographic conventions, including the use of grids, icons, and symbols, as well as how scale is used to highlight some places and minimize others (Propen 11). As Nedra Reynolds writes, maps are deemed valuable by how they represent "reality," or what a culture establishes as significant (81). Maps can also "chart resistance" by emphasizing how geography magnifies the social inequalities that Black women experience (Butler 29). For rhetoric and writing scholars interested in critical method/ologies, maps and map-making can provide a way to view our relationship with power and land. For this reason, I found countermapping as a helpful method/ology to consider the role of spatial representations of countermemory.

COUNTERMAPPING

To begin to understand countermapping as a method/ology, we need to begin first with a definition of countermemory. Countermemory is a rhetorical practice that refutes and disrupts whitestream, American Exceptionalist, and racist forms of public memory (O'Brien and Sanchez). It may be helpful to compare mainstream forms of public memory with countermemory. Where a Stonewall Jackson monument is an example of mainstream public memory, the National Memorial for Peace and Justice—the first site to remember individuals who were lynched in the United States—is an example of countermemory. The same process is apparent with mainstream mapping and countermapping as well. If a traditional atlas in a middle school classroom shows Greenland and Africa as the same size (evidence of the Mercator Projection), then Indigenous artist Jaune Quick-to-See Smith's various map series demonstrate countermapping with her portrayal of maps with fluid boundaries, Native symbolism, and paint drippings to illustrate the blood spilled in the colonization of the land. Countermapping is a spatial application of countermemory that seeks to disrupt racist and colonial forms of spatial representation by (1) opposing dominant views of spatial history or memory and (2) visually representing public inequalities, tragedies, or injustices that have been forgotten or erased. Countermapping promotes a spatialized reckoning that visualizes an inclusive and diverse sense of place (McKittrick 949).

Since maps are so influential in shaping public perception of place, memory, and identity, I argue that it is crucial to countermap public memory—so we can visualize the memories that have been omitted and forgotten. Historically, though, maps have hindered decolonization and anti-racist efforts by communicating false spatial knowledge and undermining the contributions of people of color in human geographies. Jim Enote, an A:shiwi farmer and tribal member, makes this compelling argument: "More lands have been lost to Native peoples through mapping than through physical contact" (qtd. in Steinauer-Scudder). Enote's statement underscores the impact of maps and mapping on the survivance and sovereignty of Indigenous people in the United States and throughout the Global South. While maps have contributed to the colonization and displacement of Indigenous people, maps and map-making practices have also marginalized Black communities and their geopolitical concerns through geographies of exclusion (McKittrick and Woods 4).

As a result, scholars, activists, and artists have taken up disruptive mapping practices to resist dominant spatial narratives—a practice called countermapping. Sarah Radcliffe, a cultural geographer who specializes in decolonial geographies in Ecuador, describes how Shuar, Achuar, and other Indigenous people employ "map-making as a critical tool in their struggles for postcolonial justice" (129). Likewise, artists like Terrance Guardipee, Chris Pappan, and Jaune Quick-to-See Smith create "spatial disruptions" and recenter Native geographies in their work (Barnd 110). Jeff Littlejohn, a historian and scholar who focuses on public history, composed an interactive map/website called *Lynching in Texas*, which incorporates a map of hundreds of lynchings in Texas along with archival information about the events. James Chase Sanchez and I created a countermap of East Texas using Arc-GIS story mapping; this countermap allows users to see the spatial relationships on an interactive map, as well as learn about East Texas's violent history towards its Black community. These artifacts, which include interactive maps, paintings, and websites, illustrate the various ways in which countermapping can be employed.

The shift from chora/graphy to countermapping was gradual, and I will tell this story in three parts that are punctuated by punctum moments. Each of these punctum moments also teaches a corresponding lesson about shifting method/ologies.

PUNCTUM MOMENTS

There is much talk about "aha moments," where people have life-changing revelations that change the way they view themselves or the world. "Punctum" moments are kind of like that—they are moments that prick or sting our consciousness. Taken at face value, Roland Barthes's theory of punctum is a way to recognize images that prick or wound, in contrast to images of "studium" that perform a more educational and distancing role in visual rhetorics (26–27). However, when applied in a more expansive context, punctum can be understood as anything seen, heard, felt, or experienced that pierces one's consciousness. By applying punctum to any material-rhetorical spaces, places, or things, the link between affect and invention is forged (if not foregrounded). Employing punctum in research practices is a deeply personal journey, especially when story is/functions as a research practice. In many cases, it is through this function of story that the punctum itself becomes intelligible, where we bring to light the obtuse or "third meaning" (i.e., that element beyond communication and signification) ("The Third Meaning" 52–53). According to Sarah Arroyo, the third meaning is something that can only be found in the chora, what she calls a "holey" or sacred space (62). Arroyo, drawing from E.V. Walter, argues that a sacred place is not merely where the "literal remains of the dead 'remain'"; rather, sacred places have the ability to generate, create, and invent (Arroyo 62; Walter 120). Thus, punctum moments are those significant moments where my consciousness was "pierced" and my method/ology began to evolve.

Lesson 1: Method/ologies are Impacted by Place

My first lesson as a dissertation-writing graduate student was that method/ologies are impacted by place. As Nedra Reynolds explains, ". . . Memory and place, location and argument, walking and learning, are vitally and dramatically linked in our personal histories and personal geographies" (2). I have often returned to this story as my origin story—the beginning of my research—and how it connected to changes in my geography. After living in Pendleton, South Carolina, for a few months, I attended the town's annual Fall Festival. Amidst the scarecrow competitions, pumpkin-painting, and apple cider donuts, I noticed an advertisement on a store window. The flier advertised "The Ghosts of

Pendleton—Where the Spirits Come to Life!" which were nighttime Halloween tours inside the local plantation houses, Ashtabula and Woodburn. Immediately, I was struck by the images and text in this ad, and I started to ruminate about the implications for using violent and oppressive spaces like plantation houses as tourist destinations. Although this was early in the research process, as well as the fact that I recently moved to the area, I was almost immediately aware of the disconnection between Pendleton's public narrative and how it erased and misused Black histories. This was a punctum moment for me—I knew that this was a story that I needed to understand.

In Practice: Research

Where I lived impacted my research method/ogies, and my relationship with geography continues to influence my scholarship. In "Mapping and/as Remembering," I describe a VR countermap project in Pendleton, South Carolina. The VR project, which I collaboratively composed with community members, used "punctum to map erased memory sites (O'Brien "Mapping"). In this case, I describe being haunted by the absence of truth-telling in the town's public memory and their refusal to address the role of slavery in the town's formation, the impact of racial terror, Jim Crow laws, and segregation on the town's development. Working with the Pendleton Foundation for Black History and Culture, I collected oral histories and archival information, a process that provided education about various details that were not communicated by the town's historical foundation. Some of this information included details about lynchings, fear of violence from white residents if Black residents left the West side of town, the role of the NAACP in fighting for civil rights during integration, and several Black entrepreneurs. The disparity between Pendleton's public memory and these stories was vast; it was nothing short of complete erasure of Black history in the town. The VR countermap was a response to dominant cultural memory, which refuses all truth-telling efforts and suppresses any memories that diverge from the accepted view of history that centers white men.

The VR project, which is called *Counter-Tour: Remembering Black History in Pendleton, South Carolina*, expands cartography to incorporate more interactivity and embodiment. As Derek Alderman et al. argue, by "restricting cartographic to a narrow academic understanding forecloses the geospatial significance of . . . activism" (74). *Counter-Tour* does not fit within the parameters of a conventional map, but it still functions to tell a spatialized story. Likewise, *Counter-Tour* is an artifact of activism; it responds to the purposeful gaps in public history in Pendleton and forces people to a reckoning of racial violence and inequalities that existed in the past and persist within the town. The VR project is composed of a series of VR images that flow into each other.

Figure 7.1. Screenshot from Counter-Tour: Remembering Black History in Pendleton, South Carolina.

For example, the map begins at the center of town in the Village Green. Users can click on informational bubbles within that space or click on a bubble that takes them in various directions that branch off from the center of town. The result is a completely interactive map-like experience where users can spatially experience the town. Unlike a traditional map, though, this countermap educates users about the gaps in Pendletons' public memory and functions as a truth-telling apparatus. This information is populated through the oral histories that I collected; and in each space on the countermap, the user learns about the stories and experiences that have been erased by dominant cultural narratives.

As Katherine McKittrick and Klyde Woods remind us: "Black places, experiences, histories, and people that no one knows do exist within our present geographic order" (4). In other words, as users (particularly users who live in the Pendleton area or are familiar with the landscape) engage with the countermap in all the spaces and places, they can see the stories that have been erased and how they are superimposed on top of the places that they know well. "No one knows"? Yes, by all accounts, no one knows many of the Black histories in the United States because they have been deleted from public memory. The work of countermemory is to recover what has been erased, and countermaps allow people to leverage geography for these purposes. Where "bodies, emotions, and subjectivities have been [removed] from traditional framings of geospatial technologies," countermaps redress these inequalities, these absences, and promote a more socially just cartographic practice (Kwan 30).

Elise Verzosa Hurley reminds us, "I am/was in the spatial turn: space, place, location, embodiment—all of these things matte[r]" (94). As we pay attention to the spaces and places where we live, we can begin to ask questions. What stories do these places tell? Whose stories are visible and whose are missing? What is my relationship with these places? How can I listen to the landscape? These questions have the capacity to create method/ologies—both the theoretical frameworks that inspire our work as well as the practices that we use to understand and answer our research questions.

Lesson 2: Method/ologies are Fluid

The second punctum moment occurred a few years after the first. At this point, I had already defended my dissertation, had accepted a tenure-track assistant professor position, and was working on an article I was submitting to a journal (the paired reading for this chapter). It was a warm spring day in South Carolina, and my husband was packing boxes for our impending move to Texas. I, on the other hand, was working on an article based on part of my dissertation. I sat outside on our screened in front porch, my laptop in hand. On this sunny morning, I came across Jim Enote's work with other A:shiwi artist-activists in Emergence. The article and video highlighted how A:shiwi artists were telling critical spatial stories for years, and I was reminded of my positionality as a white settler-scholar and humbled by my limited knowledge about spatialized resistance. The A:shiwi countermaps challenge Western ways of knowing and making and seek to "reclaim the names of Zuni places and depict the land of the A:shiwi as they know and see it . . . with culture, story, and prayer . . . [because] modern maps do not have a memory" (qtd. in Steinauer-Scudder). In this section, I trace how discovering Ronnie Cachini and Jaune Quick-to-See Smith's countermaps compelled me to re/think how people can visualize countermemory through various spatial practices. This particular method/ological shift impacted how I taught countermapping as well, as I will explain.

Indigenous countermaps look nothing like Western maps or atlases. Rather, they are composed of colorful, textured images and stories. One of the artists, Ronnie Cachini, medicine man for the Eagle Plume Down Medicine Society and a head rain priest, created a map called *Ho'n A:wan Dehwa:we (Our Land)*. Cachini explains what makes Zuni maps unique: "A conventional map takes you to places—it will tell you how many miles and the fastest route. But the Zuni maps show these significant places that only a Zuni would know." Cachini adds, "especially if you're in a religious leadership position: you see the prayers that we say, the prayers that we hold . . ." (qtd. in Steinauer-Scudder). Cachini's contention directly refutes the notion that maps represent Truth and objectivity:

> [Modern maps] are widely assumed to convey objective and
> universal knowledge of place. They are intended to orient us,
> to tell us how to get from here to there, to show us precisely
> where we are. But modern maps hold no memory of what the
> land was before. Few of us have thought to ask what truths
> a map may be concealing, or have paused to consider that
> maps do not tell us where we are from or who we are. Many
> of us do not know the stories of the land in the places where
> we live; we have not thought to look for the topography of
> a myth in the surrounding rivers and hills. Perhaps this is
> because we have forgotten how to listen to the land around
> us. (Steinauer-Scudder)

As Enote and the Zuni artists reject maps that circulate a settler colonial narrative, the process of counter-mapping demonstrates the importance of drawing from the community to align social justice practices with mapping practices.

Jaune Quick-to-See Smith, an enrolled member of the Confederated Salish and Kootenai Tribes of the Flathead Nation in Montana, illustrates a subtle yet powerful commentary on land reclamation, broken treaties, name changes, and relocation. At its heart, Quick-to-See Smith's work attends to what Barnd calls "postcolonial spatial tension" in a way that compels viewers to rethink how they view cartographic public memory in the US (2). While her oeuvre is vast and diverse, I will focus on one of her map series: *Echo Maps*, where Quick-to-See Smith "centralizes the map as form or container that can be emptied and then refilled" (109). Her countermaps are not limited to these geographic regions, though, and she examines large portions of North American, including the US and Canada. Quick-to-See Smith uses mixed media and oil, and she frequently incorporates boxes, photos, sticks, and papers to the canvas—what she considers a "'narrative landscape' [that] becomes a map of stories told to fill what has been emptied [by colonization]" (Rader 51). Her choice of materials is intentional, also, to encourage viewers to recognize the "materials, methods, and methodologies of colonization, indigenous histories, and identity" (51).

Echo Map I, II, and *III* utilize a dripping technique, which smears state and national borders and blurs the layered images on the canvas. Also apparent on I and II are variations of the word "Hello" in Spanish and other languages, especially *hola* and *allo*, and clippings from global newspapers within the state boundaries. Quick-to-see Smith focuses on the relationship between language and land in this series and reminds her viewers that the US is a diverse country where multiple languages are spoken, which is a direct rebuttal to white nationalism's cry for a country of white, English-speaking residents. Since Spanish is one of the dominant languages represented in these countermaps, Quick-to-See-Smith also presents a commentary about the significance of Latinx socio-cultural influences not just at the border of the US and Mexico, but around the nation. This series of countermaps contains several different types of echoes, including the repetition of greetings (*Hola, Allo,* and *Nin hao*), newspaper articles, advertisements, and other images. The repetition indicates that language is in flux, as are the people who speak these languages. In *Echo II,* the Chinese greeting *Nin hao* is scattered throughout North America and Cuba, which reminds the viewer that state and national boundaries have no bearing on language—it continues to move, evolve, and impact the people and land. Rader also notes the impact of the aural/visual connection in these countermaps: "Smith's maps use their visuality as an aural reminder that voices do not exist in a vacuum; language is concatenated by repetition and renewal" (58). Through the echoes of languages and images, Quick-to-See Smith again disrupts the objectivity of the map and by re/imagining the traditional US map through these repetitions, she causes the viewer to question the ownership of land and the composition of these spaces and places. Quick-to-See Smith's countermapping enacts the primary goals of Indigenous Geographies, namely, to demonstrate how Native people make space, to re-narrate place, and to confront settler-colonialism (Barnd 1–2). She accomplishes these purposes by employing artistic and mapping practices to resist dominant narratives about Native people, including the attempts to make Native memory, identity, and land ownership as invisible.

In Practice: Teaching

As a result of learning from these Indigenous artist-activists, I began to incorporate countermapping in my teaching. In an upper division rhetoric course on Public Memory and Countermemory, I introduced the idea of countermapping to undergraduate students and provided various Indigenous artists' work throughout the course. In the beginning of the semester, I used Quick-to-See-Smith's *Browning of America* as a starting point to understand rhetoric. As students analyzed the painting, they not only understood how rhetoric is much more than words or speech, but they began to learn Indigenous ways of knowing and expressing the violence of colonization. Students responded to the painting in our class discussion:

> "The brown paint dripping down the canvas is like old dried
> blood. It's making the violence enacted towards Native Ameri-
> cans visible."

"The blurred state and national lines show that our entire idea of the U.S., Canada, and Mexico is something made up by white people to control people of color."

"The petroglyphs in the background tell a story about a variety of Indigenous people who lived here and still live here even though their stories are erased."

The students' analysis, which again occurred early in the semester, demonstrated a nuanced understanding of rhetoric but also of countermemory and countermapping.

Later in the semester, students created their own countermaps of people or events in East Texas that have been effaced from mainstream public memory. This project occurred after students wrote a countermemory narrative based on the *Lynching in Texas* interactive map. When students use the interactive features of the *Lynching in Texas* map, they often observe for the first time how many Black Americans were lynched in their own hometowns. One student, who I will call "J," created a countermap of Vidor, Texas, a historically racist sundown town.[3] In his words, the countermap is modeled after the A:shiwi's countermaps that showed paintings on the natural landscape.[4] J's countermap was created digitally and demonstrates the A:shiwi's more fluid practice of countermapping that does not attempt to model or mirror Western maps. Rather, J's countermap tells a multi-layered story about several historical events: the failed government housing desegregation project that took place at Vidor, Texas in 1993, a map of Vidor and the I-10 US 90 highway that runs through it, the KKK and the White Nationalists at the "Victory at Vidor" hate rally, Black residents who experience residential segregation and discrimination, and Bill Simpson, who left Vidor after months of violent threats in the early 1990s.

J's countermap demonstrated his understanding of the A:shiwi countermaps and his ability to transfer that knowledge to a new composition of a local East Texas site. In J's artist's statement, he explained his thought process:

> Enote and his project members hope to highlight an alternative view to the landscape that has been suppressed by the highways and modern buildings with English names attached to them. For my art piece I attempt to accomplish a similar

---

3   I received written permission from J to use their countermap in two ways: (1) To use as an example for other students, and (2) to incorporate in future publication to explain pedagogical applications of countermapping.

4   To view Cachini's countermaps, please see https://emergencemagazine.org/feature/counter-mapping/.

achievement by highlighting a mostly forgotten event by highlighting it on top of the map of Vidor, a town that was at one point a "sundown town."

Figure 7.2. J's countermap of Vidor, Texas.

Andrea Riley-Mukavetz reminds us that our relationship with knowledge changes as our relationship to time, space, and our bodies change. As a result, we should "make knowledge and pay attention to how the meaning and the knowledge itself changes as the relationships do" (546). Perhaps I was not ready for this new knowledge while I was still writing my dissertation. Perhaps I just never encountered a perspective like Enote's. Either way, as our geographies change or our existential positioning system (EPS) change (what is my relationship with where I live), our method/ologies are fluid and have the capacity to evolve as well.

Lesson 3: Method/ologies are Embodied

In the summer of 2018, I went on a funded research trip with my teenage daughter to visit several sites of countermemory in Alabama, Louisiana, and Georgia. While each site was significant to me, my visit to the National Memorial for Peace and Justice (NMPJ) impacted me in a way that I still struggle to express. I will never forget the immediate sense of heaviness that pierced me, how my daughter grasped my hand as we walked along the gravel path towards the memorial, or the shiver that I felt as I saw the magnitude of the memorial. When I visited the NMPJ, I learned a vital lesson about the embodied nature of method/ologies. This lesson then went on to impact a later community-engaged project.

The memorial is situated on a large parcel of land; when I first entered the gates past the garden area, I was struck by its scale. I had viewed parts of the memorial online and via an interview with Bryan Stevenson, but I was not prepared for how small I felt in comparison with the size of the memorial and its surrounding space. My body became a part of the experience in comparison with the immensity of the issues, our history, and my whiteness. As I've written about elsewhere (see O'Brien and Sanchez, "Racial Countermemory"), the spatiality of the memorial is intentional, and the "route" that the creators intended for visitors to take tells one continuous narrative about violence perpetuated towards Black Americans since the beginning of the slave trade to our current epidemic of mass incarceration and police violence. There is a long walkway from the main gate that takes visitors past sculptures, artwork, and narrative on the walls. Once I entered the main part of the memorial I was overcome by the sheer number of hanging Corten steel memorials, where I was able to view the names of more than 800 men, women, and children who were lynched in the United States. While I walked through the memorial, I tried to locate myself among the exhibit. I walked the line of hanging steel structures for "South Carolina" until I found the county where I lived. I read the names of individuals who were lynched in that county. I searched to find the names of those who were lynched in New York, where I am originally from. I looked to see if there were lists of names in the county in Florida where my parents lived at the time. I was intent on locating myself and my family within the larger narrative—or the larger "map" of lynching. At that moment, I realized that the NMPJ was also a countermap but one that represents the embodied nature of countermapping.

This type of countermap "releases cartography from its bonds of convention" (Alderman et al. 76) by bringing bodies, materiality, and affect into conversation with map-making efforts. As geographers Rob Kitchin, Justin Gleeson, and Martin Dodge explain, scholars are beginning to move from creating/critiquing maps from an ontological framework to an ontogenetic one. This shift in focus alters the primary questions from what things are to how things become (494). Furthermore, Kitchin et al. argue that as we shift from a "scientific" notion of mapping to a "processual" approach that considers the process and meaning behind map-making. In doing so, we can recognize that maps are ecological and constantly in a state of flux (Edbauer 9). While some of the countermaps that I have described defy traditional cartographic principles, the NMPJ completely rethinks the boundaries of cartography. These types of maps are characterized by their interactivity that encourages viewers and visitors to become a part of the experience. This interactivity can be achieved digitally, via an immersive virtual reality (VR) interface as well as by physically moving through a space. Whether experienced digitally or in-person, these countermaps anticipate and encourage human interaction.

Maps can also chronicle the spatialized memory of land, people, and events, but they can also render these concepts in subjective, expressive ways to communicate socio-political worldviews. As Dean Rader asks in his analysis of Jaune Quick-to-See Smith's map paintings, "To what degree do the original names for things linger in memory and embodiment? How does one map the invisible?" (49). Rader's questions remind us of the forced invisibility of Native people in the United States and the overarching goal of Indigenous Geographies that asserts the vast number of tribes that still exist throughout the country—in short, they "have neither been vanquished nor have they vanished" (Sasse and Smith 8).

In Practice: Community Engagement

This concept of remembering forced invisibility is something that I have been working on with an Equal Justice Initiative (EJI) Community Remembrance Project (CRP). My visit to the NMPJ showed me how countermapping can move past the boundaries of traditional mapping, in fact, with each punctum moment, my conception of countermapping continues to expand. It expanded to impact research, teaching, and now community work as well. In 2020, I began working with faculty at Sam Houston State University (SHSU) and the EJI on forming two CRPs—one for Montgomery County and one for Walker

County (local counties where I live and work). The purpose of these CRPs is to promote truth-telling about racial terror lynching in spaces and places where these stories have been suppressed by historical commissions. EJI works with local coalitions to provide the funding and creation of historical marker text (HMT) so that communities can avoid the traditional system through historical commissions, which often avoid placing markers that address the violence towards Black Americans (O'Brien "Exclusionary"). In addition to the historical marker placement, a CRP also uses two other tactics to "map" public memory: via soil collection and a racial justice essay contest (O'Brien and Walwema). In Walker County, research from the Lynching in Texas project revealed the murder of an entire family, the Cabiness family, in 1918,[5] The Walker County CRP was formed to memorialize the lynching via a historical marker, collecting the soil where the family was lynched, and heading up a racial justice essay contest at Huntsville High School.

The CRP is composed of a few faculty from my university, descendants of the Cabiness family, Huntsville town council members, high school teachers, and students from SHSU and Huntsville High School. The job of a CRP is to promote an atmosphere of geographic truth-telling via research and community work, and this is a geographic project because the CRP must first locate where the individual(s) were lynched and be as accurate as possible. They also must get approval to place an EJI-funded HMT on the land as close as possible to the site. The Soil Collection is a material reminder of where the person was lynched and is intended to be shared with the community, just as EJI shares the soil collection of people who were lynched at the Legacy Museum in Montgomery, Alabama. The overarching purpose of a CRP is not to force truth-telling efforts on a community but to slowly engage and involve a community. These CRPs are an example of embodied countermapping. The collection of soil, the research of the site, and the racial justice essay contest at a local school compels both CRP members and local community members to map themselves in relationship to the violence that occurred in their communities. The soil is a material reminder of this memory, as is the HMT.

APPLICATIONS FOR RHETORIC AND WRITING STUDIES

These depictions of countermaps illustrate the interdisciplinary nature of countermapping, as well as the span of countermapping. As I've shared my journey

---

5   On June 1, 1918, seven members of the Cabiness family were lynched by a white mob in Huntsville, Texas including Bessie, George, Sarah, Tenolar, Lena, Pete, and Cute. All but Bessie were shot and burned.

with countermapping, I've also examined the punctum moments that shifted my method/ology. While I hope that my story resonates with readers, I also want to provide pathways for rhetoric and writing scholars to apply counter-mapping to their scholarship, teaching, or community work. As Hurley reminds us, critical spatial perspectives belong in writing classrooms (103). Fortunately, there are entry-level platforms where students can begin to tell spatial stories via Geographic Information Systems (GIS). Google Maps is a great starting place for students to consider their spatial positionality: Where am I from? What are significant sites in my life? Students can drop pins in all relevant sites, which is something that I model in "(Digital) Objects with Thing-Power." Along with using Google Maps, students can study Native Land Digital, an interactive web-site that allows users to plug in a location and learn about whose land they reside (or the university resides). Pairing Google Maps with Native Land Digital is a helpful way to introduce countermapping principles to students. Once students are ready to tell their own spatial narratives, ArcGIS Story Maps provide tem-plates and examples that incorporate interactive maps with drag and drop text, video, and images. These are just a few ways that students can use countermaps.

For scholars who are concerned with decolonial or anti-racist outcomes, countermapping provides a different way of considering their research. Telling critical spatial stories is a way for scholars to consider the relationships that exist between themselves and spaces and places. In "Mapping and/as Remembering," I describe the process of how I "write place," or how I do chora/graphy. Software and platforms are really the starting place for applying countermapping as a method/ology. This chapter, along with the various scholars I have cited, func-tion as the methodological foundation for countermapping, but when we get to the point of putting countermapping into practice, this is where options and platforms come into the equation. A note, too: each of these software options are intended for beginners. None of them are intended to gatekeep individuals who are not used to using digital technologies to tell stories.

> 1. ArcGIS Story Maps—While ArcGIS can be as complicated and data-driven as is required for geographers, it can also be as simple and straightforward for non-geographers who are unfa-miliar with creating data sets that can be plugged into maps. Enter Story Maps. Story Maps are just as their name implies: Basically, a story map is a stand-alone website that users can use to tell spatial stories. Templates are provided that provide visual differences including typeface and layout. The best part about Story Maps is the drag-and-drop capability. The creator begins by creating a title and then the content can be added

as they scroll, which includes text blocks, images, and videos. Since this platform is about telling spatial stories, though, the map options are what sets it apart from other website templates. Users can add maps with varying topographical and colored features, as well as add way points and informational text.

2. Google Earth—By entering a location, users can create a flyover map of a specific area as part of a larger spatial story. While Google Earth by itself would not lend itself to longform storytelling, when used in conjunction with other software, adds a spatialized element. For example, students in my Public Memory & Countermemory class have created web pages about sites of countermemory and have embedded Google Earth links so that viewers can see where the site is located and how it interacts with the surrounding space.

3. Thinglink—The VR countermap that I discussed earlier demonstrates a use of Thinglink. Thinglink is a web-based site that allows users to create VR spatial stories by uploading regular and 360 images to the site. From there, users can add informative text bubbles. I talk about this process more extensively in "Mapping and/as Remembering."

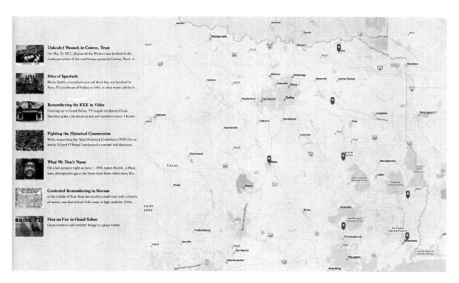

Figure 7.3. Screenshot from O'Brien & Sanchez's story map, "Resisting Erasure: A Countermemory Tour of East Texas" from their forthcoming book, Countermemory.

While there are many ways to use countermapping as a method/ology, each demonstrates the possibilities for spatialized resistance. Map-making is a critical tool used to promote truth-telling efforts, to fight for postcolonial justice, and to make visible that which has been erased from public memory (Radcliffe 129). Countermaps can declare subaltern presence, as with many of the decolonial artistic maps, or they can communicate data and facts about lynching and continuing racialized violence towards Black individuals. Countermaps can even defy conventional cartographic principles, as with interactive embodied maps. As Jeremy Crampton and John Krygier contend, "Maps are active; they actively construct knowledge, they exercise power, and they can be a powerful means of promoting social change" (15). Because it is a method to enact a rhetoric of countermemory, countermapping is a practice that is particularly active, that in its nature constructs and communicates new knowledge, and inspires social change.

WORKS CITED

Alderman, Derek, et al. "The Mapping Behind the Movement: On Recovering the Critical Cartographies of the African American Freedom Struggle." *Geoforum*, vol. 120, 2021, 67–78.

Barnd, Natchu Blu. *Native Space: Geographic Strategies to Unsettle Settler Colonialism.* Oregon State UP, 2017.

Barton, Ben, and Marthalee Barton. "Ideology and the Map: Toward a Postmodern Visual Design Practice." *Professional Communication: The Social Perspective.* Edited by Nancy Roundy Blyler and Charlotte Thralls, Sage Publications, 1993, pp. 49–79.

Butler, Tamara. "Black Girl Cartography: Black Girlhood and Placemaking in Education Research." *Review of Research in Education*, vol. 42, 2018, pp. 28–45.

Cosgrove, Denis. *Mappings.* Reaktion Books, 1999.

Crampton, Jeremy W. and John Krygier. "An Introduction to Critical Cartography." *ACME*, vol. 4, no. 1, 2006, pp. 11–32.

Edbauer, Jenny. "Unframing Models of Public Distribution: From Rhetorical Situation to Rhetorical Ecologies." *Rhetoric Society Quarterly*, vol. 35, no. 4, June 2009, pp. 5–24.

Harley, J. B. *The New Nature of Maps: Essays in the History of Cartography.* Johns Hopkins UP, 2002.

Kitchin, Rob, et al. "Unfolding mapping practices: A New epistemology for cartography." *Transactions of the Institute of British Geographers*, vol. 38, no. 3, 2013, pp. 480–496.

Kwan, Mei-Po. "Affecting Geospatial Technologies: Towards a Feminist Politics of Emotion." *The Professional Geographer*, vol. 59, no. 1, 2007, pp. 22–34.

McKittrick, Katherine. "On Plantations, Prisons, and a Black Sense of Place." *Social & Cultural Geography*, vol. 18, no. 8, 2011, pp. 947–963.

McKittrick, Katherine and Klyde Woods. *Black Geographies and the Politics of Place*. South End Press, 2007.

O'Brien, April. "Exclusionary Public Memory Documents: Orientating Historical Marker Texts within a Technical Communication Framework." *Technical Communication Quarterly*, vol. 31, no. 2, 2021, pp. 111–125.

———. "(Digital) Objects with Thing-Power: A New Materialist Perspective of Spaces, Places, and Public Memory." *Trace*, vol. 4, 2020, http://tracejournal.net /trace-issues/issue4/03-obrien.html. .

———. "Mapping and/as Remembering: Chora/graphy as a Critical Spatial Method-Methodology." *Enculturation*, no. 31, 2020, http://enculturation.net/mapping _as/and_remembering.

O'Brien, April, and Josephine Walwema. "Countering Dominant Narratives in Public Memory." *Technical Communication*, vol. 69, no. 3, 2022, https://www.stc.org /techcomm/2022/07/29/countering-dominant-narratives-in-public-memory/.

O'Brien, April, and James Chase Sanchez. *Countermemory: A Rhetoric of Resistance*. Forthcoming.

———. "Racial Countermemory: Tourism, Spatial Design, and Hegemonic Remembering." *Journal of Multimodal Rhetoric*, vol. 5, no. 2, 2021, http://journalof multimodalrhetorics.com/5-2-issue-o-brien-and-sanchez.

Powell, Malea. "2012 CCCC Chair's Address: Stories Take Place: A Performance in One Act." *College Composition and Communication*, vol. 64, no. 2, pp. 383–406.

Propen, Amy. *Locating Visual-Material Rhetorics: The Map, the Mill & the GPS*. Parlor Press, 2012.

Radcliffe, Sarah A. "Third Space, Abstract Space and Coloniality: National and Subaltern Cartography in Ecuador." *Postcolonial Spaces: The Politics of Place in Contemporary Culture*, edited by Andrew Teverson and Sarah Upstone, Palgrave Macmillan, 2011, pp. 129–145.

Rader, Dean. *Engaged Resistance: American Indian Art, Literature, and Film from Alcatraz to the Nmai*. University of Texas Press, 2011.

Reynolds, Nedra. *Geographies of Writing*. Southern Illinois UP, 2004.

Riley-Mukavetz, Andrea. "Developing a Relational Scholarly Practice: Snakes, Dreams, and Grandmothers." *College Composition and Communication*, vol. 71, no. 4, June 2020, pp. 545–565.

Sasse, Julie, and Jaune Quick-to-See Smith. *Postmodern Messenger, Jaune Quick-to-See Smith*. Tucson Museum of Art, 2004.

Steinauer-Scudder, Chelsea. "Counter Mapping." *Emergence Magazine*. https:// emergencemagazine.org/story/counter-mapping/. Accessed 15 Apr. 2022.

CHAPTER 8.

DOING, AND UNDOING, QUALITATIVE RESEARCH: A STORY OF THEORY, METHOD, AND FAILURE

Stephanie Abraham

Rowan University

Paired readings:

- Abraham, Stephanie, et al. "Creating a Translanguaging Space in a Bilingual Community-Based Writing Program." *International Multilingual Research Journal*, vol. 15, no. 3, 2021, pp. 211–34.

- Abraham, Stephanie. "Paradigmatic Fronteras: Troubling Available Design and Translanguaging with Sticky Literacy." *Journal of Early Childhood Literacy,* 2021.

In this chapter, I delve into a moment during a project at a community writing center that served the children of the Latinx community in South Philadelphia. Beginning at the end, I trace the theoretical failures of my Translanguaging and New Literacy Studies framework and methodological failures of ethnographically-grounded critical discourse analysis. In my musings, I ponder the location of the linguistic repertoire and the notion of available design to rethink language and literacy from something "out there" and "in there" to something waiting with potential to be made. I end with some thoughts on research failures and how failures, too, present opportunities for messy research that can surprise and move us forward.

In this chapter, I delve into a moment during a research project when my theoretical framework and research methodology failed me. Working backward, I begin this story on the last day of a bilingual poetry writing workshop I had been teaching at a community writing center in South Philadelphia.

As part of a larger research project on the translingual writing practices of Latinx emergent bilinguals, this workshop was one among many writing workshops

I taught at the center that was meant to promote the bilingualism and biliteracy of these children. At the end of the workshop, the children and I decided to host a poetry gallery, where their family members and the wider community were invited to the center to view the poesía bilingüe the children had written during the workshop. The children were prolific poets, writing in a variety of bilingual poetry genres such as shape poems, found poems, and parallel poems. On the day of the gallery, I brought in a variety of materials to help the children hang and display their poetry: tape, glue, and mounting putty (see Figure 8.1).

After the children had finished arranging their poetry on the wall (see Figure 8.2), some of them roamed about the center until the gallery started. Left on the circular worktables were the remaining materials, and two of the children started to play with the mounting putty.

They rolled the putty out. They rolled the putty in. Soon the putty formed into various objects and characters. One child shouted, "Hey, I made a snow-man!" As the children's play progressed, more objects formed and emerged. They, too, began to travel around the room, and we traveled with them. Held up toward the sky with proclamations of their creations, La Virgen (see Figure 8.3) appeared, gathering us around her.

And one little sculpture was even attached to the wall alongside the other displayed poetry, becoming poetry, too (see Figure 8.4).

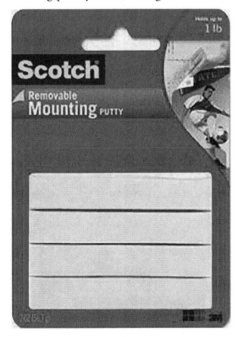

Figure 8.1. Mounting Putty

Figure 8.2. A Display of One Child's Poetry

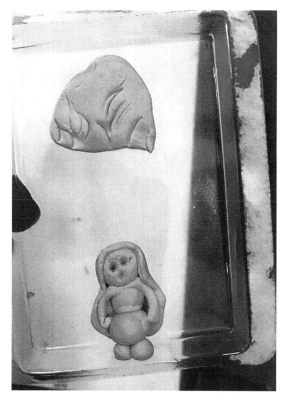

Figure 8.3. La Virgen

Figure 8.4. Putty Becomes Poetry

METHODOLOGICAL UNDOING

It's here my methodological undoing began, a moment of qualitative research unbecoming. It was an undoing of the ways, both the theory and method, I used to make sense of literacy and language, and my expectations and intents of what language and literacy should and could become were being undone.

I designed the workshops using my pedagogical framework of translanguaging and genre-based writing. These frameworks fueled intent and design as to what poetry should look like and become by the end of the writing workshop. For instance, I had planned for the children to read examples of bilingual poetry published by Francisco Alarcón and Jane Medina. Then, inspired by these mentor texts, they would craft their own versions of these bilingual poems, all the while pulling from their entire linguistic repertoire. However, my pedagogical design was interrupted and even refused by the children as this putty also began to *feel* poetic. As the children animated the putty, or the putty animated them, soon it also became attached, literally, to the walls, alongside the other more expected poetry.

So, what did this mean for me methodologically? How could I capture literacy and language given its emergent and slippery state? And here is where method left me. I could not rely on my accustomed ethnographic methods to *collect* this language and literacy data, then transcribe it, and then analyze it with the tools of critical discourse analysis. So, I turned to the ideas circulating in the "post human" turn in language and literacy studies (Kuby, Spector, and Thiel), which is exploring how language and literacy studies can decenter the human as the sole actor in a literacy act, pushing to consider the material workings of matter with the human. Moreover, the notions of the "post" method and the "post" qualitative were also fueling this inquiry, and it's here the work of Betty St. Pierre and her pedagogically and methodologically frustrating question pushed me forward. What would post-qualitative research look like? She used to always ask. She never gave an answer, but only continued to ask the question.

THE ORIGINAL RESEARCH PROJECT

This community writing center sits amidst vegetable stalls and restaurants in South Philly's Italian Market. It is one location among several sites of this community writing organization, founded in 2013 specifically to serve the diverse Latinx community of South Philly. The center hosts a variety of free educational programming, including an afterschool writing program for children between the ages of six and seventeen, weekend writing workshops, and summer writing camps. In 2015, I was a new assistant professor at Rowan University without any institutional relationships to conduct research. Because of my interest in community language and literacy practices, I approached the center's director about a research partnership, who enthusiastically replied to my request with, "Finally! Someone wants to research us." Thus beginning an ongoing relationship with the center.

Initially, in our partnership, I drew upon several qualitative methodologies to shape the research design including linguistic ethnography (Creese), participatory research (Kinloch, Larson, Orellana, and Lewis), and critical discourse analysis (Rogers). Theoretically, I turned to Translanguaging Studies (Li Wei), the New Literacy Studies (Gee), and genre-based writing pedagogies (Hyland) to create and teach a series of bilingual writing workshops that covered a variety of written genres and topics, including poetry, family stories, graphica, and community language mapping. I focused on understanding how the children drew upon their entire linguistic repertoire to write and create these genres. For instance, how did the children use their Spanish and English knowledge to craft bilingual poetry? My overarching research questions focused on how the children translanguaged in their speech and writing, how they responded to a translanguaging pedagogy, and how translanguaging was an act of resistance and linguistic restoration for them.

This chapter specifically focuses on the event with the mounting putty that occurred during the writing bilingual poetry workshop, which I taught on Saturdays during the spring of 2018. During this workshop, each week, the children and I read examples of different types of poems: shape poems (see Figure 8.5), found poems, and parallel poems (see Figure 8.6). Then, the children used those examples as mentor texts to inspire the creation of their own versions of these poems.

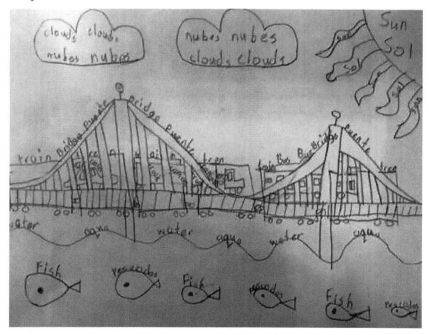

Figure 8.5. A Bilingual Shape Poem of the Benjamin Franklin Bridge in Philadelphia

Figure 8.6. A Bilingual Parallel Poem

Undoubtedly, the children and families who attended the center had experienced linguistic and political violence. To that end, in my work at the center, I hoped my research would shape the center as a temporal escape from this violence, a space where the children could practice their languages and literacies more freely with recognition of their brilliance.

UNDOING A METHODOLOGY: ETHNOGRAPHICALLY GROUNDED CRITICAL DISCOURSE ANALYSIS

Up until this point, I had grounded my research in the linguistic ethnographic methods of participant observation, cultural immersion, and naturalistic interviews. As a researcher, I believed I could learn about the world and people by watching them and talking to them, and subsequently, I could share my conclusive findings through academic publications. Moreover, I located my qualitative research on the threshold of the interpretive and critical paradigms, which also shaped my assumptions as to the ontology and epistemology of the world, specifically of language and literacy.

Ontologically, I assumed language and literacy existed out there, albeit in all its messiness. Epistemologically, I assumed language and literacy could be captured through ethnographic methods and applied tools from critical discourse analysis to interpret and critique this language and literacy that I had captured. For example, I created transcripts from the audio recordings of the bilingual poetry writing workshop sessions, then I analyzed the transcripts using concepts, such as appraisal, from Systemic Functional Linguistics (SFL) (Rose and Martin). For clarity, appraisal is a theory of language that examines how people use language to evaluate and construe the worth or value of things, ideas, and people. Most importantly, SFL imbues an overwhelming amount of agency upon the human and posits that the human always creates language full of intent and a defined purpose. My analysis was retroactive, and I would produce a finding after the language and literacy event had happened. Finally, more or less, this analysis was meant to be a faithful representation of what had occurred during such an event.

However, the mounting putty/into/poetry event was not something I had planned for. I had not designed a research or pedagogical project with an expected outcome of putty becoming poetry. I had not brought putty to the center that day to become part of our gallery. The putty had been full of my own intent, meant only to affix the expected and intended poetry to a wall. Moreover, because putty had seemingly nothing to do with my answerable and plausible research questions concerning translanguaging, bilingual poetry, and writing, I could have ignored the mounting putty, the snowman, and La Virgen. They weren't something I had intended to document. Yet, I decided to pay attention as putty came together "catching [us] up in something that [felt] like something" (Stewart 2).

Because theory and method are twinned, my data collection methods were also becoming undone, I could not capture this literacy and language like my other data. I could not clearly record the audio and easily transcribe it into words with line numbers and some added-on transcription techniques. St. Pierre called this "methodological enclosure," or retreating safely and comfortably to the methodologies and methods we have been taught, which enable us to "do" real research (606).

Scholars working the posthuman turn in literacy studies have attempted to decenter the humanist "human" in literacy research, rather than focus on only the acts of a human participant, they center the agency of the things, objects, and the non-human with which humans intra-act. Assemblage is one concept often put to work in literacy studies situated in the post human ontologies, or the "coming-together of heterogeneous materials (bodies, things, signs), held together in ways that might allow for durability but also for dividing up and reorganizing into new assemblages" (Ehret and Leander 6). Moreover, in Kimberly Lenters' critical instance case study of 11-year-old Nigel and his stick figure drawings, assemblage theory showed how Nigel's seemingly off-task stick figures were examples of how literacy unfolds in unpredictable ways, and rather than off-task behavior, his drawings were examples of possibility and agency. Kevin Leander's and Gail Boldt's rereading of a pedagogy of multiliteracies (NLG) showed literacy unfolded with Lee, a 10-year-old boy, and his manga; in turn, Lee's literacy defied the definition of literacy as intentional, planned, and rational, but rather his manga literacy was full of affect, spilling over into his bodily movements. Other important concepts that inform post human thinking about literacy are the rhizome, intra-action, and entanglement. Kevin Leander and Deborah Rowe used a rhizomatic analysis of a single literacy performance by three students of the book, *The Jungle*, in a secondary school to show how materiality, spatiality, and multiple resources and shifts in footing demonstrate that literacy performances go beyond mere language. Candace Kuby and Shonna Crawford used intra-action and entanglement to examine how when three second-graders studied the solar system, their literacy shifted away from alphabetic print that is passively read to "an entanglement of materials and people that call into being, in the process of becoming" (28).

Others who have been working the posthuman turn in literacy studies have also posed related questions of quandary: What do we do when print loses its privileged place in literacy studies? Likewise, I began to wonder if a snowman made out of mounting putty could also be poetry. Even though, in retrospect, it appears the children had already decided that, yes, putty could become poetry when they definitively attached it to the wall, to be openly displayed in our poetry gallery.

WHEN THEORY FAILS

I'll turn to two particular concepts within the theoretical frameworks, Available Design and the Linguistic Repertoire, to unpack the failings of my theoretical framework and the methodologizing of language and literacy.

Available Design

The first concept is Available Design, which emerged from the New Literacy Studies as a way to account for the possibilities of how literacy exists and could exist in the world (NLG). The notion of design posits an embedded intent toward a specific purpose or shape of literacy. One where literacy is and could become a recognizable part of an already existing system of designs. For example, Roblox is a human-created online gaming platform and within the platform, there exists a variety of worlds or games. Within those games, there are certain possibilities for the creation of avatars, names, and places, which are the available designs to the players.

Available design is further informed by genre theory and genre-based pedagogies, and I thought of literacy as creations and participation in a preestablished genre. Importantly, these genres already preceded us and could be appropriated by us, albeit in some new and dynamic ways, but any literacy would still be the replication of the genre and its forms and rules. Because literacy existed out there and beyond us, then, epistemologically, it could also be captured during research. Moreover, these stances also shaped how I taught literacy to the children who attended this workshop (see Figure 8.7).

Figure 8.7. A Comic Illustrating My Ontological and Epistemological Stances of Language and Literacy

Furthermore, the New Literacy Studies had troubled my print-centric definition of literacy, and I held to the idea that literacy was a socially-mediated, multi-modal meaning-making process. I knew that literacy included modes beyond the textual, such as the gestural, the aural, the oral, the tactile, and the spatial. However, admittingly, I still paid most of my scholarly and pedagogical attention to the textual mode. In other words, I paid attention to and valued print. But when putty became poetry, I wondered how could I know about literacy if no one was reading or writing anything.

The Linguistic Repertoire

I was also working the *trans* of language, pulling from translanguaging theory (Li Wei). I held to the idea that instead of humans having one or two specific languages, we have a linguistic repertoire that we use as we see fit in any given communicative context. As a researcher who turned to translanguaging theory, a critical theory of language, to explain the dynamic and vibrant language practices of young emergent bilinguals, I needed to capture spoken and written language as means of knowing about their linguistic repertoire. But my knowing of language was also slipping. How could I know anything about language if no one was saying anything? Jasmine Ulmer had already claimed that language, alone, has always been an insufficient representation of us and our things, and how we intra-act among them. So, too, I was looking to make sense of things beyond translanguaging from "language-to-language," talking and writing without so many palabras (Zapata, Kuby, and Thiel 493).

The notion of the linguistic repertoire is a critical heuristic put forward by translanguaging scholarship. It has helped to disrupt positivist and deficit notions surrounding multilinguals, particularly those who come from minoritized backgrounds. However, for the most part, the linguistic repertoire has been located solely within the cognition of the individual. More simply, our linguistic repertoire is inside our heads. At the time of this research project, I held onto this ontological belief that this linguistic repertoire was firmly located within the individual's cognition. Again, we have it; we can expand it; and we use it. Throughout the scholarship on translanguaging and translanguaging pedagogy, the linguistic repertoire is referred to as something teachers can "leverage." It is to be incorporated into classroom pedagogies and to be used; it's a place where words reside and can be retrieved from.

But during this moment between the children/mounting putty/I, just a little bit of language was used, and it wasn't clear to whose linguistic repertoire these words belonged or from whose linguistic repertoire they came from. Language felt out there, in a distributed repertoire, emerging among us, instead of coming from just one us. When one child held up her snowman before me, I stammered, "He looks like . . . he looks like . . ." She immediately completed my sentence with, "Olaf!" As she crafted another little body, the rest of us were called around to gaze down at the new figure that had just emerged. Upon seeing it, I wondered aloud, "¿La Virgen?" (See Figure 8.8.) In response, the child only nodded. To whose linguistic repertoire did these words belong? Instead of belonging to the child or me, in our individually-possessed linguistic repertoire, they emerged among and between us. In turn, some translanguaging scholars are also pushing the linguistic repertoire out of the head and into the shared space between bodies and things (Canagarajah; Pennycook), presenting a spatialized and multi-semiotic linguistic repertoire.

Figure 8.8. La Virgen Emerged Among Us

DOING AND UNDOING RESEARCH: THEORETICAL AND METHODOLOGICAL FAILURES

Was this a failure or a blip in research and pedagogical design? Perhaps. Certainly, it was a departure from the research agenda, the learning outcomes, and the research questions. It was something the theories and methods I employed could not explain or capture. But failures in research are not new. Even experimental and positivist research is hinged on the idea of replicate, fail, replicate, fail. But in qualitative research, failure feels different. It often comes with doubt as to why this project didn't work. Why couldn't we answer our research questions? Or perhaps why we weren't able to do what we had planned to do according to our research design. But maybe, a more hopeful view of failure would be to let it surprise us and reflect on our inability to make sense of something, of data, because our current theory and methods just don't know what to do with it. Yet.

In a way, all of my research projects have been failures. In an early teacher research project, I also failed to accomplish the one thing I had intended to do. Initially, I set out to conduct a Bilingual Family Stories Writing Project in my fifth-grade classroom, where I would include the "entire" linguistic repertoire of my students in a narrative writing unit. Near the end of that teacher research project, and after the children had published their final family stories, one of my most precocious students, Juan, asked to use my phone to call his dad. Although I can't remember why he needed to call his dad, I do remember, very clearly, when Juan's dad answered the phone, and he began to talk. A language that wasn't English or Spanish came out of his mouth. When the call ended, I asked Juan, "What language were you speaking?" He answered somewhat nonchalantly, "Oh, just the language of my dad." Later, I found out that Juan, who was originally from Guatemala, spoke both the Indigenous Mayan languages of his mother and father, in addition to his Spanish and English. It was then I realized I had failed to include those languages in a teacher research project intended to include the *entire* linguistic repertoire of my students. Importantly, when I tried to publish this detail in academic journals, I was asked by reviewers to delete it because it was deemed irrelevant, or it would have been just too difficult for me to have included all of Juan's languages anyways. Erase the failure and the data that didn't fit, so the findings could be neat and tidy.

So, what should we do when our research, theories, and methods have failed? One, we write about it. Two, we must also think about failure differently.

BEGINNING WITH FAILURES

When theories fail, so do methods, so when mounting putty became poetry, I could no longer hold on to my methodological approaches. While the data took on new life, I stepped back as mounting putty swung and splat. As a snowman appeared on the walls of the community center. As La Virgen se juntaba, something emerged among us that no longer fit within my research design. As putty circled the room, becoming language and literacy, a flood of ideas washed over me, mostly from my readings of the posthuman turn in literacy studies. I recalled the theoretical and methodological work that had been coming from other scholars (Kuby, Spector, and Thiel) who were pushing the post-human turn in language and literacy studies. Concepts like affect, assemblage, and a flat ontology came to the forefront. So, I started to think about them, read about them, and then think *with* them (Jackson and Mazzei). Affect is what "sticks" together, and it caused me to take up how I felt during the literacy event and what was it they had affected me. Assemblage is the coming-together or the throwing together of humans and things, causing me to look at the new formations of a snowman and La Virgen as capable of moving, acting, and becoming. And a flat ontology reduced the distance between us, humans, and our reality, redirecting my gaze from looking out there to in there, at how we made reality happen from moment-to-moment.

Letting go of my groundings in interpretative and, gulp, the critical paradigms, I lost myself in the thoughts of the posthuman. Not only do humans matter, but the things with which we intra-act also matter, and maybe can matter more. Just as we animate things, so do things animate us. No longer was a linguistic and literate reality out there waiting for me to capture it, not waiting for me to find and analyze it. Instead, it was waiting, with potential and possibility, to be made. This also problematized my focus on only the human child and their subsequent language and writing, and my focus on only the end of their writing and not the process of it, which was already full of material intra-actions.

Soon other concepts would further undo my theory/methodology when I began to think about desire, bodies-without-organs, and the rhizome. Instead of relying on research questions, I started to ask what is being affected. What moves? I abandoned the idea of design and intent in both pedagogy and research, and I started to ask the Deleuzian and Guattarian questions of desire. Of what could become? Of what might happen?

Instead of focusing only on the actions of the humans, I looked to these tiny little bodies-without-organs forming, The Snowman and La Virgen, wondering how they had come to appear among us. Why did they move us? Why did it move me? Instead of focusing on the children's individually held linguistic repertoires, I asked how that repertoire was shared among us, instead of only within us. Instead, of linearly created poems that could be easily published with expected formats, I thought of the rhizome, splintering and poking up and out, where poetry might grow haphazardly in an unplanned trajectory. I began to linger on what language and literacy could become, instead of what it is or should be (Buchholz).

So, I had to ask of this work, if I cannot apply critical discourse analysis to this un-transcribable data, then what will I do with it? As I began to read more, Jane Bennett offered up some answers to these questions. She suggested perhaps poetry is more fitting for representing the mattering of matter, for animating the inanimate, and for granting, or maybe letting, things have a little agency that they have always been previously denied. So, too, I decided to write poetry about putty becoming poetry during a bilingual poetry writing workshop.

Rather than capturing, enclosing, and accurately representing what had happened among us with mounting putty that day, I wondered if I could poeticize it, accompany it, and bring others into the moment. Would poetry do that? Would poetry, in its aesthetic appearance, already indicate that what was being read about this mounting putty becoming poetry wasn't a perfect or even faithful representation of exactly what had happened that day during the poetry gallery? Instead, writing poetry left what was still to be found intentionally open.

UNMETHODS: NOT COMING TO A CLOSE, BUT ANOTHER OPENING

My intent in this chapter is not to call for a new turn to posthuman thought, nor even a return to the critical; instead, it is a call to allow for more research that undoes design, theory, and methods, without tidy findings, ending with more questions than answers. Importantly, this theoretical and methodological messiness only happened because I was reading outside of my paradigmatic and methodological comforts, something I encourage all researchers to do. In turn, I'm sure many other "messy" things occurred in this research project, and during others, that I did not pay attention to. St. Pierre, among others, has pushed us to work against methodology, against a linearly designed plan when conducting research. To do research, then it becomes more about thought than methodology, about thinking differently toward and about people, language, and things.

Even as my methodology failed me, and my ontological and epistemological stances could no longer make sense of what I saw, said, heard, and felt, I remained and remain committed to doing ethical research toward the end of social justice. Questions are always more important than answers. So then, what does all this have to do with more ethical research and acts of social justice? Again, my research projects have fallen within the interpretive and critical paradigms. I have looked for how people, usually young children or teachers, are agentive or not, when can they make choices, or when they cannot. As a language and literacy researcher, I looked for an ontology of language and literacy as out there, something we could find and do, collect and analyze. I took up an epistemological grounding that I could interview and observe as children spoke and wrote, identifying specific times and places for their knowing and learning of language and literacy. Through this, I began to rethink ideas of power and agency, all central notions in discussions of ethics and any kind of justice.

Recalling this research was located among children who had no doubt had power continually exerted upon their bodies, their languages, and their literacies, always shaping them. In another way, I, too, was exerting power over and on the literacy and language practices of the children during this bilingual poetry workshop. I also began to wonder who or what is agentive. And what does agency have to do with language and literacy? And then what does it have to do with equity and social justice? For me, if the ontology and epistemology of literacy and language are relocated from "out" there and "in" there, and instead emerge between and among us through intra-actions of child and material, then this opens up new questions as to how to do more equitable research, and importantly for me, on how to create more ethical language and literacy classrooms. So, when the children picked up the mounting putty that day, when they made something that would let go and move out and beyond us, I felt power being relocated from *over* and *on* them to something that they began to *have* and to *do*.

Moreover, there are many reasons to resist methodological enclosure, but for me, one of those reasons that came to the forefront was to decenter the "human" in my research, because of who *He,* the human, is. Arguably, the human we have always been centering in the social sciences is the White, the Straight, the Man, the Abled, and the Christian. Even when we try to focus on those who are not Him, we are left endlessly comparing and contrasting *Them* to *Him.* This human-centeredness has bled into language and literacy studies, and despite many workings to undo this disbalance, there remains a singular valued literacy and language. Moreover, those who do not practice those kinds of literacy and language connected to the *Human* are left to something else: *literacies, language variations, home language,* and *out-of-school literacy practices.* To abandon and decenter the human is not to abandon humanizing, rather it is to abandon how the human has always been defined.

Another reason to resist methodological enclosure was to trouble my pedagogical framing of critical literacy and leveraging the linguistic repertoire, such as teaching critical literacy *to* children or leveraging their *entire* linguistic repertoire. Rather, it moved this to different ontological and epistemological assumptions. Moving away from teaching criticality to embracing spaces that *let* children be critical and *let* their linguistic repertoires emerge among them. Criticality is, instead, found in the letting and the waiting for language and literacy to take flight into something else, into something unexpected.

Finally, research in flexible, outside-of-school learning spaces, like this one, is full of potential for informing studies of language and literacy practices, especially among children who come from backgrounds that are typically excluded and erased in official schooling. In turn, methodologically those who are doing research in schools could learn from these methodological undoings, especially given the tight and tidy research designs that often constrain and restrict research in schooling spaces.

We, as qualitative researchers, must make sure that we are, at least at times, doing some messy research, not just writing about doing it, telling others to do it, or teaching about doing it in our qualitative research courses. Do it, then share it. It's about locating research in a possible and pedagogical opening into the unexpected. However, doing this kind of research also needs recognition from multiple angles, from the writer of the research to the reviewers of such.

WORKS CITED

Abraham, Stephanie. "A Critical Discourse Analysis of Gisela's Family Story: A Construal of Deportation, Illegal Immigrants, and Literacy." *Discourse: Studies in the Cultural Politics of Education*, vol. 36, no. 3, 2015, pp. 409–423.

———. "Paradigmatic Fronteras: Troubling Available Design and Translanguaging with Sticky Literacy." *Journal of Early Childhood Literacy*, 2021, https://doi.org/10.1177/14687984211021944.

Abraham, Stephanie, et al. "Creating a Translanguaging Space in a Bilingual Community Based Writing Program." *International Multilingual Research Journal*, vol. 15, no. 3, 2021, pp. 211–34.

Bennett, Jane. *Vibrant Matter: A Political Ecology of Things*. Duke UP, 2010.

Buchholz, Beth A. "Drama as Serious (and Not so Serious) Business: Critical Play, Generative Conflicts, and Moving Bodies in a 1:1 Classroom." *Language Arts*, vol. 93, no. 1, 2015, pp. 7–24.

Canagarajah, Suresh. "Translingual Practice as Spatial Repertoires: Expanding the Paradigm Beyond Structuralist Orientations." *Applied Linguistics*, vol. 39, no.1, 2018, pp. 31–54.

Copland, Fiona, and Angela Creese. *Linguistic Ethnography: Collecting, Analyzing, and Presenting Data*. Sage Publications, 2015.

Fairclough, Norman. *Critical Discourse Analysis: The Critical Study of Language*. Routledge, 2013.

Gee, James. "The New Literacy Studies." *The Routledge Handbook of Literacy Studies*, edited by Jennifer Rowsell and Kate Pahl, Routledge, 2015, pp. 35—48.

Guatarri, Felix, and Gilles Deleuze. *A Thousand Plateaus: Capitalism and Schizophrenia*. U of Minnesota P, 1987.

Hyland, Ken. "Genre-Based Pedagogies: A Social Response to Process." *Journal of Second Language Writing*, vol. 12, no. 1, 2003, pp. 7–29.

Kinloch, Valerie, et al. "Literacy, Equity, and Imagination: Researching with/in Communities." *Literacy Research: Theory, Method, and Practice*, vol. 65, no.1, 2016, pp. 94–112.

Kuby, Candace R., Karen Spector, and Jaye Johnson Thiel. *Posthumanism and Literacy Education*. Routledge, 2018.

Leander, Kevin M., and Gail Boldt. "Rereading 'A Pedagogy of Multiliteracies': Bodies, Texts, and Emergence." *Journal of Literacy Research*, vol. 45, no. 1, 2012, pp. 22–46.

Leander, Kevin M., and Deborah Wells Rowe. "Mapping Literacy Spaces in Motion: A Rhizomatic Analysis of a Classroom Literacy Performance." *Reading Research Quarterly*, vol. 41, no. 4, 2006, pp. 428–460.

Lenters, Kimberly. "Riding the Lines and Overwriting in the Margins: Affect and Multimodal Literacy Practices." *Journal of Literacy Research*, vol. 48, no. 3, 2016, pp. 280–316.

Li Wei. "Translanguaging as a Practical Theory of Language." *Applied Linguistics*, vol. 39, no. 1, 2018, pp. 9–30.

Jackson, Alecia Youngblood, and Lisa Mazzei. *Thinking with Theory in Qualitative Research: Viewing Data Across Multiple Perspectives*. Routledge, 2011.

Martin, James, and David Rose. *Working with discourse: Meaning Beyond the Clause*. Bloomsbury Publishing, 2003.

The New London Group (NLG). "A Pedagogy of Multiliteracies: Designing Social Futures." *Harvard Education Review*, vol. 66, no. 1, 1996, pp. 60–92.

Pennycook, Alastair. "Reassembling Linguistics: Semiotic and Epistemic Assemblages." *Crossing Borders, Making Connections: Interdisciplinarity in Linguistics*, edited by Allison Burkette and Tamara Warhol, De Gruyter Mouton, 2021, pp. 111–128.

Rogers, Rebecca. *An Introduction to Critical Discourse Analysis in Education*. Routledge, 2004.

St. Pierre, Elizabeth Adams. "Writing Post Qualitative Inquiry." *Qualitative Inquiry*, vol. 24, no. 9, pp. 603–608.

Stewart, Kathleen. *Ordinary Affects*. Duke UP, 2007.

Ulmer, Jasmine B. "Posthumanism as Research Methodology: Inquiry in the Anthropocene." *International Journal of Qualitative Studies in Education*, vol. 30, no. 9, 2017, pp. 832–848.

Zapata, Angie, Candace R. Kuby, and Jaye Johnson Thiel. "Encounters with Writing: Becoming-with Posthumanist Ethics." *Journal of Literacy Research*, vol. 50, no. 4, 2018, pp. 478–501.

PART 4.
RECONSTRUCTING METHOD/OLOGICAL TENETS

CHAPTER 9.

RISKY PROJECTS & RESEARCHER WELL-BEING: LOCATING NEW METHODOLOGICAL TRADITIONS IN RHETORIC & WRITING STUDIES

Bridget Gelms

San Francisco State University

Paired reading:

- Gelms, Bridget. "Social Media Research and the Methodological Problem of Harassment: Foregrounding Researcher Safety." *Computers and Composition*, vol. 59, 2021, https://doi.org/10.1016/j.compcom.2021.102626

In rhetoric and writing studies, we necessarily put great emphasis on developing research projects that are meaningful and inspire change in the world—work that interrogates structural inequalities in pursuit of a more equitable and just future. Yet there are often unique challenges that come with taking on such high-stakes work. This chapter offers reflections on these challenges while locating researcher well-being as a rich site of understanding the hidden costs of pursuing high-stakes research. Throughout, the author reflects on her experiences as an online harassment researcher—a topic notorious for provoking researcher harm—and how her relationship to method/ ologies evolved over the course of a specific project. In reflecting on the entire lifecycle of this project all the way to publication, the author argues that a messy research process—one that is disrupted, emotional, and deviates from the processes typically celebrated and taught in rhetoric and writing studies—is not a failure on the researcher's part but instead a natural piece of taking on challenging query topics. The chapter concludes by offering tangible steps the field can take to prioritize researcher humanity and thus sustain high-stakes research in rhetoric and writing studies.

Lying in bed, the light from my phone illuminating my face, I frantically googled the name of the sender of an email I'd received late at night about my dissertation. Researching gendered forms of online harassment, I'd recently started publicizing a survey I'd designed as the primary form of data collection, and the sender of this email—who self-identified as a "well-connected male troll"—wanted to "help" me with my project. He turned out to be more than just a troll. Search results revealed a sordid and litigious past, including a lawsuit involving hacking and his non-consensual distribution of women's private photos. He wanted to speak to me. I wanted nothing to do with him.

This uninvited email was just one of several experiences throughout my dissertation research that caused me to question whether I could even continue with my work. Violent, misogynistic, and invasive comments from strangers on the internet filled my social media feed in the days immediately following the survey going live, rendering these spaces unusable to me. Between the exorbitant amount of time spent blocking users and safeguarding my digital presence, I found myself wondering whether I was willing to experience this kind of stress and anxiety for potentially years to come as I, an early-career scholar not yet out of graduate school, built a research agenda around online harassment. Was my research worth jeopardizing my well-being? Nothing I'd learned about academic research or methodologies prepared me for this.

As a relative newcomer to the field at the time, I had limited training in research methodologies, and the ones I had encountered through coursework emphasized *participant* safety as the key value by which to organize my project. Because of this, I failed to consider *my own* safety, which ultimately left me vulnerable to harassment and the ensuing negative effects of it. Years later, as an assistant professor settled into a tenure-track job, I attempted to make sense of how my experience as a researcher came to bear on the process itself in my piece "Social Media Research and the Methodological Problem of Harassment: Foregrounding Researcher Safety" (Gelms). Thinking through questions of how to better methodologically prepare for when research goes "wrong," I found that I still have many questions related to how we can prioritize our own humanity at every messy turn a project may take.

In this chapter, I'd like to offer an extension of our thinking about ways that methodologies enable research in rhetoric and writing studies—an extension that locates researcher well-being at the center to understand the hidden costs we face when we pursue the sort of high stakes, risky, and emotionally challenging topics that can inspire upset or damage to the researcher. Throughout, I'll reflect on my own experiences as an online harassment researcher—a topic notorious for provoking harm—and how my relationship to method/ologies evolved over the course of a specific project. This chapter won't exhaustively detail every inherent risk in taking on a risky research project, but I will touch on certain risks that creeped their way into my process. It's my hope that by narrativizing some of my own research experiences, this chapter can offer affirmation that a messy research process—one that is disrupted and deviates from those typically celebrated and taught in rhetoric and writing studies—is not a failure on the researcher's part but instead a natural piece of taking on challenging topics in an inquiry.

HIDDEN LABOR COSTS OF RISKY RESEARCH

A distinct value of rhetoric and writing studies as an organized field of inquiry is that we necessarily put great emphasis on developing research projects that are meaningful and inspire change in the world—work that interrogates structural inequalities in pursuit of a more equitable and just future, whether in the classroom or in our broader communities (Kirsch). Yet there are often unique challenges that come with taking on such high-stakes work. In my dissertation project, for example, as I investigated online harassment experiences and their effects on one's ability to participate in public discourses, my challenges extended well beyond typical hurdles researchers face. Instead, I found myself having to make decisions around personal safety and my commitment to seeing the project through to the end (Gelms).

Researchers working on feminist interventions of internet cultures often face extreme harassment from misogynistic agitators (Jane), and my project was no different. Once my survey went live, harassment arrived swiftly, in large quantities, and across multiple platforms. From name-calling to violent threats, this experience was both overwhelming and terrifying. I assessed things on the fly, weighing multiple aspects of the situation including goals of the project, bureaucratic deadlines to finish my dissertation, and my own comfortability level with being on the receiving end of intensifying harassment. Ultimately, I decided to close down the survey and pivot towards interviews as my main source of data—something that deviated from my original research plan but a decision made necessary by the threats to my safety and privacy. I also went into a full digital lockdown, changing all of my passwords and privacy settings . . . even going so far as to disconnect my devices from the internet for several days, just to be safe. In the end, I successfully completed the project in a form I was proud of, passed my defense, and graduated. But the experience of having plans go awry mid-project and feeling lost in a dark void when it came to my own well-being has stayed with me since.

Evidenced by my story, researching challenging or risky topics can introduce a lot of precarity and vulnerability into the research process that threatens the well-being of the researcher (Mallon and Elliott; Vincett). Despite this, researcher well-being is often absent from methodological discussions. Sharon Mallon and Iris Elliot note, "the idea of researchers as potentially being vulnerable participants in the research process is a relatively new concept" that has only been sporadically examined in methodology scholarship (2). Indeed, in rhetoric and writing studies, method/ologies addressing risk mitigation typically focus purely on participant safety. But what happens when the researcher's safety is threatened due to the nature of their work? How can we develop methodological frameworks in our discipline that support risky research projects and the unpredictability that may come with such inquiries? To start, we would do well to recognize the varied and abundant hidden labor costs of pursuing challenging research.

One such cost is the potential of suffering second-hand trauma—a serious condition in which a person experiences trauma indirectly, such as through witnessing or hearing about someone else's traumatic experience. There are a variety of terms that are used to describe this phenomenon—secondary trauma stress, vicarious trauma, exposure trauma—each with nuanced differences but all describing the general experience of distress brought on by sharing in the pain of someone else's experience through prolonged bouts of empathy. As one can imagine, clinicians, therapists, doctors, and other professionals who work in healthcare are at an extraordinarily high-risk of second-hand trauma (Honig; Ludick and Figley). Recently, scholars have begun to note how *researchers*, even those outside of healthcare fields, are also a group of people who shouldn't be discounted in conversations about risks of second-hand trauma, as bearing witness to participants' traumatic stories through observation, survey, or interview data can have significant and long-lasting consequences (Adonis; Berger; Drozdzewski and Dominey-Howes; Newell & MacNeil).

Second-hand trauma can manifest in a variety of ways. In their study of field researchers interviewing survivors of violence, Amelia van der Merwe and Xanthe Hunt find that researchers commonly feel "preoccupation with thoughts of the traumatized person outside of the interview session, reexperiencing clients' trauma in memories, and distressing emotions such as grief, depression, anxiety, dread and horror, fear, rage, or shame" (15). These researchers "were deeply affected by participants' traumas and reported that they themselves felt traumatized most often because of an empathetic response to participants" (17). Similarly, in their study of sexual violence survivors, Jan Coles et al. find that researchers experience "anger, guilt and shame, fear, crying, and feeling sad and depressed" as a result of their research work (100). Laura Shannonhouse et al. also report the prevalence of second-hand trauma among researchers working on projects that are traumatic in nature—in this case, researchers were interviewing parents of children who died in a fire at a daycare. Every researcher reported evidence of second-hand trauma, with many going so far as to say they questioned their choice of profession given the immense difficulties they faced in doing this research. The authors ultimately conclude that the enduring effects of second-hand trauma are too great to ignore, noting that many researchers in this study needfully sought out counseling as a result of their research.

Of course, the amount of risk one faces in experiencing second-hand trauma has much to do with their level of empathy, world-view, positionality, as well as the nature of the traumatic material being discussed (van der Merwe and Hunt 12). These factors account for the variance in how a researcher experiences second-hand trauma, if at all, along with its severity and duration. But when experienced, it can cost a researcher their time and their health. For example, the amount of time I lost from having to take extended breaks from my work due to the traumatic nature of the topic itself is remarkable. Reading through narratives, survey responses, and other data about traumatic harassment experiences such as rape and death threats, doxxing, and stalking kept me in a heightened state of anxiety and sadness, which only worsened while conducting, transcribing, and coding interviews. Disruptions to my sleep in the form of nightmares also became more frequent and intense the longer my project went on.

This phenomenon is known as "researcher saturation," or the specific immersion a researcher finds themself in through data gathering, transcribing, coding, analysis, or any of the steps germane to their methods, and can cause second-hand trauma (Coles et al. 96; Wray et al.). Nikki Kiyimba and Michelle O'Reilly, too, note that transcribing specifically, a task that requires careful and repeated listening, puts researchers at risk of experiencing trauma. This kind of immersion—a deep dive into stories of trauma—often made me question whether I wanted to continue on with the project and, more broadly, the profession at all. I remember feeling a deep sense of regret in selecting this research trajectory, as another dissertation topic I considered pursuing was much less emotionally-heavy in nature.

The researchers in van der Merwe and Hunt's study of second-hand trauma reported dissociating or "zoning out" in the days following an interview with a traumatized participant, which tracks heavily onto my own experience. In addition to the general research fatigue many of us face when working on a large-scale project such as a dissertation, I found myself becoming extremely physically exhausted after conducting interviews in which participants recounted a traumatic experience. I took prolonged breaks from working on my project and found myself dreading and avoiding transcription tasks or time spent analyzing my data. For obvious reasons, this made staying on track incredibly difficult.

Joanne Vincett, who interviewed immigrants undergoing indefinite detainment as part of her research, had a similar experience. She writes, "By the fourth month of fieldwork, deep in the dark depths of women's horror stories and atroc-ities, I hit rock bottom," in that she started experiencing depression, cynicism, anger, inability to sleep, and a loss of interest in the things that once brought her joy (50). She identifies this as an extreme form of compassion fatigue, whereby someone suffers because of their relative inability to tangibly help a person in need. Natascha Klocker describes how researchers seeking to inspire structural changes that would positively intervene in a traumatized person's life face many emotional pitfalls when they aren't able to affect the change they had hoped to. She writes that for researchers pursuing high-stakes and risky research, "there's a great deal of pressure to achieve *something*" (Klocker 18). But "successful" or long-lasting change isn't always achievable or realistic. For researchers with ide-alistic expectations, this realization can be difficult to accept.

Of course, Vincett and I experienced instances of second-hand trauma, researcher saturation, and compassion fatigue because we cared deeply about our work and our participants. Given that many researchers begin a project from a place of care, selecting an inquiry topic that they feel passionate about and invested in, it's difficult to imagine anyone is able to truly maintain the emo-tional distance that might wholly safeguard us against these costs. This is not to say that every researcher working on a risky topic will experience the conditions described in this section, but it is important to take stock of how our time and well-being may be affected in the process, and the probability of early-career scholars working on emotionally challenging work abandoning their projects, or worse, leaving the field altogether as I almost did.

TAKING RESEARCH PERSONALLY: RESEARCHER IDENTITY & POSITIONALITY

Despite many celebrated methodological traditions that privilege a fictitious researcher neutrality in the name of objectivity (Acker et al.; Ackerly and True), research is deeply personal for many rhetoric and writing studies scholars, par-ticularly when our work is entangled in our own communities and identities (Manivannan; Ray; Sparby). Threats to personal safety—physical, emotional, and everything in between—as a result of our work become compounded when we find ourselves personally close to the project, our very being wrapped up in the contours of our inquiry. As Mallon et al. note, researchers "are not unat-tached and objective instruments." Instead, "research is personal, emotional, and reflective" (518).

Research is also highly situated within structural, cultural, and rhetorical contexts. In this way, risky research becomes further complicated when navi-gating the contentious relationship we may have with our institutions and the

Academy writ large. Encapsulating this tension, Santos F. Ramos writes about his identity as a non-Black Xicano activist and scholar whose research centers around issues of social justice. Given the nature of his work, he writes about how participating in, for example, a Black Lives Matter action "could technically be considered part of my 'research,' though I still often cringe when using this word to describe what I do." For Ramos, the word "research" signifies "the transformation of people into objects, centuries of colonial violence against Indigenous peoples, and the foundation of capitalist enterprise. 'Research' suggests that I am not an activist, but an academic who enters activist spaces in order to collect data, to bolster my career, and to improve the reputation of my institution." As he explains, understanding our personal and professional relationships to power as well as our situatedness within unrelenting institutions deeply rooted in colonialism, racism, and subjugation is crucial to research that seeks to enact material change in our communities.

Similarly, Esther Ohito discusses her experiences as a Black African immigrant navigating a tenure-track position in academia—a profession, culture, and monolith designed for exclusivity and that which relies on exploitation to function. "A perpetual outsider" (516), Ohito struggled to grieve the loss of a loved one while having to navigate the "dehumanizing confines of the output-obsessed neoliberal academy," (517) and demonstrates how the labor and cultural conditions of academia promote decay, stagnation, and indifference to the embodied experiences we have as compassionate human beings. Ohito advocates for embodied reflexivity in Black feminist research traditions of memory work as a method for "resisting, recovering from, and surviving the deadening trap/pings of neoliberal academia" (517). Her approach necessarily requires centering the self and personal affective experiences in order to bring attention "to where and how our positionalities and intersecting identities intertwine" with our bodies and our memories (521). Locating ourselves within a project is something that Lois Presser has identified as being a crucial part of inquiry. Like Ramos and Ohito, Presser argues that we should contextualize our identities, positionalities, and the conditions of our research as much as we are able to (2069). In this way, the aforementioned authors position methodology as something that communicates our *values*, distinctly as they relate to identity and the work we want to produce in the world.

Recent scholarship in rhetoric and writing studies has complicated our notions of what methods and methodologies can and should do for our work, demonstrating how research frameworks establish values that guide both our scholarship and our civic lives too. In *Race, Rhetoric, and Research Methods*, Alexandria L. Lockett, Iris D. Ruiz, James Chase Sanchez, and Christopher Carter demonstrate how antiracism can act as a methodology for research, particularly in the context of our "ethical obligation to confront the epistemological, social, and political ramifications of living in a capitalist white supremacist patriarchal society" (16). Throughout the book, the authors use narrative and personal storytelling in order to unsettle "the idea of a 'neutral,' aracial point of view" (23). Incorporating their own lived experiences, the authors thereby provide a rich context for how antiracist methodologies can operate within rhetoric and writing studies research as well as our everyday lives.

Laura Tetrault also acknowledges her personal positionality in relation to her scholarly work and voices a commitment "not just to an examination or summary of my own positions and privileges, but also to finding ways to advocate for oppressed communities across differences in positionality" (459). In her methodology for rhetorical analysis of activist rhetorics, Tetrault advocates we center the notion of accountability so as to "*enact* social justice principles through our research by building accountability to vulnerable communities" (463). Much like Ramos, Ohito, and Lockett et al., Tetrault demonstrates how methodology can be used to advance a specific value, both of a personal nature and one of the rhetoric and writing studies field.

As a whole, these scholars remind us that our identities as researchers cannot be easily divorced from our identities as human beings, despite methodological traditions in the academy that ask us to do so. Their work describes entanglements with methodologies that not only seek ethical and just approaches to the research, but also to *themselves* as researchers and humans. Asserting our values through methodologies and locating the self within research allows us to demonstrate how our work extends beyond the confining pages of any single publication or conference talk. For me, I had a strong commitment to feminist research principles and wanted to undertake a project that could have real impact, and while I did feel broadly connected to the topic by interest, my personal involvement became more textured and layered once I started being harassed, experiencing the very thing I was studying. An unwilling participant in my own project, I suddenly had to pivot in ways that were unexpected and felt insurmountable.

In retrospect, there is much I could have done at the outset of designing my study to prepare for the likelihood that I might be harassed in conjunction with my work. However, any sort of plan I might have prepared wouldn't have changed my standing at my university and in the profession, and factoring the potential costs to well-being into our research plans also requires an acknowledgment of how our risks as researchers fluctuate across institutional positionalities. Access to resources that are necessary for well-being—things like time, money, healthcare, and job security—are insufficient for graduate students and lecturer faculty, thus making the pursuit of sensitive research topics among these groups even riskier. As Vincett notes, "the practicalities of how to prepare and cope with [research] predicaments that may affect emotional and mental health are limited," particularly among early-career scholars (44). Building networks of support, both emotional and professional, is important to sustaining and guiding a researcher through a challenging project. For graduate students, early-career faculty, and lecturer faculty, access to these networks can be difficult and insubstantial. Renee Ann Drouin, for example, notes how her own experience with harassment stemming from her work on fandom rhetorics mirrored mine (158). Like me, Drouin also suffered immediate hardships, while the threats to her well-being made her question her desire to continue researching, pursue publishing, or even graduate from her Ph.D. program altogether (159).

Drouin notes that her institutional status as a graduate student left her with limited resources to effectively handle the threats to her well-being brought on by her research (159). Time, for example, is a resource that is incredibly scarce, and institutional hierarchies make access to it inequitable. During my dissertation work, I knew that the threats to my well-being required, at the very least, time—time away from my work, time to process, and time to rest. Of course, as anyone who has navigated a Ph.D. program knows, academia is not an environment known for the promotion of health and wellness—a cultural norm greatly exacerbated under the conditions of risky research. Encountering story after story and the constant immersion in accounts of women being threatened, swatted, doxxed, stalked, and abused left me absolutely exhausted on every physical and spiritual level. As a graduate student going deeper into debt every semester I was enrolled in school, I didn't have the luxury of time that most risky research projects require. Taking additional time to complete my project and Ph.D. meant more money spent and further delays to opportunities for advancement in my career. And so, I pressed on.

Additionally, the "publish or perish" culture of academia feeds into this untenable model whereby scholars are expected to consistently engage in research at an excessive pace (Ohito), leading to "burnout, stress, dysfunction, career-dissatisfaction and lack of support for researchers," particularly among graduate students and others who find themselves in precarious institutional positions (Drozdzewski and Dominey-Howes 175). For scholars working on consequential research who may need more time to address their own capacity and well-being, the publication expectations can feel even more grueling, especially when accounting for the amount of emotional labor that goes into these kinds of projects. After defending my dissertation, I was confronted with excited questions about how and where I might get my work "out into the world," and I met these questions with total panic. Not only did the emotional toll of my research completely eliminate any desire to continue thinking about my work, but I was also fearful of the prospects that publishing might trigger new waves of harassment. I was extraordinarily depleted.

A pervasive worry still hangs in the atmosphere today that wide circulation of my research about online harassment could invite more harassment and threats. Leigh Gruwell describes her experience being featured on a disingenuous yet popular Twitter account devoted to highlighting academic work that its anonymous moderator finds disagreeable. As a result of this wide circulation—certainly wider than its original publication—and into networks of audiences who were inherently hostile to feminist academic work, Gruwell was subjected to attacks on her character, loss of privacy, and even worse: threats of physical violence (Gruwell 97–98). No matter the severity or style of outsider agitation, it is difficult to predict exactly when and how it may manifest in a research process. As proven by her experience, "feminist scholars need not even actively publicize their research to become targets," (Gruwell 96).

In 2021, I published "Social Media Research and the Methodological Problem of Harassment: Foregrounding Researcher Safety" because I knew I had something to say about researcher identity and safety. Reflecting on my own vulnerabilities helped me to see where and how my institutional standing as a graduate student came to bear on my project. Despite now having more institutional power and having had literal years to reflect on the experience, revisiting those events still stirred up a lot of anxiety and generally complicated feelings that I have about publishing and publicizing my work about online harassment. Would self-promotion or wide circulation—things encouraged and even demanded by the tenure process—invite trouble for me? Would I be targeted again, potentially on a larger scale?

I was even further conflicted by an opportunity to publish my piece open-access. I value knowledge-sharing and the democratization of information, but I also wondered if the potential for harassment would be made worse if my piece was readily available for anyone on the internet to read and circulate. I went back and forth about this dilemma for a long time before ultimately deciding that my want to have my work read and shared outweighed my concerns, and so I published it open-access. Perhaps my distance from the initial harassment experience helped me feel comfortable with the decision. But then the piece started getting picked up and promoted by various entities with varying degrees of visibility—my campus's newsletter spotlighting faculty research; a European investigative journalism network's story about online harassment and the costs to democracy (Gjocaj); The Kinsey Institute for Research in Sex, Gender, and Reproduction . . . These outlets have different sizes of audiences, but having my work publicly circulated outside of my immediate disciplinary field put me back in a headspace of feeling anxious that harassment and threats would arrive once again at my digital doorstep, and potentially even my physical doorstep, as is the case for some women who speak out against harassment.

Thankfully, so far, harassment hasn't arrived. Though in highlighting the affective experience of even considering publishing my risky research, I hope to demonstrate that taking up sensitive research topics, regardless of how much institutional power or time the researcher has, will likely affect the researcher emotionally. It's important to normalize, validate, and manage negative emotions that arise in these scenarios (Dickson-Swift et al.; Holland), and equally important is understanding how many factors beyond the self are integral to the research process. As rhetoric and writing studies scholars continue to work within systems that structure our labor conditions and material realities, we have to appraise how we might make systemic interventions that support a sustainable pursuit of risky research.

SUSTAINING RISKY RESEARCH: PRIORITIZING OUR HUMANITY

There are no fast or easy answers to how we can reasonably support risky research in any given project considering the highly contextual nature of this kind of work. However, the concept of self-care is often posited as a primary method of addressing the many challenges brought on by emotionally demanding research (Kumar and Cavallaro; Rager; Theidon). Self-care is indeed an important piece of a holistic approach to well-being, but it is repeatedly positioned as a panacea to all which ails researchers working on sensitive topics. There are a few problems with this framing. For one, there is an incredible amount of privilege that comes with being able to engage in the kinds of self-care that promote long-term wellness. Self-care, in many of its iterations, is a luxury. As an activity, it can require time, money, and other resources that are scarce, particularly for academic researchers who may be overworked, underpaid, and have little worker protections, especially depending on institutional status. Additionally, advising a researcher facing risks to their well-being to simply practice self-care seems to put the onus on the researcher alone. Understanding well-being as a largely personal responsibility fails to acknowledge the very real systemic causes of emotional damage, trauma, or burnout and the conditions that make the practice of self-care so challenging.

While giving a conference talk early on in my dissertation process, an attendee asked an excellent question that jolted me into an awareness of how little I was doing to address my own well-being. She asked, "what do you do to take care of yourself while working on such an intense project?" After taking a moment to absorb the question, I answered something to the effect of, "not much, to be honest." Myself and others on the panel talked our way to the topic of self-care as an important sustaining feature of working on emotionally challenging research, describing the value of going on walks, spending time with loved ones, and engaging in hobbies that are totally disconnected from the work . . . I don't wish to diminish those strategies or position them as being wholly unimportant, but in retrospect, I'm less convinced that "self-care" is the answer to this question.

Thinking about how to care for ourselves beyond what we may typically think of when we hear "self-care"—bubble baths or a good book—can be an important piece (*just one piece*) of a larger strategic network for preparing to do risky research. Of course, predicting what might happen during the course of a project that will cause harm can be exceedingly difficult. That's part of what makes some research topics risky: you don't quite know what might arise. Risk assessment is integral to sustaining our work, and while it's something we do as researchers in a variety of contexts, risk assessment is often discussed as an activity necessary to determine the risks our research poses to participants and not necessarily to ourselves as researchers. Taking the time at the outset of a project to think about potential risks and subsequently codify how you plan to take care of your emotional and physical needs during a demanding project gives you a systemized plan to refer back to if conditions begin to feel untenable. Vincett points out that no matter your research area, "there is inconsistency in offering researchers training and support in emotional well-being and mental health. When issues develop, people rarely speak up about their struggles to cope" (54). That was certainly the case for me (and perhaps my writing this chapter is my way of rectifying that).

As I've noted throughout, my failure to assess the risks to my own well-being in the design phase of my research ultimately became detrimental to my work and, more importantly, my well-being. But I did recognize the value of spending considerable time carefully attending to plans for protecting the well-being of participants. My advisor and I, knowing the sensitive nature of online harassment, had numerous lengthy conversations about how to ensure participants didn't just *feel* comfortable and safe but actually *were* comfortable and safe—an important distinction that I wanted to make sure I addressed. This meant taking a trauma-informed approach to my work with participants, remaining sensitive to what they may have experienced and taking care not to retraumatize them with how the discussion was framed or how individual questions were worded. Designing my project with participant safety in mind was made easier by both mandated human-subjects training as well as my graduate coursework, which included a required class on methodologies. While I didn't encounter any frameworks used specifically for risky or sensitive research, the curriculum of this class did include robust units on person-based methods with attention towards ethics, accountability, reciprocity, community, and institutional critique (Cushman; Grabill; Lamos; Lather; Porter et al.; Stoecker)—all topics that are important when thinking about risky research.

Of course, participant safety is necessitated by our Institutional Review Boards (IRB) as well, but compelling arguments have been made about the value of going beyond those minimum standards of ethics, especially when engaging in digital research (Eble and Banks; McKee and Porter), like I was. While IRBs are a necessary and important function of the university, they can't possibly consider the entire multidimensional context of any research topic, let alone ones that may be emotionally complicated for the researcher. However, the IRB review process allows us to secure "considered peer feedback based on the ethical principles of autonomy, beneficence, and justice" (Phelps 3), and is thus "a key avenue for pursuing greater recognition of researcher trauma" (Drozdzewski and Dominey-Howes 176). This review process presents an incredible opportunity for researchers to develop the theoretical self-awareness and the practical plans necessary to adequately prioritize our own well-being amidst risky projects, regardless of whether the IRB requires this information or not.

Even more locally than the IRB, we should also consider the significant role that mentors play in shaping an early-career scholar's research project. Mentorship is particularly important and valuable in risky research contexts (Coles et al.; Drozdzewski and Dominey-Howes; Mallon and Elliott), and to harken back to methodology as an articulation of values, we should understand mentorship as having the same function. Mentors have a responsibility to an individual mentee in one-on-one support, but outside of these activities, mentorship should also involve advocacy for structural, institutional changes that support the researcher—things like greater access to healthcare and wages that sustain a high quality of life. Such mentorship practices are a commitment to prioritizing the care and humanity of the *people* who comprise our field, not just their ideas.

Many scholars also call for a standard practice in research mentorship whereby mentors receive training on how to support students working on sensitive or emotionally challenging research projects. Sharon Mallon, Erica Borgstrom, and Sam Murphy, for example, highlight the incredible influence mentors have on their mentee's work and affective experience (520). In my case, while my advisor didn't have specific training on mentoring researchers working on risky projects, I was able to lean on them for guidance during especially tricky times. For example, the morning after receiving the strange email that set me on edge, we talked on the phone for some time and they carefully guided me towards a decision about my work that prioritized my humanity over my responsibilities to the Ph.D. program. For me, this care and attention promoted psychological safety in that knowing I had an advocate I could turn to—someone who saw me as a whole human being as opposed to just a graduate student who needed to finish their degree—really allowed me the emotional space to commit to acting in the best interest of my personal well-being. My project was better for it.

LOOKING AHEAD: MAKING THE PROCESS VISIBLE

As a graduate student working on risky but important research, I felt like I had somehow failed in my inability to foresee the threats to my safety. I had spent many hours carefully assembling a methodology and methods for my work, paying close attention to the aspects of each that would ensure I created a sound research design. Having to rework my research project mid-data collection in light of the harassment I experienced felt like something that wasn't supposed to happen. In retrospect, I wonder if these feelings were made worse by methodological traditions that privilege rigidity and present objectivity as a gold standard in research. Taking on a challenging problem like online harassment was sure to inspire the need to be methodologically flexible and attend to roadblocks as they arose, because a researcher can't possibly predict the twists and turns a project might have in store for us.

The meta-aspects of the kind of research that we do in rhetoric and writing studies are just as important as the research itself. In looking ahead at the future of the discipline, I hope rhetoric and writing studies researchers find more opportunities to document the emotional and psychological aspects of our work, especially that which could be considered risky in some kind of way. Of course, as Vincett points out, "incorporating researchers' emotions in reflexive accounts is often a retrospective activity and a response after an emotional upheaval has occurred" (45). What could we learn about our values and approaches to research as a field if attention towards researcher well-being happens throughout *all* stages of research, rather than just in retrospect?

In my story and others', we can recognize the need to develop greater support for researchers taking up this kind of work on myriad levels—individual, departmental, institutional, and within the broader field. In rhetoric and writing studies specifically, the concepts of care and well-being vary from community to community, and thus it's important we normalize methodologies that attend to these concepts while listening to the varying perspectives, experiences, and institutional positionalities that make up our field. Articulating a value through methodology of locating the researcher within the project can inform our choices throughout the entire lifecycle of risky research, thus sustaining our commitment to work that is impactful, meaningful, and of consequence.

WORKS CITED

Acker, Joan, et al. "Objectivity and Truth: Problems in Doing Feminist Research." *Women's Studies International Forum*, vol. 6, no. 4, 1983, pp. 423–35.

Ackerly, Brooke A., and Jacqui True. *Doing Feminist Research in Political and Social Science*. 1st ed., Red Globe Press, 2019.

Adonis, Cyril K. "Bearing Witness to Suffering—A Reflection on the Personal Impact of Conducting Research with Children and Grandchildren of Victims of Apartheid-era Gross Human Rights Violations in South Africa." *Social Epistemology*, vol. 34, no. 1, 2020, pp. 64–78.

Berger, Roni. "Studying Trauma: Indirect Effects on Researchers and Self—And Strategies for Addressing Them." *European Journal of Trauma & Dissociation,* vol. 5, no. 1, 2021, pp. 100–149.

Coles, Jan, et al. "A Qualitative Exploration of Researcher Trauma and Researchers' Responses to Investigating Sexual Violence." *Violence Against Women*, vol. 20, no. 1, Jan. 2014, pp. 95–117.

Cushman, Ellen. "The Rhetorician as an Agent of Social Change." *College Composition and Communication*, vol. 47, no. 1, 1996, pp. 7–28.

Dickson-Swift, Virginia, et al. "Researching Sensitive Topics: Qualitative Research as Emotion Work." *Qualitative Research*, vol. 9, no. 1, 2009, pp. 61–79.

Drouin, Renee Ann. *"Fans are Going to See it Any Way They Want": The Rhetorics of the Voltron: Legendary Defender Fandom*. 2021. Bowling Green State University, Ph.D. dissertation.

Drozdzewski, Danielle, and Dale Dominey-Howes. "Researcher Trauma." *Research Ethics in Human Geography*, edited by Sebastian Henn et al., 1st ed., Routledge, 2021, pp. 168–81.

Eble, Michelle, and William Banks. "Digital Spaces, Online Environments, and Human Participant Research: Interfacing with Institutional Review Boards." *Digital Writing Research: Technologies, Methodologies, and Ethical Issues.* Edited by Danielle DeVoss and Heidi McKee, Hampton Press, 2007, pp. 27–47.

Gelms, Bridget. "Social Media Research and the Methodological Problem of Harassment: Foregrounding Researcher Safety." *Computers and Composition*, vol. 59, 2021. https://doi.org/10.1016/j.compcom.2021.102626.

Gjocaj, Shqipe. "Delete Profile: Online Abuse of Kosovo Women Costing Democracy." *Balkan Insight: Reporting Democracy Project*, 25 Aug. 2021.

Grabill, Jeffery T. "Community-Based Research and the Importance of a Research Stance." *Writing Studies Research in Practice: Methods and Methodologies*. Edited by Lee Nickoson and Mary P. Sheridan, Southern Illinois UP, 2012, pp. 210–19.

Gruwell, Leigh. "Feminist Research on the Toxic We: The Ethics of Access, Affective Labor, and Harassment." *Digital Ethics: Rhetoric and Responsibility in Online Aggression*, edited by Jessica Reyman and Derek M. Sparby, 1st ed., Routledge, 2019, pp. 87–103.

Holland, Janet. "Emotions and Research." *International Journal of Social Research Methodology* vol. 10, no. 3, 2007, pp. 195–209.

Honig, Caryn Alyce. *Compassion Fatigue in Registered Dietitians Who Treat Patients with Eating Disorders*. 2019. Walden University, Ph.D. dissertation.

Jane, Emma A. "'Back to the Kitchen, Cunt': Speaking the Unspeakable about Online Misogyny." *Continuum*, vol. 28, no. 4, 2014, pp. 558–570.

Kirsch, Gesa E. "The Challenge of Making Our Work Matter in Dark Times: Afterword." *Making Future Matters*. Computers and Composition Digital Press, 2018. https://ccdigitalpress.org/book/makingfuturematters/kirsch.html.

Kiyimba, Nikki, and Michelle O'Reilly. "The Risk of Secondary Traumatic Stress in the Qualitative Transcription Process: A Research Note." *Qualitative Research*, vo. 16, no. 4, 2016, pp. 468–76.

Klocker, Natascha. "Participatory Action Research: The Distress of (Not) Making a Difference." *Emotion, Space and Society*, vol. 17, 2015, pp. 37–44.

Kumar, Smita, and Liz Cavallaro. "Researcher Self-Care in Emotionally Demanding Research: A Proposed Conceptual Framework." *Qualitative Health Research*, vol. 28, no. 4. 2018, pp. 648–658.

Lamos, Steve. "Institutional Critique in Composition Studies: Methodological and Ethical Considerations for Researchers." *Writing Studies Research in Practice: Methods and Methodologies*. Edited by Lee Nickoson and Mary P. Sheridan, Southern Illinois UP, 2012, pp. 158–70.

Lather, Patti. "Research as Praxis." *Harvard Educational Review*, vol. 56, no. 3, 1986, pp. 257–278.

Lockett, Alexandria L., et al. *Race, Rhetoric, and Research Methods*. The WAC Clearinghouse, 2021. https://doi.org/10.37514/PER-B.2021.1206.

Ludick, Marné, and Charles R. Figley. "Toward a Mechanism for Secondary Trauma Induction and Reduction: Reimagining a Theory of Secondary Traumatic Stress." *Traumatology*, vol. 23, no. 1, 2017, pp. 112–23.

Mallon, Sharon, and Iris Elliott. "The Emotional Risks of Turning Stories into Data: An Exploration of the Experiences of Qualitative Researchers Working on Sensitive Topics." *Societies*, vol. 9, no. 3, Aug. 2019. https://doi.org/10.3390/soc9030062.

Mallon, Sharon, and Iris Elliott. "What Is 'Sensitive' about Sensitive Research? The Sensitive Researchers' Perspective." *International Journal of Social Research Methodology*, vol. 24, no. 5, Sept. 2021, pp. 523–535.

Mallon, Sharon, et al. "Unpacking Sensitive Research: A Stimulating Exploration of an Established Concept." *International Journal of Social Research Methodology*, vol. 24, no. 5, Sept. 2021, pp. 517–521.

Manivannan, Vyshali. "'Maybe She Can Be a Feminist and Still Claim Her Own Opinions?': The Story of an Accidental Counter-Troll, A Treatise in 9 Movements." *Digital Ethics: Rhetoric and Responsibility in Online Aggression*, edited by Jessica Reyman and Derek M. Sparby, 1st ed., Routledge, 2019, pp. 104–122.

McKee, Heidi A., and James E. Porter. *The Ethics of Internet Research: A Rhetorical, Case-Based Process*. Peter Lang Publishing, 2009.

Newell, Jason M., and Gordon A. MacNeil. "Professional Burnout, Vicarious Trauma, Secondary Traumatic Stress, and Compassion Fatigue." *Best Practices in Mental Health*, vol. 6, no. 2, 2010, pp. 57–68.

Ohito, Esther O. "Some of Us Die: A Black Feminist Researcher's Survival Method for Creatively Refusing Death and Decay in the Neoliberal Academy." *International Journal of Qualitative Studies in Education*, vol. 34, no. 6, July 2021, pp. 515–533.

Phelps, Johanna L. *Engaging Research Communities in Writing Studies: Ethics, Public Policy, and Research Design*. 1st ed., Routledge, 2021.

Porter, James E., et al. "Institutional Critique: A Rhetorical Methodology for Change." *College Composition and Communication*, vol. 51, no. 4, June 2000, pp. 610–642.

Presser, Lois. "Negotiating Power and Narrative in Research: Implications for Feminist Methodology." *Signs: Journal of Women in Culture and Society*, vol. 30, no. 4, June 2005, pp. 2067–2090.

Rager, Kathleen B. "Self-Care and the Qualitative Researcher: When Collecting Data Can Break Your Heart." *Educational Researcher*, vol. 34, no. 4, May 2005, pp. 23–27.

Ramos, Santos F. "Building a Culture of Solidarity: Racial Discourse, Black Lives Matter, and Indigenous Social Justice." *enculturation*, vol. 21, Apr. 2016. https://www.enculturation.net/building-a-culture-of-solidarity.

Ray, Caitlin. "The 'Shit' that Haunts Us: Disability in Rhetoric and Composition Research." *Making Future Matters*. Computers and Composition Digital Press, 2018. https://ccdigitalpress.org/book/makingfuturematters/ray-response-essay.html.

Shannonhouse, Laura, et al. "Secondary Traumatic Stress for Trauma Researchers: A Mixed Methods Research Design." *Journal of Mental Health Counseling*, vol. 38, no. 3, July 2016, pp. 201–216.

Sparby, Derek M. "Toward a Feminist Ethic of Self-Care and Protection When Researching Digital Aggression." *Methods and Methodologies for Research in Digital Writing and Rhetoric: Centering Positionality in Computers and Writing Scholarship Vol. 2*, edited by Victor Del Hierro and Crystal VanKooten, The WAC Clearinghouse, 2022, pp. 45–64. http://doi.org/10.37514/PRA-B.2022.1664.2.11.

Stoecker, Randy. "Are We Talking the Walk of Community-Based Research?" *Action Research*, vol. 7, no. 4, 2009, pp. 385–404.

Tetrault, Laura. "Learning from The Identity Project: Accountability-Based Strategies for Intersectional Analyses in Queer and Feminist Rhetoric." *Peitho Journal*, vol. 21, no. 2, 2019.

Theidon, Kimberly. "'How was your trip?' Self-Care for Researchers Working and Writing on Violence." *Drugs, Security and Democracy Program Working Papers on Research Security*, vol. 2, 2014.

van der Merwe, Amelia, and Xanthe Hunt. "Secondary Trauma among Trauma Researchers: Lessons from the Field." *Psychological Trauma: Theory, Research, Practice, and Policy*, vol. 11, no. 1, Jan. 2019, pp. 10–18.

Vincett, Joanne. "Researcher Self-Care in Organizational Ethnography: Lessons from Overcoming Compassion Fatigue." *Journal of Organizational Ethnography*, vol. 7, no. 1, Apr. 2018, pp. 44–58.

Wray, Natalie, et al. "'Researcher Saturation': The Impact of Data Triangulation and Intensive-Research Practices on the Researcher and Qualitative Research Process." *Qualitative Health Research*, vol. 17, no. 10, 2007, pp. 1392–1402.

CHAPTER 10.

WHAT WE THOUGHT WE KNEW: SNAPSHOTS ALONG THE DEVELOPMENT OF A CULTURAL RHETORICS METHODOLOGICAL PHILOSOPHY

Aja Y. Martinez

University of North Texas

Paired readings:

- Martinez, Aja Y. "Core-Coursing Counterstory: On Master Narrative Histories of Rhetorical Studies Curricula." *Rhetoric Review*, vol. 38, no. 4, 2019, pp. 402–416.

- Martinez, Aja Y. *Counterstory: The Rhetoric and Writing of Critical Race Theory*. NCTE, 2020.

This essay presents a retrospective related through snapshot narrative vignettes. Because this collection focuses on questions of methodological approaches that reflect on choice, examines overlooked and/or undervalued research sites, and challenges traditional frameworks, this essay illustrates through storytelling a methodological education that has served as foundation toward the development of a Cultural Rhetorics Methodological Philosophy.

SNAPSHOT I: THE DUDE

I attended a school-to-prison pipeline high school, but because I was a student tracked into the minimally offered AP and Honors courses, I was considered part of the "college-going track." As such, once my senior year began, I was summoned out of class one day to my guidance counselor's office. The guidance counselor for college-bound seniors was an old hippie who clearly emitted "The Dude" vibes in his very chill, laid back, and lackadaisical approach to planning for the unknown futures of anxious college-bound teens. I remember arriving to this appointment with a well-rehearsed script in my head, a script heavily informed and influenced by my parents, both of whom were not four-year college grads, let alone professional school or graduate school grads. I was prepared to inform this counselor of my plans to go to law school, plain and simple. As far as my family was concerned, I was always good at reading, writing, and researching, so naturally, I should aim for a well-paying legal career. It only made sense. And as the diligent first generation and first-born daughter of my Mexican American parents, I agreed this was a reasonable career objective. I announced my plans to "The Dude," not fully comprehending there were four (at minimum) years of undergraduate learning I would have to clear before embarking on this law school ambition. In turn, "The Dude" casually informed me I would have to choose a major and earn my bachelor's degree first. When I asked what he recommend I major in as a good foundation for my plans, he placed the social sciences degree listings before me and replied, "It's really up to what you feel your flow is, man. But truly, for law school anything [with a whimsical sweep of his hand up and down the list] in the social sciences will do."

I scrutinized the list, feeling a bit panicked at the thought that my well-rehearsed law school plan and script were nowhere to be located on this list. All I saw on this line up were lots of unfamiliar words that ended in "ology" and because I was feeling the vice grip of anxiety begin to close in around me, I pointed at the first word listed alphabetically on the list: Anthropology.

It wasn't until about three years after this experience and well into coursework as an anthropology major that I began to learn about methodology. I relate the above story because it introduces the unifying thread that has led to what is now a twenty-plus-year academic career concerning legal studies and methodology. In retrospect, I can now say I was always in pursuit of a methodological outlet for my academic interests that centers minoritized ways of knowing and storying. But here again, as any novice learner, I didn't know this at the start of my academic journey, so this essay is very much a retrospective related through snapshots, narrative vignettes (fully aware that I am mid-career, so there is still much ahead of me to learn). And because this collection focuses on questions of methodological approaches that *reflect* on choice, *examine* overlooked and/or undervalued research sites, and *challenge* traditional frameworks I present vignettes that display for audiences a methodological education that has served as foundation toward the development of my own Cultural Rhetorics Methodological Philosophy.

SNAPSHOT II: THE BAHAMAS

I was sitting in Dr. Richard Stoffle's Ecological Anthropology course and perked up when I heard him close class one day by asking "anyone interested in going to the Bahamas for some research?" Prior to this posed research possibility, I was simply a third-year anthropology major wading through several semesters' worth of overwhelmingly confusing prerequisites. Two and a half years into my undergraduate studies, I still had no clear idea what my major "anthropology" *really* was, nor how this would prepare me for the ever elusive and increasingly hazy goal of law school. And yet here I sat in Dr. Richard Stoffle's elective course on Ecological Anthropology with an offer to go to paradise.

I jumped at the opportunity to join Dr. Stoffle's cultural/applied anthropology research team comprised of undergraduate and graduate student research assistants. I didn't know what I was doing, but figured I could learn along the way, and through the scaffolded system Dr. Stoffle established of graduate students training undergrads, and advanced undergrads training new undergrads, I was soon plunged into the methodological ecosystem of an applied cultural anthropologist. At this point in my education, I wouldn't say I had a grasp on frameworks in a named theory sense—although because of Dr. Stoffle's body of work and research interests I was receiving an education on the theory of co-adaptation (Stoffle et al., "Landscaping") and Indigenous epistemologies that involved consulting and publishing with elders and other community members of which the studies were concerned (e.g. Stoffle et al., "Ghost Dancing"; Stoffle et al., "Shifting Risks"; Stoffle et al., "Nuvagantu"). As such, I began learning the methodological ropes of qualitative approaches such as ethnography, transcription, and field and site visits. This education also involved learning about the immense amount of detailed and necessary preparation to conduct such studies ranging from IRB application and approvals/denials/revisions, crafting of the interview instrument (demographic information, questions, follow ups, etc.), recruiting participants, researching and purchasing of field equipment such as tape recorders and tape, and then the necessary training to prepare for the study. At this point in the project I was only a volunteer (I would eventually be hired on as an undergraduate research assistant, which meant I'd be paid a small stipend for this labor—I think an important point in terms of compensating student labor); but for the time being, I was voluntarily spending whatever extra time I could eek out of my day on this project—a day already filled with a full undergraduate course load, a job as a receptionist at the student health center, and being a single mom to my then two-year old. What I learned on this project is the undeniable foundation for the work I continue to pursue to this day.[1]

---

1   I have discussed aspects of my involvement in the Bahamas biodiversity and marine protected areas project in previous scholarship (Martinez 96) and anyone interested in detailed and intricate specifics of this project can (and should!) consult any of the associated reports from this project written by my colleagues (Van Vlack; Stoffle and Minnis, "Marine"; Stoffle et al., "Two-MPA"; Stoffle et al., "Sustainable").

What has proven methodologically formative *and* transformative for me was not anything I learned in the classroom or from books but what I gained from the embodied work of preparing for and experiencing site visits as an anthropologist. What became clear to our team upon realizing we were enlisted by the Bahamian government for the *second* phase of the marine protected areas project was that the government had conducted a preliminary study with leading marine biologists and ocean biodiversity specialists but had left people, the very people invested in sustainable community-oriented generations deep fishing practices and sea stewardship, *out* of the initial study. No one thought to speak to local and native fishers—because what would a people who have stewarded the Bahamian seas (in non-commercial ways, no less) since emancipation from the British Crown, and according to some local sources, since the Arawak times, know about biodiversity and sustainability anyway? As I'm sure my audience can guess, the local people know a lot. But what fascinated me as a novice researcher, is that the Bahamian government had more faith in our team of mostly white anthropologists from the land locked deserts of Arizona to travel the 2,200 miles from Tucson to Exuma, Bahamas, to speak with their own citizens, and in turn document, transcribe, and compile a report to let the government know how much their people know about stewardship toward sustainability of the Bahamian sea. And herein lies a kernel toward the development of my Cultural Rhetorics Methodological Philosophy:

> Why talk for or over a people when you can talk to the people
> and let the people relate their experiences on their own terms?

SNAPSHOT III: WHAT'S GRAD SCHOOL?

Somewhere within the time I was immersed in my budding identity as an applied anthropologist and ethnographic methods researcher, one of my research team members asked what my plans were for graduate school.

"Graduate school?" I asked, "what's graduate school?"

I had spent the better half of three undergraduate semesters on this research team and of course knew there was a hierarchy within our ranks, with Dr. Stoffle as our Principal Investigator (PI) and lead, Alex Carrol the Graduate Research Assistant (GRA) (full disclosure, I hadn't yet connected the dots that the "G" in this stood for graduate), and then a whole array of undergraduate research assistants (URAs) like me. Admittedly, most of my education in methodology coincided with my education as a first gen student. As I learned from the team about research tools I likewise learned about institutional terminology and navigation strategies. Another URA peer of mine, Kathleen Van Vlack, was kind enough to fill me in on what exactly grad school was.

"It's a continuation and extension of sorts of the kind of work we are already doing on the Bahamas project," she simply stated.

"You mean I can get degrees beyond my bachelors in anthropology? I can keep doing this research? I don't have to go to law school?"

"Yup," Kathleen confirmed, "you can keep doing this research."

As I neared my final undergraduate year, I began seriously contemplating this graduate school prospect, ever still aware of my assumed duty to my family to become a lawyer. As I prepared to select my final courses before graduation, I went ahead and scheduled an appointment with a family friend who happened to be an attorney—just to see if his answer would differ any from "The Dude" all these years later in terms of best course of preparation for law school. I assumed he would also say "anything in the social sciences would do," and that I could leave his office with the peace of mind that I had done my best to prepare for eligibility to law school and had inadvertently discovered a passion for applied anthropology and ethnographic research methods instead. So, I was more than floored when he responded, "English. If I could do it all over again, I would have majored in English."

~~~

Ever the dutiful daughter, but also by this point a worried single-mother, I wasn't ready to lean fully in to the decision of grad school and the pursuit of advanced degrees in anthropology when I had been so conditioned to this point in my life to identify as someone meant for a career in law. And as first gen logics go, what viable career options are there for an anthropologist anyway? I truly didn't know. No one in my family had *ever* mentioned becoming an anthropologist. So, I decided to keep the law school option in my back pocket, true as it was that my heart was with this qualitative research I was learning about and conducting. In a Hail Mary move, I went ahead and added English as a double major at the start of my fourth year of undergraduate study. This move added a *fifth* year to my degree program, but I had a toddler's mouth to feed and familia to make proud, and I felt I better have more options for career possibilities than less at the end of this college experience. And while I stayed rigorously involved in my work as a URA for Dr. Stoffle, I also embarked on my coursework as an English major and encountered my first tastes of rhetorical methodologies.

SNAPSHOT IV: THE RHETORICAL TURN

As an English major I undoubtedly experienced the array of required core courses representing the old dead white guy canon trifecta: Shakespeare, Milton, Chaucer. But it was the two rhetorical studies courses with Dr. Edward M. White and

Dr. Roxanne Mountford that sparked my interests. Particularly, in Dr. Mountford's class, we were assigned Sonja Foss's textbook *Rhetorical Foundations*, where I learned two major lessons that further contributed to the development of my Cultural Rhetorics Methodological Philosophy:

> There are *many* methods of rhetorical analysis—not just the too often unnamed/unidentified Neo-Aristotelian approach;

and

> Our stories, our embodied and lived stories, are valid and important rhetorical artifacts.

The above related revelations were in fact revelations to me because prior to encountering Foss's text and Dr. Mountford's course my only other interaction with "rhetoric" as a defined concept was in my first-year writing course where the (presumably literature) graduate student teacher assigned us *Gone with the Wind* to read and discuss for the entirety of the semester and then asked us to "rhetorically analyze" the entire book as a timed written final. Details about what this instructor actually taught us about rhetoric or rhetorical methods are fuzzy for two reasons, (1) who can remember anything else when their mind is weighed down by a semester's-worth of Margaret Mitchell's epic tome, and (2) I took this first-year writing course during a particularly barfy first trimester of my pregnancy and am astounded I managed to make it to class at all.

As we proceeded with Foss's book in Dr. Mountford's class, I was astonished to learn there were *many* more methods of rhetorical criticism beyond the singular approach I was provided in first-year writing (FYW). In fact, as it turned out, the FYW method we learned is most attributable to Aristotle, and as Foss specifies, it is *Neo*-Aristotelian—therefore nodding to the Enlightenment's influence on the resurgence of our attention to what the Greeks had to say about rhetoric. As Dr. Mountford instructed, this method is indeed useful for rhetorical studies, but she encouraged us to apply it as a tool best suited to analyze artifacts such as political speeches. This method-to-artifact mapping continued throughout the semester as we traversed the various other methodological options in Foss's book such as Ideological Criticism, Feminist Criticism, Generic Criticism, and (as important to my work as an undergraduate then as it is now) Narrative Criticism.

By the time we arrived at Narrative Criticism I had worked up the courage to approach Dr. Mountford with an idea I had for an artifact: my grandfather Alejandro's stories. I had a small sepia colored photo of my grandfather as a young man kneeling on a dirt road, one knee propped up, dressed in what looked like military fatigues, holding a rifle of some sort, upright and against his propped knee. And I knew, from his stories, stories I was quite literally raised on (Martinez xxv–xxix), this photo represented more than just WWII-era military propaganda. And I knew, again because of my knowledge of the narratives, Aristotle's method would not be a sufficient enough method to fully encompass and piece apart the intricacies and complexity of this visual artifact in relation to the accompanying narrative artifact, a uniquely Mexican American border narrative that made this photo so much more than what could ever be gleaned by the eye. But Narrative Criticism, as presented by Foss, with its methodological tool set that centers the voice, the teller, would work, I only needed to make sure my chosen artifact, these family stories by my Indigenous-Mexican American grandfather would be accepted as a valid rhetorical artifact by my academic context. Before this point in my academic career, I had not ever merged my rich family stories/cultural rhetorics and ways of knowing with my work in the academy because I had not ever been offered the opportunity. Before this point in my academic career no teacher, professor, curriculum, or assignment had ever communicated to me that my stories, my embodied and lived stories, were valid and important rhetorical artifacts.

Happily, Dr. Mountford loved the idea of me centering my Grampa Alejandro's stories as rhetorical artifact for Narrative Criticism, I got an A on the assignment, and long story short, both Dr. Stoffle and Dr. Mountford wrote me letters of recommendation for graduate programs to anthropology and rhetoric and writing studies graduate programs—clearly rhetoric and writing studies won out—funding, ya know? I never ended up applying to law school. I did, however, end up writing a book founded in legal studies that makes a case for a narrative methodology that centers the voices of minoritized peoples.

PART V: SOME TEACHERLY RETROSPECT

I could spend time in this section reviewing the difficulties and joys I experienced throughout graduate school in pursuit of a methodological outlet for my embodied commitments to minoritized peoples and storytelling—but I won't. My existing body of scholarship[2] already demonstrates much of this process, so for fear of sounding repetitive I will instead jump into a discussion about learning to be a Cultural Rhetorics scholar and teacher of rhetorical methodologies in turn. In my 2019 *Rhetoric Review* essay, "Core-Coursing Counterstory" I recount my first opportunity to teach a survey of rhetorical histories course—a course similar in conceptualization to the rhetoric course I experienced with

---

2   See particularly Martinez, "A Plea for Critical Race Theory Counterstory"; Martinez, *Counterstory*; and Martinez, "The Catharsis for Poison: A Counterstory Retrospective."

Dr. Mountford as recounted above. At this point in my career, I was a new tenure-track professor, but not a new teacher, having spent the past seven years of my graduate education teaching FYW and, of course, many units' worth of Neo-Aristotelian rhetorical criticism. Now that I was fresh out of grad school, well placed in a hands-off English department who essentially handed me the reigns of this rhetoric survey to do with as I pleased, I felt a curricular freedom not typical of the graduate student teaching experience; of course, this freedom was simultaneously thrilling and daunting. While on one hand I had matriculated from a program that was known at the time for espousing a mainstream canonical "The Rhetorical Tradition" curriculum, on the other hand I had forged post-coursework pathways that built a network amongst scholars specializing in the new (to me) direction for our field: Cultural Rhetorics. Since this was the direction I wanted to continue to pursue, the question became how do I incorporate the rhetorical education I did have with the rhetorical education I was continuing to pursue? I found my answer where I was taught to find it from the moment I began conducting applied anthropologic research with Dr. Stoffle's team: go to the field, go on site, talk to the people—and in this case the field was the Cultural Rhetorics community (in-person and in-text), the site was the classroom, and the people were my students.

Over the course of ten years with time spent at three universities, I have shaped and honed a course that has many aliases: "Rhetorical Foundations: A Focus on Intercultural and Non-Western Rhetorics," "Rhetoric and Ethics," "Contemporary Rhetorics," "Studies in Modern Rhetoric: Contemporary Rhetorics—Cultural Rhetorics." Despite the variety of names, what has remained consistent for me through the span of these courses is my commitment to a Cultural Rhetorics Methodological Philosophy:

> Instead of talking for or over a people let people relate their experiences on their own terms.
>
> There are *many* methods of rhetorical analysis/critique—not just the too often unnamed/unidentified Neo-Aristotelian approach.
>
> Stories, the embodied and lived stories of multiply minoritized and marginalized peoples, are valid and important rhetorical artifacts.

Moving from and through these guiding principles I have spent the better half of ten years crafting curriculum (see syllabi in Martinez "Core-Coursing" and *Counterstory* for examples) that offers students primary texts by rhetors and

Cultural Rhetorics scholars whose voices and experiences are not traditionally centered in the rhetorical canon. Inspired by my formative experiences with Foss's text, I have adopted portions of this book because I continue to believe it models for teachers a solid multiple-methods rhetorical curriculum.

Now in its fifth edition, there is surely room for critique of Foss's book (that lends itself to revisions worthy of perhaps a sixth edition?) such as her choice to continue placing Neo-Aristotelean Criticism in the first part of the book, describing this method as the "genesis" of rhetorical criticism, which of course indicates an Enlightenment-influenced Euro-Western orientation of the book/ author to the rhetorical canon that Cultural Rhetorics scholars (e.g. Cedillo and Bratta; Cobos et al.; Cultural Rhetorics Theory Lab; Sackey et al.) before me and beyond me have done a thorough job of critiquing. In previous scholarship (Martinez 68, 97–98, 121–125) I have joined the call Lisa A. Flores ("Between Abundance") makes for a centering of Racial Rhetorical Criticism, and I believe incorporation of this method into Foss' offerings would greatly enhance the impact and significance of her text, especially within our contemporary times when racial rhetorical methods are more necessary than ever. Recently, upon teaching the Foss text and finding myself critical and wistful for inclusion of chapters that would instruct students on frames like Racial Rhetorical Criticism, I realized something I was interested to try out with my students—something we could very well do ourselves.

PART IV: LET'S WRAP IT UP ALREADY! A FINAL PHILOSOPHICAL THOUGHT

As I mention above, I never really shed my applied anthropology roots. To this day I research from and make meaning from my classroom as a site. For a few years now and a couple publications' worth (Martinez, "Core-Coursing"; Martinez, *Counterstory*) I have argued it is no longer methodologically enough to simply assign "diverse" or Cultural Rhetorics scholarship and read these texts for what they offer as primary texts alone. No matter how nicely the multicultural model is packaged, if you're still assigning students the same tired old Neo-Aristotelian application of tools to every text you assign, it will never matter how diverse, how cutting edge, how fresh your primary texts are—you'll still miss important insights due to the limitations of this lens. If my methodological work as a critical race theorist and counterstoryteller has taught me anything at all, it is that *tools matter*. I know also that tools/methods can be embedded within what may seem to the undiscerning reader just a primary text, when in fact the author is offering insight into analysis of an interesting rhetorical artifact AND the tools/method by which they did the analysis all along. It is then up to us as rigorously engaged rhetorical teachers and/or scholars to *read these essays two-fold*. Let me offer an example.

Angela M. Haas's 2007 essay "Wampum as Hypertext" is a highly regarded, assigned, and cited essay in rhetoric and writing studies—an essay many curriculum builders include on their syllabi as a nod to either American Indian rhetorics, cultural rhetorics, digital rhetorics, or some combination of these three. Haas' essay is excellent in its introduction for an unknowing audience to an Indigenous multimedia and hypertext called wampum (77). While this essay is well loved and, in many cases, widely incorporated into rhetorical studies curriculum, it is most often not fully appreciated for all that Haas offers. Beyond teaching us the rhetorical importance, and for many, the very existence of wampum as a rhetorical artifact worthy and valid of analysis (see the connection here to my own grandfather's stories as artifact?), Haas also offers us a meticulously crafted method of analysis. Her critique engenders aspects of Indigenous epistemologies, digital rhetoric, visual rhetoric, and storying, all braided together to create a methodological lens that she in turn provides the audience toward comprehension of the importance of wampum. At this point of my example, it is important to point out the neo-Aristotelian method is not present in *any* aspect of Haas' analysis of wampum. Why? Because as method-to-artifact associations go, Aristotle (neo or otherwise) has no business framing wampum. Not because it's impossible to conduct a neo-Aristotelian critique of wampum but because details will be *missed*. Epistemologically speaking (and ideologically too for that matter) there are cultural intricacies and complexities to wampum, as Haas so meticulously illustrates throughout her essay, and as much as primary texts are ideologically informed, so too are our methods. Which brings me to my final (for this essay) Cultural Rhetorical Methodological Philosophy:

> Read cultural rhetorics texts rigorously and two-fold. Make
> efforts to learn from cultural rhetorics texts what they offer as
> rhetorical artifact and as rhetorical method.

~~~

In all, my journey as a student, researcher, anthropologist, critical race theory counterstoryteller, and cultural rhetorics teacher-scholar has been storied. So, I tell stories. It is my hope that these snapshots provide you, my audience with some insight into a path forged sometimes by chance, mistake, and confusion, but that always seemed to right itself due to supportive mentorship and a steady passion to hear from those who are not often listen to. I know I still have much to learn and room to grow, but as things stand, I believe I am on a steady continuum towards realizing my passion as I add to and expand my:

Cultural Rhetorics Methodological Philosophy

Instead of talking for or over a people let people relate their experiences on their own terms.

There are many methods of rhetorical analysis/critique—not just the too often unnamed/unidentified Neo-Aristotelian approach.

Stories, the embodied and lived stories of multiply minoritized and marginalized peoples, are valid and important rhetorical artifacts.

Read cultural rhetorics texts rigorously and two-fold. Make efforts to learn from cultural rhetorics texts what they offer as rhetorical artifact and as rhetorical method.

WORKS CITED

Cedillo, Christina V., and Phil Bratta. "Relating Our Experiences: The Practice of Positionality Stories in Student-Centered Pedagogy." *College Composition and Communication*, vol. 71, no. 2, 2019, pp. 215–240.

Cobos, Casie, Gabriela Raquel Ríos, Donnie Johnson Sackey; Jennifer Sano-Franchini, and Angela Haas. "Interfacing Cultural Rhetorics: A History and a Call." *Rhetoric Review*, vol. 37, no. 2, 2018, pp. 139–154.

Cultural Rhetorics Theory Lab. "Our Story Begins Here: Constellating Cultural Rhetorics." *Enculturation: A Journal of Rhetoric, Writing, and Culture,* vol. 18, 2014.

Flores, Lisa A. "Between Abundance and Marginalization: The Imperative of Racial Rhetorical Criticism." *Review of Communication*, vol. 16, no. 1, 2016, pp. 4–24.

Foss, Sonja K. *Rhetorical Criticism: Exploration and Practice*, 5th ed., Waveland Press, 2018.

Haas, Angela M. "Wampum as Hypertext: An American Indian Intellectual Tradition of Multimedia Theory and Practice." *Studies in American Indian Literatures*, vol. 19 no. 4, 2007, p. 77–100.

Martinez, Aja Y. "The Catharsis for Poison: A Counterstory Retrospective." *Composition Studies,* forthcoming, 2022.

———. "Core-Coursing Counterstory: On Master Narrative Histories of Rhetorical Studies Curricula." *Rhetoric Review*, vol. 38, no. 4, 2019, pp. 402–416.

———. *Counterstory: The Rhetoric and Writing of Critical Race Theory.* NCTE, 2020.

———. "A Plea for Critical Race Theory Counterstory: Stock Story versus Counterstory Dialogues concerning Alejandra's 'Fit' in the Academy." *Composition Studies,* vol. 42, no. 2, 2014, pp. 33–55.

Mitchell, Margaret. *Gone with the Wind,* Scribner, 1936.

Sackey, Donnie Johnson, Casey Boyle, Mai Nou Xiong, Gabriela Raquel Ríos, Kristin L. Arola, and Scot Barnett. "Perspectives on Cultural and Posthuman Rhetorics." *Rhetoric Review*, vol. 38, no. 4, 2019, pp. 375–401.

Stoffle, Brent, Richard W. Stoffle, and Kathleen Van Vlack. "Sustainable Use of the Littoral by Traditional People of Barbados and Bahamas." *Sustainability*, vol. 12, 2020, pp. 1–26.

Stoffle, Richard W, et al. "Ghost Dancing the Grand Canyon: Southern Paiute Rock Art, Ceremony, and Cultural Landscapes." *Current Anthropology*, vol. 41, no. 1, 2000, pp. 11–38.

Stoffle, Richard W., Rebbeca Toupal, and M. Nieves Zedeño. "Landscape, Nature, and Culture: A Diachronic Model of Human-Nature Adaptations." *Nature Across Cultures: Views of Nature and the Environment in Non-Western Cultures*, edited by Helaine Selin, 2003, pp. 97–114. Kluwer Academic Publishers.

Stoffle, Richard W., et al. "Shifting Risks: Hoover Dam Impacts on American Indian Sacred Landscapes." In *Facility Siting: Risk, Power and Identity in Land Use Planning*, edited by Asa Boholm, Ragnar E. Löfstedt, 2004, pp.127–144. Earthscan Publications Ltd.

Stoffle, Richard W., and Jessica Minnis. "Marine Protected Areas and the Coral Reefs of Traditional Settlements in the Exumas, Bahamas." *Coral Reefs*, vol. 26, 2007, pp. 1023–1032.

Stoffle, Richard W., et al. "Nuvagantu, 'where snow sits': Origin Mountains of the Southern Paiutes." *Landscapes of Origin*, edited by Jessica Christie. 2009, pp. 32–44. U of Alabama P.

Stoffle, Richard W., et al. "Two-MPA Model for Siting a Marine Protected Area: Bahamian Case." *Costal Management*, vol. 38, no. 5, 2010, pp. 501–517.

Van Vlack, Kathleen. "To Grub a Fish: Marine Protected Areas and Impacts to Community Resiliency." *University of Arizona Campus Repository* https://repository.arizona.edu/handle/10150/293239. Accessed 12 May 2022.

CONTRIBUTORS

Stephanie Abraham is Associate Professor of Language and Literacy Education at Rowan University. In her scholarship, she studies the language and literacy practices of emergent bilingual children attending a community writing center in South Philadelphia and how transnational teacher education changes teachers' ideologies toward language and literacy pedagogy and practices. Her work has been funded by The National Endowment for the Humanities, the Americas Research Network, the Spencer Foundation, and the Fulbright Organization. She has published in various empirical journals, including *Teaching and Teacher Education, Equity and Excellence in Education, The Reading Teacher*, and *The Journal of Educational Policy*. She has also published creative works, including "¡Aguacate!: Bringing Up Bebe Bilingüe" in *The Autoethnographer* and "After Reading Number the Stars" in *The Journal of Language & Literacy Education*.

Sonia C. Arellano is an independent scholar and current Director of the Migrant Quilt Project. Her scholarship broadly engages social justice issues through textiles, tactile methods and rhetorics, and mentoring of BIPOC students and faculty. You can see her scholarship in journals such as *Peitho, Rhetoric Review, Composition Studies*, and *College Composition and Communication*. Sonia was awarded the 2022 CCCC Richard Braddock Award for her research quilt and article titled "Sexual Violences Traveling to El Norte: An Example of Quilting as Method." Additionally, Sonia received the 2022 Theresa J. Enos Anniversary Award, which recognizes "Best Essay" published in Rhetoric Review, for her article "Quilting as a Qualitative, Feminist Research Method: Expanding Understandings of Migrant Deaths."

William P. Banks is Professor of Rhetoric, Writing, and Professional Communication at East Carolina University. In addition to directing the University Writing Program and the Tar River Writing Project, Will teaches courses in writing, research, and pedagogy, as well as LGBTQ and young adult literatures. His essays on digital rhetorics, queer rhetorics, writing assessment, pedagogy, and writing program administration have appeared in several recent books, as well as in *College Composition and Communication, College English*, and *Computers and Composition*. He has edited five recent collections of scholarship, including *English Studies Online: Programs, Practices, Possibilities* (2021) and *Re/Orienting Writing Studies: Queer Methods, Queer Projects* (2019). His co-authored monograph *Failing Sideways: Queer Possibilities for Writing Assessment* has been recently published by Utah State UP (2023).

Bridget Gelms is Associate Professor in the English department at San Francisco State University (SFSU), where she teaches courses in professional writing, social media rhetorics, document design, collaboration, and writing theory. She is also the co-director of the College Undergraduate Research Experience in SFSU's College of Liberal and Creative Arts. Additionally, Bridget teaches and tutors at Mount Tamalpais College—a fully accredited Associate of Arts degree and college preparatory program inside San Quentin State Prison. Her work has appeared in *Computers and Composition, Technical Communication Quarterly, Composition Forum,* and *enculturation,* among other journals and edited collections. She was the recipient of the Ellen Nold Award for Best Article in Computers and Composition Studies for her 2022 piece on research methodologies and social media harassment.

Ashley J. Holmes is Professor of English and Interim Director of the Center for Excellence in Teaching, Learning, and Online Education (CETLOE) at Georgia State University. She teaches undergraduate and graduate courses in composition theory and pedagogy, research methods, public and visual rhetoric, writing program administration, and digital writing and production. Her recent research explores student writing beyond the university, best practices for curriculum development and program design, and experiential and place-based pedagogies. Her first book *Public Pedagogy in Composition Studies* (2016) was published through the Conference on College Composition and Communication's Studies in Writing and Rhetoric Series, and her work has also appeared in *College English, Composition Forum, English Journal, Community Literacy Journal, Reflections, Kairos,* and *Ubiquity,* as well as several edited collections. Holmes serves as managing co-editor of *Composition Forum.* Her monograph *Learning on Location: Place-Based Approaches for Diverse Learners in Higher Education* was published by Routledge in 2023.

Elise Verzosa Hurley is Associate Professor of Rhetoric, Composition, and Technical Communication at Illinois State University, where she teaches graduate and undergraduate courses in rhetorical theory, technical communication theory and pedagogy, multimodal composition, feminist rhetorics, and visual/spatial rhetorics. She is also the editor of *Rhetoric Review.* Her scholarship has been published in *Technical Communication Quarterly, Kairos, Res Rhetorica,* and various edited collections.

Jerry Won Lee is Professor in the Department of English at the University of California, Irvine, where he currently serves as Director of the International Center for Writing & Translation and Director of the Program in Global Languages & Communication. His recent book publications include *Locating Translingualism* (Cambridge University Press 2022), *The Sociolinguistics of Global Asias* (Routledge 2022), *Language as Hope,* co-authored with Daniel N.

Silva (Cambridge University Press 2024). He is currently co-editing, alongside Li Wei, Prem Phyak, and Ofelia García, the *Handbook of Translanguaging* (under contract with Wiley-Blackwell) and, alongside Sofia Rüdiger, *Entangled Englishes* (under contract with Routledge), which explores the globalization of English in relation to its multiple, complex, and oftentimes unexpected entanglements.

Meagan E. Malone is Assistant Professor of English at the University of Alabama at Birmingham. In her research, she seeks to understand how rhetorical theory and practice must change in response to online, multimodal composing. Takeaways from this research suggest new technologies and methods to pioneer in the composition classroom that prompt students to consider all the semiotic resources at their disposal in some composition. She also studies and writes about embodied rhetoric and transgender theory.

Aja Y. Martinez is Associate Professor of English at the University of North Texas. Aja is author of the multi-award-winning book *Counterstory: The Rhetoric and Writing of Critical Race Theory* and is co-author, with Robert O. Smith, of several forthcoming titles on the storied histories of CRT.

April O'Brien is Assistant Professor at Sam Houston State University. Her research and teaching interests include public memory, countermemory, technical and professional communication, and social justice. She has published in *Technical Communication Quarterly, Technical Communication, Technical Communication and Social Justice, enculturation*, and elsewhere. Her current coauthored book project theorizes a rhetoric of countermemory. She is available at aprilobrien@shsu.edu.

Sarah Riddick is Associate Professor of Professional Communication at Worcester Polytechnic Institute, where she researches and teaches courses in rhetoric and writing. Her research explores rhetorical methods and methodologies, digital publics and cultures, emergent media and technology, and rhetorical audience studies. Her work has been published in *Rhetoric Review, Computers and Composition,* and *Media and Communication*, among other journals and edited collections.

Crystal VanKooten is Associate Professor at Michigan State University, where she teaches courses in the Professional and Public Writing major and in first-year writing, and also serves as co-managing editor of *The Journal for Undergraduate Multimedia Projects* (*JUMP+*). Dr. VanKooten's work focuses on digital media composition through an engagement with how technologies shape composition practices, pedagogy, and research. Her publications appear in journals that include *College English, Computers and Composition, Enculturation*, and *Kairos*. VanKooten's digital book, *Transfer across Media: Using Digital Video in the Teaching of Writing*, was funded by a Conference on College Composition and Communication Emergent Research/er Award and is available online from

Computers and Composition Digital Press. The book is a qualitative research project that provides an in-depth look at the experiences of eighteen first-year students as they completed different kinds of video composition assignments in their writing courses.

Stephanie J. West-Puckett is Assistant Professor of Professional and Public Writing at the University of Rhode Island where she directs the First Year Writing Program. Stephanie's research focuses on equity, access, and diversity in writing curricula and assessment, and she specializes in writing program administration and digital, queer, and maker-centered composition and assessment practices. Her scholarship has been published in *College English, Journal of Adolescent and Adult Literacy, Contemporary Issues in Technology and Teacher Education: English/Language Arts Education, Education Sciences, Journal of Multimodal Rhetoric, and Community Literacy Journal* as well as in several edited collections. The monograph *Failing Sideways: Queer Possibilities for Writing Assessment*, which she co-authored with Nicole Caswell and William Banks, was published in April 2023 by Utah State UP.